NEWGATE'S
Knocker

Greg W. Peterson

[signature]

GREG W. PETERSON

The Second Edition released in March of 2020 includes condensed passages, and some minor changes to dialog and storyline.

Newgate's Knocker — Newgate Prison in England, first constructed in 1188, housed the most vile members of society, many meeting their end by public hanging. Over the years, the prison gate and its black iron knocker have become synonymous with extraordinarily dire expectations.

CHAPTER 1

Gila Belly, Arizona
14:00 Mountain Time
September 9, 2006

Squinting into the morning sun, gazing across the barren rockscape, Robert Bennetti watched a long trail of dust grow from a spot on the horizon where the rutted road intersects highway 69 about twenty miles south of Prescott. Most travelers view the saguaro cactus, mesquite, and tan sandstone rocks as endless miles of desert wasteland. Arizona natives know the flat barren land as Gila Belly, and to the old-timers, Estómago de Gila. Locals recognize the brilliant flashes of light west of the highway as reflections from a glass-walled corporate compound. A retreat owned by the Tomlinson Financial Group, more specifically, the Bennetti family.

Robert Bennetti raised a white coffee cup embossed with a gold Tomlinson logo to his lips. "They're here," he stated flatly.

He was flanked by his two brothers. The three suits fit the large bodies tightly, especially around the shoulders and biceps. John and Robert's once black hair is now dusted gray and conservatively trimmed. Tony's is full, covering the top of his ears and a portion of his jacket collar in the back.

John placed a beefy hand on Robert's shoulder. It rested there for nearly a minute, a calm endorsement to what was about to take place. He said softly, "Volente o nolente." *Willing or unwilling.*

Robert, expressionless, nodded a sanction of understanding, but remained transfixed on the growing trail of dust advertising the advancing cars. He counseled his two brothers, "These gentlemen are not ignorant. They know what they're doing. We need to be careful."

"Why so many cars?" Tony asked.

"Paul Porter and Ed Romano met up with Nicholson at the airport and are driving the other cars. We don't have enough vehicles here for the test. They'll be parked at either end of the ranch for the experiment." He took a sip of coffee. "I told them they could stay here for a few extra days and do some hunting."

John reached into his inside jacket pocket, removed a short, dark brown cigar, a Belicoso. He studied it as though assessing the wrapper for flaws, then pulled it slowly across his upper lip and breathed in deeply. He turned and poked the end of the stubby Puro towards Tony and said, "They'll be at each end of the ranch? What, twenty miles? Are you telling me it'll work that far away?"

Robert said, "I know it's hard to comprehend, I'm not sure I'm convinced, but Nicholson swears it works perfectly, just as he described it. Come on, let's go meet our guests."

Tony and John followed Robert across the expanse of the large room. The hard leather soles on the Italian marble echoed in the empty space. Tony stepped from behind and opened the massive glass door for his brothers.

"Gonna be hot today. We should get this done quickly."

They walked in tandem, Robert in front, down a steep flagstone walkway toward the main parking area at the base of the small hill below the house. Three luxury cars sped between two stone monoliths defining the entrance. As they slowed, a thick cloud of dust and sand swirled forward, obscuring the occupants inside. The brothers waited for the air to clear.

The seven guests exited the cars quickly. Four passengers from one of the vehicles wore sandals, turbans, and long white robes made of a single sheet of handspun linen and known in their native country as chesch, jellaba, and baboosh. The tallest man carried a black attaché. They had dark features that distinguished them from the passengers in the other cars.

Two men emerged from the adjacent vehicle and moved forward to greet the foreigners. They wore business attire, white shirts and ties, dark suits, and expensive shoes. They guided the foreigners to the Bennetti brothers and made introductions. Mike Nicholson, a tall, blonde-haired Empire Airlines captain, exited the end vehicle. He reached across the seat to pick up an object before getting out. He joined the group and together they climbed the walk and entered the house.

An hour later, the three Bennetti brothers and their seven guests left the residence. They returned to the parked vehicles. Three cars sped off and the dust cloud came alive. Twenty minutes later there were four vehicles parked miles apart. Two at the north property line, one at the south, and one remained at the complex. Three cars continued to idle.

The Bennetti brothers, Mike Nicholson, and the foreigners parked two vehicles at the far north corner of the ranch. They set up various instruments, radios, and briefcases on a folding table. The tall, blonde-haired man, Nicholson, stepped from the group and placed a small black box on the table. The four Mid-Eastern men assembled nearby and watched silently. Robert began to speak, assuming control of the activities. He provided instructions to Nicholson.

Using a brass key, Nicholson opened the box.

Shortly, the eight men in the clearing became still and attentive. Robert picked up a hand-held radio and began operational checks with Paul and Ed, parked miles away

After confirming communication and ensuring that everyone was ready, Robert nodded to Nicholson, indicating the test could begin. The blonde-haired airline captain moved closer to the table and reached for the box. There was no movement or sound from the others. A light breeze swirled his white hair and several long strands danced on his ashen face. He remained focused on the box as his fingers found a toggle switch on the inside. He glanced to Robert and without waiting, he flipped the switch.

The idling car behind Robert Bennetti choked, misfired, and stopped running. The smooth lugging of the car's well-tuned engine had been the only sound in the remote desert location and the instant silence drew the attention of those nearby. The three brothers stood mesmerized. The tall man moved the toggle switch back to its original position with a faint click. The dark men in white robes remained silent, staring at the disabled vehicle.

The pause in activity was short-lived. Only seconds passed before sound returned and movement within the group resumed. The radio in Robert Bennetti's hand crackled with Paul and Ed's excited voices. They tried to talk during breaks in the transmission. As the radio chatter subsided, Robert Bennetti keyed his microphone and spoke.

"Quiet, you both can't talk at once. Ed, what

happened?"

"Just like Nicholson said. A few seconds after you gave the word, a sputtering noise, like a spitting sound...hard to describe...came from the box inside the trunk. The engine started to cough like it was running out of gas. It just stopped running. Do you want me to try and start it back up?"

"No, stand by. How about you, Paul?"

"Pretty much the same thing. Kind of a pulsating noise from the box, the engine began to misfire, then it stopped. Incredible."

CHAPTER 2

Motel Casa de Grande
Five Months Later
Midland Texas
February 1, 2007

My left arm uncoiled like a striking snake in response to the obnoxious buzzing of the alarm, targeting the snooze button with the accuracy of a cruise missile. I hated the first five minutes of the day and the guessing game of what motel and city I was in.

Boston?

No. Not even close.

New Orleans?

No. Our New Orleans motel always has an unmistakable musty odor.

Maybe it's the late hours. Next time, I'm going straight to the room and get a decent night's sleep.

A two-story, Spanish style, stucco place. The picture is coming into focus, small courtyard, a pool, an empty lounge. All seven of us had met downstairs last night for a drink before turning in.

Midland. That one came to me pretty quick.

Midland, Texas.

Sometimes I have to open the door and take a look outside.

Subtle clues, like the sticky tropical humidity or the salty smell of the ocean, might mean Miami or West Palm Beach. A cold and drizzly overcast morning could be Seattle. Regardless, it's always the same, I invariably need to escape the generic surroundings of the motel room and look to outside clues for orientation. I seldom react to the alarm after waking in a strange motel knowing where I had spent the night.

There are a couple of reasons for the confusion. I've been under a good bit of stress the last few months. Nothing serious, no women problems, except, I guess, not having had a date in over a month could be considered a problem, and not having a serious relationship in, damn, I guess about two years. Okay, maybe there are a few issues with my sex life. That's not the issue. I've worked hard to get to this stage in life, that is, this point in my career. With a good bit of luck and fortunate timing things seem to be working out. But the stress of making a mistake or waking up and realizing this is all a dream, might be a factor. Maybe I've just got too much on my mind with the new job. Mostly though, I think it's the constantly changing towns we fly into. Getting up in a different room every morning makes it difficult. When you're half asleep, it takes a minute to recall exactly where you are. I wonder if the rest of the crew struggles with this each morning.

Anyway, this is Midland, Texas. No doubt about it. I recall drinking the water in the lounge last night. Tasted just like oil. I believe you could put Midland water in your crankcase and drive for a year without engine damage.

It's an interesting life, flying for a major airline. Even though I'm new with the company and, as a flight engineer, I don't get much stick time, it's still incredibly challenging and fulfilling. The French might say, Je voudrais vous voir a poil, which means the ultimate experience. Maybe it means, I would like to see you naked. I really wasn't that good in high school French. Anyway, this month has been a little less than ideal. I'll be a bit relieved when it's over.

I'm Mac McIntyre. My real first name is Vernon, but I've gone by Mac since my early navy days. I'd gotten used to Vern and having heard the name my entire life I never gave it much thought although, as you might imagine, it was somewhat of a character builder, much like the boy named Sue. Nikki, one of my longer lasting relationships, brought it to my attention a few years back that Vernon is actually a weak eponym. She explained that it could negatively impact my future and how I might be perceived in the business world. She was convinced that Vernon is not a strong name. She cited research on the subject. I wasn't too sure. I told her there were three Pee Wees I could think of who did pretty well, although one did have a rather unfavorable image. And, what about an adult male being called Sonny? Now there's a name that says, "I'm intelligent". Yet, I can name several very respectable Sonnies. I let it go.

I've been flying for Empire Airlines for two years and I'm just getting to where I'm starting to feel at home in the large jets. I say large, but the Boeing 727 is really considered a pretty small commercial airliner by the more experienced pilots. To me it's a big plane. I flew small props in the navy, mostly as a flight instructor, and some transports, but I've never flown what you'd consider a "heavy" or really big aircraft. I've flown into most of the cities serviced by Empire and the mystery associated with new destinations has become less of a concern. I'm starting to relax more now. It makes a big difference who I'm flying with. I feel comfortable with most of the crewmembers based in Minneapolis, except for Captain Kiley. No one's comfortable around him.

Kiley doesn't present the image one would expect from an airline captain. He's in average shape for sixty-five, short, thinning gray hair, and more often than not his face speaks for him. It says to me, *"Don't speak to me or I'll hire someone to burn your house down."* Most people avoid conversation with him unless absolutely necessary.

I can't avoid him. The job pretty much demands we converse.

He's an experienced aviator though. He's flown more types of planes and has held more positions with the company than probably anyone working for Empire. Recently, I've begun to question his ability to focus and handle cockpit contingencies. If it weren't for the exceptionally proficient first officers in the right seat, I might refuse to fly with him. We've only been paired together a few times during the last two years, so I hadn't noted the change. Until now.

Looking back, I think that I was either more tolerant or just concerned about making a good impression the first few months on the job. That was back in two-thousand five. I think, back then, I might have attributed some of his meanness to my own inabilities associated with being a "new-hire." I was certainly a little slow in the beginning, completing checklists and performing cockpit duties, that have since become routine. Most of the other captains recognized this and have been indulgent and understanding those first few months. Kiley never was. As I recall, he's always been short-tempered and somewhat arrogant. Almost like he's looking for a way to find fault in my performance. Even though he's been this way since I've known him, there's no question he's deteriorated. Recently, I've noticed a lot of people commenting on his behavior, whereas a year or two ago it was seldom discussed openly.

Kiley has no close friends or family who could have observed this change, otherwise someone might have interceded to straighten him out. After next month he'll retire, and my guess is that he'll withdraw to his farm in Sauk Centre and provoke his cows into giving sour milk.

This morning I skipped breakfast, not wanting to start the day off with an attempt at conversation with Kiley. Usually the three of us, Kiley, Ted Lawrence, the first officer, and I, gather in the motel restaurant prior to leaving for the terminal. We generally start off the day listening to Kiley complain about the cold eggs he had for breakfast and the cheap mattress he slept on.

I entered the motel lobby a few minutes before I expected the rest of the crew to assemble for our ride. The glass door leading to the foyer swung open easily and slammed hard against the rubber stop. The resulting clank echoed through the empty space and Ted, the only one in sight, instinctively looked in my direction from the registration desk where he stood.

He leaned against the counter, trying to balance a Styrofoam cup of coffee and the morning paper in one hand while picking up his flight bag with the other. His hat was lying on the counter and I wondered how he planned to pick it up. Ted lives in Minneapolis, he's married and has two kids, a very pleasant person and professional aviator. This month with Kiley has been stressful however, and the edge in his demeanor has become increasingly evident.

"Morning, Mac, Where's Kiley?" he asked as our eyes met.

"Don't know. Thought you two were meeting for breakfast."

"Yeah, well, we were. He didn't show and I wasn't about to wake him."

"Don't blame you," I said

"I'm sure he'd probably bitched all the way back to Minneapolis that I got him up too early. What's his problem anyway? You'd think he'd be happy about retiring. I think he's worse now than he's ever been."

The day had already begun to show signs of conflict.

"You know," I said, "I think he's terrified of going through the rest of his life without an airplane strapped to his butt."

Ted didn't look sympathetic.

I said, "He's been flying planes since before I was born. I don't believe I've ever heard him talk about anything else. It's legitimate to be upset about forced retirement. Just because you turn sixty-five doesn't mean you can't do your job."

"I believe Kiley can go through the mechanics, but there's a lot more to being a captain then flying the plane. You need to expect some leadership from the man in the left seat. Some people skills would be helpful. Kiley couldn't get a golden retriever to like him."

There was some truth in what Ted had said, and I nodded in agreement. By this time, the limo was parked at the curb. I set my flight bag against the scuffed-up Masonite counter, onto the cracked quarry tiles. This motel's cheap construction and poor upkeep was in considerable contrast to other places we stay.

"Ted, most of the other captains feel the same about giving up their wings while they're still physically and mentally sharp. Hell, we have members of Congress who are in their nineties running the country. Kiley's simply depressed."

Ted set his flight bag on the floor, retrieved his hat from the counter, and squarely positioned it over his manicured hair.

I still had to fly home with these two guys and the less tension in the cockpit the better. I couldn't help thinking that two more days and the rest of my career would be downhill. Flying with Kiley this month has been a daily challenge. Either Ted was ready to grab the yoke and wrestle control away from him or I was contemplating clubbing the old man in the back of the head with the emergency ax for treating me like an idiot. He might have a million or so more hours in the air than me, but I had excelled as a naval flight instructor and had more flight certifications than most of our captains. Kiley's snide remarks about my capabilities had become increasingly annoying, especially since he'd been making an unusual number of in-flight mistakes lately. I empathized with Ted.

Kiley was divorced several years ago. His only child, Bob Junior, had become a success only to fall into a deep bottle of scotch. He ultimately lost his family and career to bad investments and illegal stock maneuvering. All this took a toll on Bob Senior. Add to that a touch of alcoholism and a mental deterioration, possibly due to some unknown disorder, and you have a witch's brew destined for disaster. In any case, Kiley would have been reported months ago for one reason or another had he not been so close to retiring.

But where is he now?

Ted called Kiley's room from the house phone at the end of the counter. I could see from his annoyed expression that there was no answer. The fact that our captain was temporarily missing wasn't unusual. Occasionally, one of us would have personal plans and would end up taking other transportation to the terminal. This wasn't, however, something one would expect from Bob Kiley.

"Think he left?" I asked.

"Not like him," Ted frowned, "he wouldn't up and leave without letting someone know. I'm going to get the desk clerk to check his room."

As Ted turned away to find the clerk, the

flight attendants entered the lobby en masse, each pulling matching suitcases on wheels with various purses and bags deftly attached. All four are very attractive girls. Only one, Karen, is married. She's an excellent leader of the cabin crew and several years senior to the other three. I think of Claire a little differently than the rest. We haven't flown a full trip together before this week and with just the last few days to get to know each other, I think we've started to make a connection.

I greeted them as they pulled their things up close to Ted and me. "Morning, ladies."

I smiled and received a few back.

Claire, the tallest and most junior and, as I admitted earlier, my favorite, was reactive as usual. "Big Mac, I left the door unlocked last night like you asked. How come you stood me up?"

Claire was a lot of fun and of course was being a tease. She's exceptionally cute, fairly new with the airline, and lots of fun to work with. I could see some potential and played along.

"Sure Claire, all talk. Tell you what, next time we fly together I'll be on time."

I felt it a good time to use a little French and with a reasonably accurate Maurice Chevalier flair, I said, "Il y a une fete dans mon slip et je t'y invite!"

I think I suggested a romantic evening on the

beach.

"No thanks, I don't think I'll take you up on that."

"You speak French, I'm impressed."

"Fluently. If I were you though, I'd work on a more romantic line. Inviting girls to a party in your pants isn't very original."

Shoot, wrong line.

Karen said, "Where's Mr. Sunshine?"

Her sarcasm about Kiley seemed to go by the other three.

"Easy, Karen," I said, hoping to keep the disrespect to our boss at a minimum.

"Sorry. Are we all here? The limo driver looks ready to go."

"Great," I said, somewhat sarcastically. I was beginning to get a bit nervous about Kiley's delay. We were an hour or so from departure and had no captain to fly the plane. "Kiley hasn't been down. Have any of you seen him?"

The four flight attendants shook their heads in unison.

"Haven't seen him since last night," one responded.

Ted didn't seem bothered.

He said, "Someone's going up to check his room now. I'll go out with the girls and hold our ride. Will you go up and see if he's there? If his things are gone, I'm sure we'll catch him at the plane. Otherwise, if he's there, tell him we're on our way and we'll meet him at the terminal."

Ted managed to gather all his things and started for the door behind the flight attendants. He seemed annoyed but not overly concerned about the captain. He probably wished that Kiley wouldn't show up and that we would be assigned a new pilot to complete the trip. That would be fine with me.

"Sure thing. Load up my bags, will ya?"

I didn't like going up to Kiley's room and facing the possibility that I would have to wake him or interrupt him. It wasn't as attractive a prospect as Ted's self-assigned devoir of helping the four girls into the limo. I glanced back toward our ride and could see the four flight attendants standing just outside the glass entry doors to the lobby. Claire was brushing her hair and gathering it together in some kind of ponytail arrangement. They were laughing about something.

Kiley was in Room 203, several doors down from 209 where I had spent the night. Both rooms overlooked the pool. His front drapes were closed. There was a housekeeper's cart at the end of the concrete walkway where the steps led down to the pool. I could see the open door of the room she was cleaning at the end of the second level mezzanine. Otherwise, the whole area seemed deserted. The Texas early-morning air was cool, but the sky was clear. Soon, the rapidly rising sun would produce an unseasonably warm day. Heavy snow was forecast for our layover tonight in Chicago. I thought it strange to start the day with this pleasant weather and in just a few hours we'd be getting out of an airport van in a foot of snow.

Approaching the closed door of Room 203, I paused. This was one of the reasons I didn't like being the junior pilot in the cockpit. I knocked several times rather delicately, not wanting to startle Kiley if he was still asleep. No response.

"Bob," I called, as I knocked harder a second time. "You in there? Wake up."

A young Hispanic man approached from behind and touched my shoulder. Somewhat startled, I turned to face him. He looked to be about seventeen and was working on a mustache that would be a few years in the making. His white shirt was wrinkled and a size too small, as where his black shiny pants. The rumpled shirt was open at the neck and the sleeves tightly rolled to the elbows. The trousers narrowed to where they ended two inches above an unlaced pair of badly-scuffed black wingtips. He reeked of Aqua Velva. He held a motel key attached to an oblong brass tag at eye level, causing a cheap gold Timex to slide down his skinny forearm. He hooked me a wide grin, exposing shiny white teeth.

"You want me to open the door, sir?" he said, with a heavy accent. "Mr. Kiley checked out last night."

"Last night? Why didn't someone tell us that at the desk when we were down there a few minutes ago?"

I tried to impart just the right amount of anger in my voice to reflect some authority.

"Linda, our desk clerk, looked for Mr. Kiley's checkout in this morning's log but she didn't think to look at last night. We just noticed he had checked out when Mr. Lawrence asked about him. I'm sorry if it caused any inconvenience."

"No, that's okay. Open the door though and let me make sure his things are gone."

The young man had trouble getting the cheap brass lockset to turn and unlock. He wiggled the key and jerked the knob back and forth. Finally, it opened, and he stepped aside to let me through. As I entered, I stopped cold. The room hadn't been used and it didn't appear that anyone had even been in it during the night. My first thought was that the maid had already cleaned up.

"Has your housekeeper already been here?" I asked the kid with the key.

"No sir, not yet. Clara always phones in each room as she finishes so we know the status for check-ins."

Everything was in order. The four glasses with sanitary covers were neatly arranged on the counter by the sink, all the towels were squarely hung, and the soap bars and shampoo hadn't been touched. The room looked the same as mine had yesterday when I checked in. There wasn't even a wrinkle on the bedspread where he might have laid his suitcase.

"Well, he's not here and it doesn't look like he's been here," I said.

I looked around the room with the hope of finding some clue. I even looked under the bed.

I was curious and a little confused. Kiley had left the motel lounge at about ten o'clock last night. He must have gone to his room and at least flopped on the bed. I remember him saying he was beat and needed to get some sleep. We were all happy about that.

"Do you know when he checked out last night?" I asked, realizing immediately that it really made no difference.

Kiley was gone and had not used his room. He had told no one that he had plans. I'd flown this trip with him several times and knew he had no friends or contacts in Midland that would draw him away for the entire night. It wasn't like we were in San Antonio or Dallas where there might be some explanation, but Midland? There was no reason I could think of for him not to stay in the motel room.

"No sir, I don't know when Mr. Kiley checked out, but we can find out at the desk very quickly."

"Yes, please. Let's check that out, and anything else you can tell me about Mr. Kiley's stay. I'm in a very big hurry. Can you do this quickly? I'll meet you downstairs in a few minutes."

I took the stairway at the end of that

wing and turned toward the glass wall where I first made my entrance to the lobby. Looking through the glass and out the far side, I could see the rest of the crew in the limo.

Ted was reading Grisham's *The Testament* in the front seat. The girls saw me approaching and put their conversation on hold while I opened the van's sliding side door.

"I've got a date tonight in Chicago, Mac. Don't tell me we're going to be stuck in Midland today because we don't have a captain?"

Claire seemed to be the spokesperson for the others who were obviously just as curious. Even though she was the youngest and had the lowest clock number, she seemed to enjoy acting as the spokesperson.

"Could be," I said, looking at Ted. "He's gone. Checked out last night and the room hasn't been used. I've asked the desk clerk to find out when he left, and anything else he can. What do you want to do?"

"Wonderful," Ted muttered caustically. "What I'd like to do is forget about it and leave without him. You're ready to do a little flying aren't you?"

He spoke a little louder now with a serious tone. This did sound like a good idea, but I knew it wasn't possible.

"Seriously, we've got to get moving. We're an hour from departure," I said.

"I know. Look, let's go to the terminal and

see if we can track him down. If he's not around, we'll call Ops and see what they want to do. I'm not too worried about our flight but I am concerned about Bob." He folded his book and set it aside. "This is pretty strange," he added.

The Midland terminal didn't have a crew room or even an Empire office but the agent at the ticket counter could communicate with our Dallas Operations Department using a ring-down line behind the counter. Ted asked the rest of us to get the plane ready in the event Kiley showed up, or in case a new plan developed. He called Operations.

It was looking doubtful we'd depart on time.

The flight attendants and I were lucky to arrive at the gate not much later than normal but very close to boarding time. The ticket agent was checking in the last of the standbys. All the waiting-area seats were filled, and passengers stood idly near their belongings waiting for the boarding call. Others gathered their carry-on luggage and formed a long line beginning near the ticket agent at the gate area and stretching back into the main concourse.

The lone female agent, wearing a tan Empire uniform, looked relieved when she saw us. We walked quickly toward the front of the long line where I stopped and placed my bag on the floor. The girls rushed down the Jetway to begin readying the cabin. The young female agent stopped what she was doing and looked to me, I assumed for an explanation as to why we were so late. I felt I should prepare her for the possibility of the flight being delayed, but I didn't want to alarm the passengers standing nearby. I pulled her aside so we could talk in private.

"Sorry we're late."

"I'm just glad you could make it. I was about to call Stuart up front to start looking for y'all."

"Well, I don't want you to panic but there's still a problem. The captain hasn't arrived yet and we haven't seen him since last night. There's a good chance he won't make it."

"I was afraid you dragged me over here for some bad news. So, should I start herding them on or what? I don't want to have to ask them all to deplane if the flight gets cancelled," she said.

The girl didn't seem overly concerned but was looking for some direction.

I said, "Since we don't know for sure what the situation is with the captain, I think we should go ahead and board. If we have to cancel the flight, we'll worry about that when the time comes."

The agent rubbed her nose and looked around at the passengers. "This will be interesting."

I continued, "Let's hope not. Look, I'll keep you posted. There's a chance we could have a deadheading captain on the flight. Are you aware of any pilots flying with us today?"

"'fraid not. None that I know of. Maybe Stuart up at ticketing can help with that."

"Well, you should get back to the passengers. I think the worst case would be for Dallas to send us a captain down on the next flight. Do you know when that one arrives?"

"That would be Flight 605. Gets in at 10:45. You'll have to work fast to get a captain on that one. The next chance won't be until two o'clock this afternoon."

"Okay, thanks. We'll continue on as though the flight is still going out and see what happens."

She returned to the restless passengers waiting to be checked through. I got a few questioning stares when I reached down and picked up my things near the front of the line. Trying to provide a little reassurance, I caught the eyes of a few of the passengers near me and acted as though nothing was wrong. The line had tightened up somewhat during my talk with the agent. I looked for a place where my pressing through would cause the least trouble. I selected a lady and her teenage daughter. They seemed to be arguing about something.

The girl had on tight-fitting blue jeans with lacing up each hip allowing her skin to poke through. Her top probably wouldn't be legal in South Carolina, and she had enough rings stuck on her face to stock a small jewelry store. I couldn't tell what the discussion was about but figured they wouldn't mind being interrupted for a minute while I passed through.

"Excuse me," I said, as I moved ahead, leading with my flight bag and attempting to pry the two apart.

"Excuse us, Captain Midnight. We're in the middle of something here if you don't mind."

The mother was the one with the sharp tongue.

She caught me by surprise. I've never had a passenger be so rude. I tried a little diplomacy.

"I'm very sorry, ma'am, if I'm interrupting here. I just need to get to the plane so we can get you on your way."

"Well, that's right considerate, but don't you think that if you hadn't overslept this morning, we might have stood a better chance," the mother said.

The daughter seemed to be enjoying the verbal mugging I was taking from her mother. I was afraid she was about to join in so I quickly moved ahead before either could continue.

"Excuse me," I said again.

This time I forced my way ahead. The daughter moved slightly to help out but not without covering the smile on her face to keep in the laughter. At least, I think the two bonded a little.

I rushed to get my things into the cockpit, pushing ahead of the passengers who were beginning to gather at the bottom of the Jetway. Karen was temporarily keeping them from boarding while Claire and Erin finished a quick cabin inspection. I glanced back at the interior before entering the cockpit.

Claire was helping Julie set up the forward galley. She asked Erin, "How do you know when you're halfway through a date with a pilot?"

"Don't know, how?" Erin asked.

Claire, glancing over to me and smirking, said, "It's when he says, that's enough about flying, let's talk about me."

I shook my head and set my bags inside the cockpit. "Good, Claire, funny."

I was certain she timed that just for my benefit. Claire and I had only met a few times around the crew room in Minneapolis and during this trip I've really seen her in a different light. I was becoming interested in getting to know her better and wondered if she was serious about meeting someone in Chicago. I would miss not having her on the plane next month and hoped she was feeling the same chemistry I was.

Karen had confided that Claire was from a small town north of the Minneapolis-St. Paul area, or to those of us from Minnesota, "the cities", and was hired by Empire a year or so before me. She's only twenty-three and hasn't been seeing anyone special. I've been looking for the right opportunity during this trip to ask her out, but she has either sensed my impending advances and has been avoiding me, or she's just difficult to approach. Now with Kiley's disappearance, and this chaotic departure, I probably wouldn't get a chance the rest of the trip. Nuts.

Claire seemed to have finished her work and looked over to me. A crooked smile. She said, "Fait-il chaud ici, ou c'est juste vous?" sounding like a native Parisian.

What the hell does that mean? It sure sounds good. It was a question, and I recognized the words "hot" and "you". Maybe she was asking about the cabin temperature and if I thought it was too hot in the plane. Then again, maybe she said that she thinks I'm hot. Doubt it. I tried a non-committal answer and said, "Peut-être."

She laughed.

Wish I would have studied more.

Karen released the passengers before I had gotten completely through the cockpit door. *Here they come*, I thought, *better get moving*.

After a quick assessment of the cockpit, I checked the logbook and worked my way back against traffic to do a fast, outside inspection. The passengers were mostly seated when I returned. Karen told me the cabin was in order and all the seats will be filled. Karen Franklin had been with the company for about twelve years and had an impressive reputation for being thoroughly efficient and company orientated. Everything was by the book once her feet hit Empire equipment.

Upon calling Flight Ops for our take-off weights, I learned that two pilots were on their way to fill the front seats.

The last two passengers straggled down the Jetway and were trying to find room in the forward closet for their hanging bags when Ted appeared at the cabin door. Behind him, an Empire captain held his hat securely under the arm holding his flight bag. He was probably in his late forties, somewhat pale, tall, blonde hair, and his expression was like that of a bank executive faced with an unscheduled audit. I didn't recognize him, but that wasn't unusual. Empire employed about 1500 pilots. Most of them based in Dallas.

"Did you find Bob?" I asked.

I knew full well that our new captain was about to take his seat and that Bob Kiley wouldn't be joining us. I was somewhat concerned and very curious about Kiley. I immediately considered several questions but knew Ted and the new captain had some catching up to do. We were about to push back.

"Sorry, Mac. No luck. It's complicated. I'll fill you in after we get going. This is Mike Nicholson. We were lucky to get him. Mike, Mac McIntyre."

"Hello, Mac." He reached out his hand.

"Mike's based in Dallas and was planning on deadheading home with us. He's picking up the trip as Bob's replacement. Are we ready for blast off?"

"We are now," I said, while shaking the captain's hand.

The stony look vanished and he suddenly

33

seemed like a pretty good guy. Funny thing about first impressions. I had him pigeon-holed and now I had to reshuffle the files.

Both front-seat guys were moving into position with experienced precision. We were going to make it out of the gate on time but the first few minutes would be hectic.

"Too bad we have to meet under such strange circumstances. Nice of you to help out," I said to the new captain.

"Worked out well for me," he said while getting seated, and then asked, "Good bird?"

"It's got a full set of 200s, two of them newly tuned. I saw nothing major in the logbook. The right main-gear light wouldn't come on two trips ago. Looks like maybe a bad switch in the bay. That's about it."

"Okay, then."

"We're heavy and we'll need the entire runway," I said.

By the time I finished my little speech Ted had strapped in, finished positioning his equipment, and was checking the radios that I configured for him earlier. He had already filed the flight plan and was copying the current airport information from ATIS. Captain Nicholson was flipping toggle switches with one hand and positioning his seat with the other.

"Fire away when you're ready, Mac."

He spoke with the calm assurance that ninety-nine percent of the pilots master by the time they settle into the left side of the cockpit. I had been reciting the pre-taxi checklist from memory, loud enough for the voice recorder, while Ted and Nicholson checked things up front. As I got to the first item that required acknowledgment from one of them, I spoke up and waited for the right response. Having been through this routine three, four, or even five times a day for the last two years, it had become rote.

We moved back from the force of the tow truck and things began to calm down. In the cabin, the flight attendants checked seatbelts and made the standard emergency escape announcements. It was all business now and Bob Kiley was out of my thoughts. Years of training had ingrained habits that are now reflexes. During our taxi toward the active runway, we continued with the take-off checklist. Ted was directed to switch to tower frequency and hold short by ground control. With a glance upward, I located the call button on the overhead console, pressed it, and said over the PA, "Flight attendants, please take your seats."

Five minutes had elapsed since the two drivers entered the cockpit.

Everything appeared normal.

CHAPTER 3

Killey's Farm
Sauk Centre, Minnesota
07:50 Central Standard Time
February 1, 2007

February is a bitterly cold month in Minnesota, and today was no exception. The passage of a low front the previous afternoon left the nighttime sky crystal clear, releasing the warmth of the earth and allowing the cold air mass from Canada to push the mercury beyond the twenty-below mark.

On the small plot of land in Sauk Centre, the Kiley family farmhouse sat perched on a high hill in the middle of an endless blanket of freshly fallen snow. The weathered old structure was accustomed to the harsh northern winters and stood like a veteran sentinel defying the cold. From a distance, the building looked peaceful and undisturbed, oblivious to the severe drop in temperature. But inside, the building cracked and popped as the hot air from the rusty old furnace battled to maintain its assigned temperature.

Bob Kiley was raised in this farmhouse with his older brother Eddie. The times were perfect back then and Kiley grew up wishing he would never have to leave. He worked the fields alongside his father, a typical country kid who fished and hunted the unspoiled land with consistent success. The Kiley boys were raised with the same work ethic common throughout the Midwest, which Bob later drew upon to excel in school and later to become one of the first decorated pilots of the Vietnam conflict. Following his tour of duty in the Air Force, he became one of the charter members of the Empire pilot force. Over the years he worked for the company as chief pilot, training coordinator, Minneapolis ALPA union representative and, most recently, as the company safety manager representing the pilot's union.

Two years ago, his life began to change. He became irritable with his wife Debra and avoided social engagements. With her son grown, Debra became wearied and searched for ways to find fulfillment. She and Bob became increasingly distant and he became more reticent and reclusive. Finally, the following spring, Debra moved out. The divorce was unpleasant and costly. When the courts awarded her the house on Lake Minnetonka, Bob moved back to the farm. Kiley's son, Bob Junior, was imprisoned for illegal financial dealings shortly thereafter. Things had not been right on the

Kiley homestead for several years.

Bob Kiley helped with his son's legal bills which only drove him deeper into debt. The stress and expense of the trial combined with Bob Junior's incarceration increased Kiley's despair. His parent's health continued to deteriorate during this period. This past year, the couple succumbed to old age and stress within two months of each other.

Now, with his pending forced retirement, he faced a growing sense of depression, which he perceived as insurmountable, until his discussion with a fellow Empire captain two years ago.

The discussion encompassed retirement, money, discontent, and their mutual depression from unfulfilled dreams. Coincidentally, and fortunately for Kiley, the old friend had offered a solution to their mutual problems, but Kiley would have to provide an important element for the alliance to succeed.

That day, in the crowded airport lounge, the two airline flyers formed a binding covenant. Kiley had become involved in events that he knew would result in a personal struggle, one that meant choosing between salvaging what was left of his life or accepting the unbelievable pact proposed by his fellow captain. He had no choice but to accept. He wouldn't be able to survive with his current life intact, but he believed he had found a way to eliminate some of the pain.

Today, the sky behind the old Kiley farm was a clear, even shade of deep-sky blue. Beyond the tree line, hidden by a badly weathered barn, steam from a nearby electric plant rose in a perfect vertical plume as though painted on canvas. The air was tranquil and quiet, each compass quadrant to the horizon.

A black, late-model, Lincoln Town Car broke the stillness as it sped down the gravel road leading to the house, its rear wheels slinging clumps of dirt-stained snow. Had any of the local residents passed by just now, the Town Car would draw notice and comments like, "They must be lost. We should stop and see if they can use some help." But the nearest home was a mile away and few cars traveled County Road 17 past the old Kiley place.

There were two men in the car, both in their mid-forties, each occupying the better portion of his side of the seat. The black car pulled to a stop at the bottom of the drive, the driver nervous about the three-hundred-foot expanse of open ground between the road and the house. These men were not Minnesota boys and an attempt to plow through fourteen inches of virgin snow in their rented Town Car a mile from the nearest sign of life in subzero temperatures would have been foolish. They were smart to finish their journey on foot, even if it meant water damage to their six-hundred-dollar suits and Bruno Magli shoes. At least they brought gloves and overcoats.

They exited simultaneously as the car stopped. The passenger waited until the driver circled around back and took the lead. They walked quickly up the hill through the deep snow, one behind the other, breathing hard and puffing small clouds of moisture. They stomped their feet on the wooden porch planks and exchanged a few words. Both men were huge, but the leader was shorter and stockier. He was the one that kicked in the door.

They knew their way around. The shorter one, always in the lead, leapt up the steps to the bedroom. The other followed like an obedient dog. Before the follower reached the top, the leader had made his way to the bedroom closet.

Mick was standing on an oval, brown woven rug with his back to the door when Jack entered. Both men stood for a moment and studied the room. Mick moved further in, reached deep into his pants pocket, and extracted a crumpled piece of paper. He studied it momentarily before opening the closet door.

Inside was a five-foot tall black safe, with a numbered dial halfway up the front on the left side. The name of the manufacturer was written with gold-embossed lettering that formed an arch over a red and yellow painting of a railroad steam engine; it read SOUTHERN PACIFIC SAFE CO. Underneath the locomotive was the name of the city where it was made and the year. Louisville, Kentucky, 1937.

The men knew the safe would be there and that it held an extremely valuable item that they were sent to retrieve.

Jack grinned. "Well, there it is."

"Very astute, Jack, now let me concentrate and we'll get this thing open and get out of here."

"Right, Mick," Jack said, wishing he'd kept his mouth shut.

Mick shook his head and stared at his partner with contempt. He had decided long before leaving the previous morning that he didn't like Jack Esposito and he wouldn't pretend that he did.

Jack grinned.

Mick turned back toward the closet. Holding the piece of paper in his left hand, he smoothed the wrinkles out with a huge thumb and index finger. He read the numbers out loud, then spun the dial several times and stopped on the first number. After entering the second set of digits, he forgot both the next number in the sequence, and whether he should go through the number once or stop on the first pass. Normally his memory was faultless, but the importance of what he was about to do, combined with the taxing ten-hour drive with his mentally deficient partner, strained his thinking. The safe was expensive and the movement tricky.

"Damn," he snorted, and spun the dial again.

Jack observed intently.

The second attempt was identical to the first. Jack wasn't the sort of person to remain silent for very long. After watching Mick rotate the black dial several times, he was itching to speak.

"You want me to give it a try?"

Mick tried hard to maintain his composure. He was a rough individual who had lived on the extreme end of immorality his entire life. He had killed a number of men and held no remorse, even for his worst sins. His value to Tony Bennetti was his ability to intimidate anyone and carry out physical restitution however and whenever directed. He was extremely intelligent and controlled, a professional and experienced criminal. But now he was being tested and his contempt for Jack was building. He turned his body just enough to look fully at his partner.

Jack's nervousness showed. He knew he had spoken without thinking. He tried to apologize. "Mick . . . I . . . "

Too late.

Jack could see the veins bulging in Mick's neck. He looked like a bull that had been stabbed several times by a taunting matador.

"Jack," Mick said slowly and deliberately, "you would be doing yourself a favor if you didn't say anything. Don't open your mouth again."

Jack was smart enough to realize when he was in trouble. He was aware of his shortcomings, especially in the area of verbal communication. He always meant well, but his mouth generally engaged a few minutes before his brain. On this particular occasion, his brain never got involved.

On the next try the expensive mechanism fell into the correct position with a muffled click. Mick lifted the release and slowly pulled open the heavy door. Inside were several shelves holding a few stacks of envelopes and loose papers. On the floor of the safe sat the small steel box they had come for. Mick's left hand slid into his suit pocket and exchanged the crumpled paper with a shiny brass key. He lowered himself to one knee in front of the safe and used the key to open the metal box. Inside was a toggle switch. Mick clicked it to a different position before unplugging a power cord from the side of the case. He gingerly removed the box and placed it on the bed.

The two men's expressions changed as they studied the maze of electronic components on the inside. It was apparent that it was unique. There were several rows of small red lights, some of which were flashing, and circuit boards that looked like CPU peripheral cards. Black and red power supply wires connected an internal battery to a built-in charger.

Mick smiled, forgetting about his anger toward Jack. He had completed the first and most important part of the assignment. The rest would be easy. He grinned at Jack who was somewhat comforted and decided it safe to speak. "Does it look okay, Mick?"

"Yes, it looks okay."

Jack looked at the cord, which remained plugged into the wall. "Mick, do we need to bring the cord along?"

"No, Jack. Take a look at it. How do you expect to pull it through the hole?"

Jack took a second look. The hole that had been drilled for the cord was just big enough to feed the wire through the side of the safe. The fittings on each end were much too large to pass through the hole.

"I see what you mean. How did they get it through the hole to start with?" Jack asked.

"Look, we don't have all day for me to stand here and go over every detail with you. Look at the end that was plugged into the ACU. It comes apart, but we're not going to fool with it. We've got one just like it in the car. It's tucked down in the bottom of the cooler. You ready to get out of here?"

"Sure, Mick."

Mick had been only superficially told about the purpose of the box and how it worked. He remembered hearing about the test last September at the Arizona ranch. He wasn't sure how the device would be used, but he knew it was extremely significant. Mick Mallory was feeling important. He was aware of its potential and knew the implications were monumental. He was also aware that Mr. Bennetti had negotiated a use for the apparatus that would make Mick richer than he had ever dreamed. He knew that for the next eighteen hours he would be in control of a device that could change world events, and that if he failed, he would be lucky to survive the week.

"That's the cord we'll use to charge it when we get to Madison?"

"That's right. Like I told you coming out here, we have to make sure the internal batteries don't go dead. There's a built-in battery charger. All we have to do is plug it in when we get to the hotel in Madison, leave it plugged in for six hours, then finish the last couple of hours into Chicago."

"Sure wished I would have gotten in on the meeting you had with Tony. I would really like to know what this thing is."

"The less you know the better. Just don't dick with it. It's sensitive to radio signals. That's why we're not flying. If it got messed with in the air, who knows what might happen."

"No shit?"

"No shit."

CHAPTER 4

FBI Regional Field Office
Minneapolis, Minnesota
07:55 Central Standard Time
February 1, 2007

Agent Dave Blake passed the empty office cubicles and opened the glass door to his private lair a few minutes earlier than normal, hoping to get a jump on the day's events. Yet, he knew full well that the heap of manila folders tossed randomly across his cluttered desk would prevail. Today, his plan was to catch up on some of his paperwork and tidy up the office. He had started out other days with the same ambitious intention, but somehow his desk, and the entire office for that matter, never quite got organized. Cardboard boxes did get moved, but only to a different corner of the room. And the desk got cleaned once in a while but only for a few hours at best. He often started the day intending to clean up but invariably became distracted. Today was different. The place was a pit and he was determined to get organized, once and for all.

Carlson and Olsen were in the field investigating the big fish scam, as Carlson liked to call it. It had become a popular joke around the Bureau. Two trucks of sardines smuggled in across the Canadian border were somewhere in Blake's area and he wasn't exactly bubbling with excitement at having stolen fish as the top priority on his desk.

His work was becoming monotonous lately. The lack of activity in Minnesota wasn't helping his morale. At least his return to his home state allowed him to get back to his roots and enjoy the lakes during the summer. Even the harsh winters brought back childhood memories that helped to fill a void in his life.

The phone was ringing as he walked through the door at seven fifty-five in the morning. Thinking it was probably Lonnie Carlson or "Olie" Olsen checking in with an update on the investigation, he negotiated his way through the mess and picked up the receiver.

"Blake here."

The move to the smaller regional office in Minneapolis warranted adjustments that Dave still hadn't mastered. Managing incoming calls not relevant to his specific projects was at the top of his list of irritating distractions. A few official calls would come from FBI headquarters in D.C., or other law enforcement agencies during the week, but most calls to his office were from local residents who had somehow gotten his number. *This is probably just another home burglary or mailbox bashing that someone wants resolved,* he thought.

"Agent Blake, this is Steve Sergeant, County Sheriff down in Midland, Texas. Got time ta chat a bit?

"Sure, Sheriff, call me Dave. I just walked in the office. Let me excavate a bit here and find a pencil."

The sheriff spoke with a heavy Texas drawl and went on with a coolness that belied the serious nature of his call.

"Dave, glad I caught ya in yer office. You might not 'member, but we worked a case together a few years back, cupla killers, young buck 'bout seventeen, other feller 'bout twenty-five. They ended up down our way. We made 'em from a gas station camera. I think yer boys corner'd 'em down by Kingston."

"I remember."

Ennaway, sumthin' come up this morn'n. I know it's a tad early in the game but thought you might wanner git a jump on things."

"Lay it on me, Sheriff."

"Wull, we got a small motel down here, Casa De Grande, where those Empire Airline flight crews hole up on layovers. We had a cap'n disappear on us there last night."

"Uh huh."

"Don't even look like he stayed in his room. He was s'pose ta fly the morn'n flight to Dallas but was a no show an hanta bin seen since. Empire brass have bin a houndin' me all mornin'. I don't think he's in town. It looks a might fishy to me."

"How do I fit in there, Steve?"

"Wull, it just hap'ns he's one a yer hometown boys. I thought ya might wanner put one a yer men o'er ta his house, check it out. Ya know."

"Got an address for me?"

"Yep, I looked it up onna map. Seems like maybe a few hours drive for you, west-a Saint Cloud a bit. Close ta a place called Say-awk Centry."

"You mean Sauk Centre?"

"Yuh, I guess that's it. His address is 7919 County Road 17, Say-awk Centry."

"What's the captain's name?"

"Bob Kiley."

"Well, Sheriff, I owe you one."

"Ah'll keep that in mind. Good luck."

"Thanks again, I'll be in touch."

Detective Dave Blake was not unlike every other law enforcement officer in the country. If he received early information about a developing case, especially an interesting one like a kidnapped airline captain, he wasn't about to sit down and fill out a canned report to send back to Washington and waste a week to see what came back. Generally, Bureau involvement wouldn't begin until the local authorities had responded to a crime and requested support. Typically, there'd be confirmation that a Federal statute had been violated. Dave's instincts changed the rules in this case. He sensed that the information Sheriff Sergeant had offered was peculiar, and he considered it a request for assistance.

At any rate, Blake was more than curious, and he didn't intend to sit around the office and let an opportunity like this slip away. He grabbed a St. Cloud phone directory, his personal black book, and a power bank for his cell phone. He reached in his pocket for the gloves he had just placed there and headed back out the door, still not having unbuttoned his winter coat.

Detective Blake was more excited than he had been in months. His years of experience allowed him to extract details from the phone call that most detectives would have missed. He knew this was the real thing. This Kiley guy was either in trouble or causing trouble. Spring cleaning at the office would have to wait.

Interesting, Blake pondered, *how the Texas sheriff thought that something was fishy. How ironic. If he only knew what my big case was these days, he would have chosen a different adjective.*

CHAPTER 5

Tomlinson Financial Building
Chicago, Illinois
09:30 Central Standard Time
February 1, 2007

The entire twenty-second floor of the Tomlinson Financial Building on East 22nd Street in downtown Chicago was reserved for the exclusive use of Robert C. Bennetti, CEO of the Tomlinson Financial Group. Standing by the massive bronze tinted glass windows defining the north wall of the office, Robert Bennetti contemplated the lost opportunity to know his father. He thought about the early years growing up with his two older brothers and about the different paths each had taken in life.

Robert, the youngest, had become the unlikely leader of Tomlinson Financial Group through a unique serving of fate. His father, Vincent Bennetti, was a hardworking steelworker on New York's South side. He vowed, by working sixteen-hour days, six days a week, to eventually break loose the chains of labor in an unforgiving city and during an era with limited opportunities. Vincent Bennetti died of a heart attack at the age of thirty-six.

Robert's mother, Mary, raised the three boys in the city's worst conditions during the late nineteen-sixties. Robert, John, and Anthony were then seven, twelve, and fourteen respectively. Although Mary Bennetti was relentless in her devotion to raise her sons well, she was no match for the temptation of the streets. The boys were easily lured by the attraction of easy money. They knew no other life besides the run-down, two-room apartment and the constant threat of eviction.

The streets offered two possibilities. The two oldest brothers, John and Tony, took the obvious one. They started out in the usual manner, petty theft, burglary, grand larceny, and the standard assortment of minor felonies. They started life with obvious handicaps but were blessed by what their father unwittingly passed on, a natural charisma and a leadership ability that would prove invaluable in their rise to the top of the New York crime world.

John managed to survive his apprenticeship in criminal life avoiding incarceration. However, he was under constant surveillance by every legal agency within the state of New York. Tony was well into his twenties before he committed his first and last major mistake. He checked in at the Oneida State Penitentiary reception desk three days before his twenty-fifth birthday to serve fifteen to twenty for accessory to murder.

During those years in prison, Tony developed life-long bonds with many of his fellow inmates. He became a powerful authority with a reputation for producing legal documents that influenced trial arguments. Prepared by Robert Bennetti, these legal services were offered to chosen inmates, accumulating a loyal following of the state's most proficient felons.

One inmate in particular that had been assisted by the Bennetti team was Mick Mallory. Mick had served eighteen months of a twenty-year sentence for armed robbery. His trial was littered with unorthodox police tactics and questionable evidence gathering. Due to his extensive record, however, and inept legal representation, his fate was sealed before his attorney began opening arguments.

Mick's intelligence far surpassed his appearance. Early during his stay at Oneida State Penitentiary, he recognized that Tony Bennetti was indeed special. He fought hard for his approval. He eventually was accepted as a Bennetti underling. Tony learned of the circus that resulted in Mick's wrongful judgment and directly unleashed his brother's legal arsenal. Mick won an appeal and used his get out of jail free card to find lucrative work under John's wing on the outside.

While Tony served most of his twenty years upstate, John forged ahead, becoming one of the most powerful men in the city. Over a period of thirty-five years, John, now fifty-four, had cemented his position into New York's financial matrix. He was a fast learner and cashed in on his leadership qualities and dishonest money. Through the years, he accumulated legitimate businesses and important contacts. Eventually, his ties to the underground were obscured by his connections to city officials and corporate leaders. He sat on five boards and had holdings in eight major industries focused on construction, finance, and shipping. Tony extended John's business arm to his world at Oneida State Penitentiary. With Mick Mallory acting as liaison to the outside, Tony was able to tighten the screws of persuasion from his prison office, enabling John to establish a reputable identity among the city's aristocracy. Upon release from prison, Tony was charged with all business objectives requiring special resources, with Mick acting as his lieutenant.

The youngest Bennetti brother, Robert, opted for the road less traveled. He had a vision and the strength to stretch his God-given attributes beyond the streets of the city. He studied hard in school and excelled in every subject. His two older brothers saw the possibility for their sibling to escape to a better life. They made sure the wrong elements, their elements, stayed clear. After high school, Robert's near-perfect academic scores qualified him for Harvard Law

School under the auspices of a city excellence enrichment program designed for the specially gifted inner-city kids.

But acceptance was only a foot in the door and Robert still faced paying ninety percent of the tuition. By now, Tony and John had sizeable bank accounts scattered throughout the state and insisted on paying for every penny of his education. Robert graduated with honors, passed the bar on the first attempt, and at the request of his brother John was quickly drafted by Stanley, Hyde, Bingham and Essox.

Robert later became a senior partner at Bennetti, Richardson, Essox and Litenhyer, the most sought-after, and expensive legal firm in the city. Now, forty years after the death of his father, he was responsible for the Chicago division of the family empire under the title CEO, Tomlinson Financial Group.

Robert had achieved everything anyone could ever dream of in life. The three brothers had managed to maintain an undetectable bond. Robert was a genius at providing legal protection to John's assets with total anonymity. He specialized in the orchestration of perfectly engineered contracts and negotiations for the business. Things had gone well for the three gifted Bennetti brothers over the years. Their piracy had been elevated to the highest levels of sophistication, taking it beyond the reach of ordinary law enforcement agencies. Everything was going remarkably well.

Everything's wonderful, Robert Bennetti thought as he stood erect and tall, hands in his pockets, and deep in thought. He looked through the bronze tinted windows, twenty-two stories above the streets of the windy city. He was paralyzed in thought. *Why at this stage in my life have things become so complicated? No, everything is not wonderful. Everything is far from wonderful.*

CHAPTER 6

Tomlinson Financial Building
Chicago, Illinois
09:35 Central Standard Time
February 1, 2007

Within minutes Robert will meet with his brother, Tony, to discuss the developments of the past few months. Their years of manipulating company funds, disguising unreported assets, and applying egregious business tactics, finally has been unraveled by both the IRS and the FBI. The Internal Revenue Service was the first to apply pressure. During the past nine months Robert had exhausted every ounce of his legal talent to find a way out, but they had been at it too long. There was no denying the evidence soon to be revealed through current investigations. The FBI was also beginning to make its move and indictments were imminent.

Numerous options were available. They could fight the charges in the courts and, according to Robert, stood a good chance of delaying jail time for several years. Beyond that, the outlook was bleak. They could finalize the cash transfers to overseas accounts and flee the country. There was a considerable amount of money that could be preserved, in the neighborhood of twelve million. The brothers knew that wouldn't be enough.

Tony first approached John with his plan on July 17, 2006. Since then, there had been enormous pressure from the District Attorney who was petitioning for court-ordered inspections of the books. At first, John thought Tony's suggestion was ill-conceived. Tony persisted, and Robert was brought in for consultation. Several hours of discussion ended in an agreement that Tony's idea warranted further research. During the three weeks after the first meeting, John and Robert worked day and night to identify the players in the scheme. Nicholson, the electronics genius who flew for Empire Airlines, was brought in for lengthy meetings. Details were agreed upon and, unbelievably, the parts of what seemed like a viable stratagem came together.

On the morning of February 1, 2007, at 06:30 in Midland, Texas, the resolution began to unfold. Bob Kiley abandoned his flight and was headed south to the Mexican border with two million dollars in cash. Partial payment for his part in the installation of numerous Phantom Shutdown Devices in the tail sections of Empire aircraft. Mike Nicholson, the electronics genius, had been assigned to the rest of Captain Kiley's trip.

The small town of Midland provided a number of strategic benefits for the exchange. Midland's proximity to the Mexican border was most important. Additionally, the remote location all but ensured that no other Empire pilots, other than Nicholson, would be available to fill the captain's seat vacated by Kiley. Nicholson was assigned to finish the trip following Kiley's disappearance. Kiley provided the Bennettis with the exact location of the Activation Control Unit and the combination to his safe in Minnesota. The pick-up of Nicholson's invention by Mallory and Esposito in Sauk Centre was already complete, and the ACU was safely on the road toward Chicago. The plan was progressing perfectly.

For the first time in forty years, Robert was nervous about a contract. His thoughts were so intense he was mouthing the words. *It's up to me now to close this deal and get out. Get out of the business and get out of the country. This will be the end.*

A female voice interrupted the silence. "Your brother, Tony, to see you, Mr. Bennetti."

"Thank you, Carole, please send him in."

Tony entered the room flashing the broad set of teeth that had become his trademark. His many years behind bars had been devoted primarily to conducting business and developing relationships, but he had also dedicated at least an hour a day to physical fitness. He was in excellent condition, muscular and tanned. John and Robert, who had grown to enjoy the benefits of their labor, had become fashionably overweight.

Tony strode toward the glass wall and extended his hand.

"Morning, Robert."

"Hello, Tony, good to see you."

He wore nice Currutti slacks and decent-looking Florsheim Pisas, but he continued to favor t-shirts over collared dress shirts. He carried a Halliburton aluminum briefcase and fended the biting Chicago wind with a predictable black leather jacket. He rotated the hand, which held the briefcase, and glanced at a Presidential Edition Rolex.

"Sorry I'm a bit late. Someone's in my spot."

"Oh, I forgot. I let Brian Slater use your parking space. We have a lot to talk about. Have you eaten?"

Robert pointed to the long cherrywood conference table in the middle of the room, set with the company china. Plates of bacon, eggs, rolls, and fruit had been arranged for the meeting. Two coffee carafes, juice, and a pitcher of water. Water goblets had begun to dampen the white tablecloth.

They sat across from each other. Tony laid the aluminum briefcase on the table and opened it before sitting down.

"Where do you wanna start?"

"First tell me how the transfer went in Midland."

"Things went exactly as planned. Our associates met Kiley at the Midland motel around ten-thirty. No one saw him go to our room. Kiley's a flake, but he was holding out well. We counted the money twice and he was satisfied that the entire two million was there."

"Good."

"He expects the extra money for the additional units he installed."

Robert said, "He'll get it" and shook his head, "asshole."

Tony said, "Yeah, yeah. I told him. He wasn't worried."

Robert swirled two cubes of sugar in his coffee with a teaspoon, and said, "Arbari felt good about Nicholson's invention after the demonstration in Arizona. What'd he call those units in the car trunks? PSAs?

"PSDs. Nicholson called them Phantom Shutdown Devices."

"Right, the PSDs are in how many planes now?"

"Kiley says he was able to install eighty-seven, all total."

"Wew, that's a lot more than I thought he would manage. Good for him."

"His work was cheap."

"I would have offered double what he's getting," Robert said.

"Right. The extra twenty-seven units he installed increases the odds of bringing down additional planes," Tony added.

Robert said, "And each one after the first twenty, means our take increases substantially."

"Icing on the cake. I believe that when Nicholson activates the ACU from his plane tomorrow morning, we'll have better success than we first thought," Tony said.

"Let's hope."

Tony said, "I did quite a bit of research at Oneida on FCGs."

"FCG?"

"Yeah, Flux Compression Generator. Similar to Nicholson's PSDs. Russia has one which is generally considered the Mercedes of magnetic pulse generators. But it's bulky and not nearly as applicable for or purpose."

"Crazy. The guy is impressive."

"I'm just glad you and John agreed to perform the test."

"I think we were all shocked by how good it worked."

Tony said, "Well Nicholson's method of activating the shutdown devices with his ACU is like nothing else anywhere, from what I was able to find. His shutdown units, the PSDs, are small enough to use effectively and not draw attention. Nothing else like it anywhere. Using the ACU to remotely activate the PSDs is what makes his method unique."

Robert said, "Who would think that an invisible pulsating wave could be so destructive?"

"Interesting stuff, especially how it got discovered."

"Really?"

"Yeah, back in the fifties and sixties the government conducted tests on nuclear bombs. They sent one large nuclear warhead into space and detonated it over the Pacific. A lot of unexpected things happened."

"No kidding"

"Oh, yeah. They were lucky that they picked a location over the pacific, rather than the Nevada test site they normally used. There was major damage to electrical systems in the Hawaiian Islands, over 800 miles away."

Robert winced, "Good lord. If they had done that today, say over San Francisco or New York, with all the computer systems and internet... what a mess."

"No question. In Hawaii, the damage was nearly immediate. Just about everything electrical that was in operation failed, street lights, television, garage doors opened for no reason, circuit breakers popped. It was incredible. Shit, now we've got countries like China with special bombs designed just for that purpose. EMP bombs."

"And they have them now?"

"Have had them for a number of years. With the technology we have now, you can bet your ass it would be devastating."

Robert said, "Well Nicholson's little contraption will serve our purpose just fine. No one will know what happened."

Tony said, "They'll know what happened, but not how it happened."

"That's the key. After seeing it work in Arizona, I'm a believer. We just have to hope those two lumberheads get it here on time."

"Let's not revisit that. They're already on the way. It's done."

"I just wish we could have arranged to have had it here earlier."

"We all would have liked that, but you know Kiley. There wasn't any way we were going to get the ACU until he had his two million in his greedy little hands."

"Paranoid son of a bitch."

"Luckily, as one of the more senior pilots, he was able to pick the trip that laid over in Midland."

"Robert said, "That did work out nicely."

"It's going smoothly. Don't worry."

Robert said, "Nothing we can do. Did Empire assign Nicholson to the rest of flight?"

"I was just getting to that. Their co-pilot, Lawrence, notified their Operations people that Kiley was missing, as we knew he would. We had a man in the terminal watching the whole thing. Nicholson was ready to play his part and timed his entrance perfectly. They assigned him to the flight. Easy, no problems."

Tony reached for a roll and took a large bite. Robert waited for him to swallow.

Tony continued, "They left on time and will still be flying the same schedule through tomorrow. They've left Dallas by now, then Kansas City, St. Louis and on into O'Hare by five o'clock this afternoon."

"I don't know if Nicholson planned it, but the flight data recorders he changed out with PSDs were in a perfect place; really easy for Kiley to get to."

"Right, just next to the aft stairway. Nice enclosed private area behind the cabin door going to the stairs."

Tony added, "That's how D.B. Cooper made his exit."

"Oh?"

"Sure, you remember, the guy that bailed out the back of a 727 with a load of ransom money."

"Oh, yeah, those stairs will open in flight?"

"Not any more. They've since made sure they can't be opened unless the wheels are on the ground."

"Interesting."

"Anyway, the PSDs are located right next to the button that opens those stairs."

"Makes for a nice private area for Nicholson to go back and disconnect the one on his plane before he takes off tomorrow."

Tony chuckled, "Don't want him to bring down his own plane."

"This just might work out."

"He and Nicholson were smart using Kiley's status as Safety Manager to access the planes during his aircraft inspections. Making the PSDs an exact copy of the flight data recorders was brilliant."

"You have to hand it to Nicholson."

"Smart guy, but I hope he holds it together."

Tony said, "He'll be fine. His hatred for the airline has him driven. I get the impression he can't wait to start with this. What was that software they stole from him?"

Robert answered, "I guess he wrote a program that determined route schedules based on a number of algorithms. Really complicated...I guess. He told me it would have saved Empire millions of dollars a year. He planned on selling it to other airlines."

"Can Empire just take it? I mean legally?"

"It's called a pre-invention assignment. All these big companies hide it somewhere in the employment contracts."

Tony said, "That's a load of crap. I'm sure no one reads those things. Might be legal but if I were Nicholson, I'd be pissed too." He removed the napkin from his lap and wiped his mouth. "Well, too bad about Nicholson but fortunate for us."

"I have to say, I was skeptical about all this at first but I think this Nicholson guy is our ticket out."

Tony gripped the napkin with his index finger pointing in the air to emphasize what he was about to say. He rose and began to pace. "Remember, you have to make sure Nicholson initially activates the ACU only momentarily. He must keep the first wave of failures to a minimum. We'll lose our leverage with Arbari if we get too many planes on the ground before our initial payment is received. Nicholson has to make sure he receives his signal from your guy in the back that the money's been received before continuing."

"Uh huh."

"The timing is critical. Everyone must do their job. Who's that in the back again?"

"Short Eddie."

"Right...your guys still using those nicknames? We're not the Mafia, you know."

"Old habits. I know it's going out of fashion in our business, but I think those nicknames serve a purpose. It allows some of the boys to build an identity. Reputation is important to them. I think they want to be remembered. A legacy."

"I guess I've been away from it too long."

"Do you think you would ever forget Tony "The Ant" Spilotto, "Ha-Ha" Attanasio, "Golf Bag" Hunt, or Joseph "Joey The Clown" Lombardo?"

"How could anyone forget those guys. But you're right, it's those names. Golf Bag Hunt carried machine guns along with some handguns in his golf bag. What a character."

"No one messed with those guys."

"You're right, I think if you had Louie Ha-Ha Attanasio look at you sideways, it would swell your balls a little."

"There you go."

"Was this important?"

"Nope."

Robert selected a wooden toothpick from a leaded glass holder and fitted it between closed lips. He said, "You're sure Eddie is clear on his part?"

"We've had three trial sessions with him this week. He knows his part is critical to the operation. He'll call us from the back of the plane just after takeoff."

Robert interrupted, "We are certain about having good communication with Eddie?"

Tony nodded and answered, "We've held trials on Empire flights, and his cell should work fine while near Chicago. Empire still has Airphones available in first class. I feel good about being able to communicate with Eddie."

Robert responded, "Okay, as long as you're sure."

"I'm sure" Tony took a sip from his cup and continued. "When Nicholson is ready, he'll activate the ACU and make the coded PA announcement to the cabin to let Eddie know the device was enabled. He'll use the words expected turbulence in a cabin announcement. When Eddie hears those words, he'll call us and let us know Nicholson has started. Our boys will be monitoring the emergency frequencies for "mayday" calls. Nicholson will turn off the ACU after fifteen seconds and wait for Eddie to check with us. After five minutes, he'll go to the back for some type of inspection or use the restroom. Eddie will give him the go or no-go signal. If no planes were affected on the first shot, he'll go back and try again but this time for 30 seconds. We expect Flight 867, which should be in the air just behind Nicholson, to be one of the first to go in."

"Sounds like we've got the bases covered. Can you think of anything else?"

"Not right now. It'll take years for the country to recover."

"Excellent. Nice job. Now here are the three Empire tickets for Flight 867 out of Chicago tomorrow morning, the first plane that should go in. You know what to do with them. Will there be a problem?"

"It's taken care of."

"You know our futures depend on this."

"Everything's in order. The three parties are lined up. This is the perfect plan." He grinned. "Hand me some of that bacon, will ya?"

CHAPTER 7

Empire Flight 808
12,000 Feet Over Texas
10:15 Central Standard Time
February 1, 2007

The Empire 727 climbed out smoothly and silently through the opaque overcast, like a great blue whale ascending from the depths of the sea. The passengers were going about their business in the back of the plane, unaware that the pilots up front were guiding the craft with no visual reference to the outside world.

What an incredible way to make a living, I thought, as we soared through the white mass of water droplets on our climb to altitude. There had been no turbulence, icing, or note-worthy weather reported between Dallas and Kansas City today, only the sedate layer of stratus clouds on the back side of the weak occluded front we were penetrating. Breaking into the clear at 12,000 feet, the view of miles and miles of perfectly flat cloud tops was breathtaking. The instant we punched into the open, the un-ending layer of white looked as though we could land the plane and walk on its surface. It seemed like we had leapt through a Rod Sterling time warp and ended up on a planet encased in cotton. I was still taken by the eternal beauty of the sky, even after accumulating over two thousand hours of flight time.

The small molded earpiece tucked inconspicuously in the right side of my head crackled as Departure Control directed us. "Empire eight-oh-eight, climb and maintain flight level three-three-oh, direct Mercer. Contact Denver Center, one-two-seven point seven. Over."

Nicholson responded casually. "Cleared, three-three-oh, direct Mercer, Denver on one-two-seven-seven. Eight-oh-eight, Wilco."

He switched to the new assigned frequency while Ted dialed in the course to Mercer Intersection and started his turn.

"How does it look for higher, Mac?" Ted was asking if we were light enough to climb higher than 33,000 feet.

"Too soon, Ted. Three-three-oh is good for now, won't be long though."

I had just finished calculating our weight to determine the best cruise altitude. Taking the plane as high as the engines would allow based on total aircraft weight usually proved to be the most efficient, depending on other factors such as winds and temperature.

"What's your background?" Nicholson said, finally getting around to some conversation.

We had been too busy with the short turn-around in Dallas to socialize. Mike had gone into the terminal to try and find out more about what had happened to Kiley, Ted had gotten the cockpit ready, and I had taken a quick look at things on the outside. I managed to squeeze in a few minutes to check on the cabin crew in the back, hoping to get a few minutes with Claire. I only managed a quick, "How's it going?" as she helped prepare for another full plane.

I was encouraged by her response.

"Wish I had more time, Mac. Buy you a coke when we get settled down?"

"I accept. We may run into some bumpy weather closer to KC. You might want to get things done early. See ya," I replied.

"Thanks, we'll do that."

She smiled and I was disappointed we were so rushed on this trip. She's been fun, and I caught myself hoping we would wind up working together a lot more in the future.

I watched her check out the back section of the plane. Empire's uniform was a beige, calf-length skirt, and a blouse with long sleeves made from a lightweight, silky material that flattered her lithe figure. The thin fabric of her skirt danced in rhythm with her wavy hair when she walked. Everyone seemed to pick up on her contagious energy. I wondered what sort of things she enjoyed, and what I should suggest if the opportunity arose to ask her out. I think it would be best to forget the French.

Replying to Nicholson's question about my background, I answered. "Attended college at St. Cloud State University, same as Kiley. Spent six years in the Navy. Tower Officer at Norfolk, and almost three years instructing at Pensacola. Got out and collected all my tickets through ATP and was lucky to get two interviews. I thought I did well with Delta but missed the cut for some reason. Then Empire called about three weeks later. Back then, things were moving fast. Two weeks of systems in the classroom, about five rides in the simulator, a line check, and off to Minneapolis."

"I was in the Air Force; F-105's in Vietnam, Electrical Engineering degree from MIT," he said.

"Impressive."

"Well, we're all on equal footing up here, Mac, so to speak."

I shifted my scan from the view out the windows to the altimeter. Ted tickled the trim button with his left thumb, easing the yoke forward to position the nose on the horizon, stopping our ascent. The aircraft changed configuration so smoothly the passengers were unaware of the transition. I examined the instruments while we accelerated to cruise speed, then reached between the two pilots and eased back on the throttles. Ted engaged the autopilot and lowered his hand from the yoke as the airspeed stabilized.

"If it's okay with you two, I think I'll go stretch my legs. Can I bring back some coffee or anything?" I asked.

"Thanks, Mac. I could use some coffee. Black," Mike said.

Ted indicated he didn't need anything. I unbuckled my seatbelt, looked at my panel, and checked the gauges up front one last time. The airspeed had stabilized, and the 100-foot altimeter pointer locked at twelve o'clock. Ted was settled back in his seat enjoying the view, and Mike was inserting updates into his Jepsen manual. Out the front windshield, where the sky and earth converged at about one o'clock, a group of young cumulus clouds were expanding rapidly, trying to become thunderstorms. Probably eighty miles away, they indicated an unstable air mass that could mean changing weather ahead. I removed my earpiece and left the cockpit.

Karen and Julie were standing in the front galley talking as I entered the cabin. "Looks like you've got them sedated. What's in that coffee?"

"It's early, Mac. Give them a while. Do you guys need anything?"

"A couple coffees if you don't mind. I'm going to walk through the back for a bit. Is everything okay up here? How's the temperature?"

"Everything's fine, Mac, I'll make a fresh pot."

Turning toward the rear of the plane, the first thing I noticed was the lack of empty seats.

A couple of individuals appeared to be comfortably napping, others reading or talking to their neighbor. Reaching the back of first class, I pulled the curtain aside and entered the coach section to face a more chaotic picture. The small seats crammed together gave me the impression that there were more people per square foot back here, and there were. But it was way too obvious. The tight configuration made things less comfortable for the passengers and caused them to squirm and look for relief. A few folks had risen to go toward the back of the plane, either to stretch their legs or stand in line for the rest room. Both flight attendants in the back were busier than the senior attendants up front. Erin, just in front of me, was handing a cola to a young boy at a window seat. She looked up as I eased by.

"Howdy, Mac. How's the new captain working out?" Her twangy southern accent was a nice change. *Do they go to square dances on Saturday night in Georgia?* I wondered.

"He seems like a decent guy, great landing in Dallas. Air Force background though, but hey, what can you do? Everything okay back here?"

"You bet. Michael here is going to be a pilot. Think you could take him up front for a peek?"

The young boy appeared to be traveling alone and stared up at me with hopeful eyes. He was neatly dressed and sported a wide grin. He looked to be well-mannered and was very attentive to our conversation. Thin blond hair. A Jay

North look-a-like.

I said, "Hi ya, Michael. Are you going on into St. Louis with us today?"

"Yes sir, then to Chicago."

"Tell you what. When we land in Kansas City, we'll have more time. You can come up front, sit in the pilot's seat, and push a few buttons. How's that?"

"Neat! Thanks."

Sounds like him too. I hope Dennis The Menace isn't locked inside somewhere.

I continued my stroll, trying not to step on any feet, to where I could get a good view of the wings without making any of the passengers nervous. It was unlikely I would notice anything abnormal but, having experienced a loose leading-edge slat about a year ago, I now pay more attention to the parts of the plane I can see through the windows. I used care not to appear as though I'm looking for anything in particular. Passengers tend to get nervous when a pilot leans across the seats, seemingly concerned about the plane's wing. Like maybe it might come loose or something.

Claire was opening a drink for a sailor wearing dress blues who was standing near the aft galley. I noticed him and two other new recruits board the plane back in Dallas. Each wore well-pressed new uniforms with two diagonal, neon-green stripes on the left sleeves. I started out in the navy with the same two green stripes. It seemed like yesterday.

The sailor looked to be about eighteen and watched Claire intently. A little too intently. Her shoulder-length, light brown hair was pulled up in a style that flattered her long neck. Her sleeves were slid back above the elbows. She adjusted a white company apron. She was neither country wholesome nor big-city gorgeous, but she had her own unique look that appealed to me. Her face brightened, and her eyes widened as the gap closed between us.

"Captain Mac. Who's flying this thing?"

"Hi, Claire, I hope I didn't come all the way back here to see you, only to be maligned."

"You know better than that. If I weren't so enamored by that sharp uniform, I wouldn't tease you so much."

"Now you are worrying me. They treating you okay?"

"Wonderful. I've got the best spot in the house. If there's a problem, I can just open the back door here and make my getaway."

"If I feel a breeze up front, I'll know you left."

"Have you found out anything about Captain Kiley?"

"'fraid not. Maybe by now they've located him. I feel badly about the way we've connected, or rather not connected, lately. He's just so abrasive. Maybe there's things we don't know."

"You shouldn't feel bad. It seems like you're the only one who's been on his side. He's been an ass to everyone. I don't know how you've kept your composure. I hope he's okay, though," she said.

"I'm sure he's all right. I'll let you know if we hear anything. Please don't make any unscheduled exits back here, we're just getting to know each other. Besides, those open doors are hard on fuel consumption."

It was obvious that she was busy assisting the passengers. I would have enjoyed continuing the conversation and collecting my soda but I decided to wait for a more favorable time.

"I should check back up front. There's an Air Force pilot at the controls," I said.

"A drink to go?" she asked, smiling.

"You're busy, how about a rain check?"

"Okay. If you decide to collect, I'll be back here in my office."

We looked at each other a bit longer than necessary before I turned and headed back. I felt she had opened up a little and I wanted to tell her I liked the apron look but decided on a more restrained approach. Passing Erin on my way back, I got a look that I translated as, *"Any luck with Claire, Mac?"*

Maybe it was my imagination.

The plane buffeted and I wondered if the mild turbulence was an advance warning of the growing storm cells I saw out front earlier.

CHAPTER 8

FBI Headquarters
Washington, DC.
11:25 Eastern Standard Time
February 1, 2007

With his name, Bob Capone could have been the most harassed FBI agent in town, were it not for his notoriously strong presence that intimidated not only the criminals he arrested but his associates and family members as well. He had blunt, rugged features, with a fighter's nose flanked by penetrating, cavernous eyes. His menacing appearance became an asset when questioning suspects or informants. Seldom did he need to ask twice for things from anyone. He was focused and was precise in using only the words he needed. He avoided idle conversation and when he spoke, he usually had something important to impart. Bob Capone didn't attend social functions and had no time for extra-curricular activities or hobbies. He worked fourteen-hour days and spent his almost non-existent free time relaxing at home with his wife, Janet. His one child, a son, worked as a college professor in Connecticut. Capone, as he was usually referred, was a hard man to reason with, but he was sharp, both in street sense and technical expertise. He also possessed an intuitive talent that had become his trademark, and which made him one of the most effective investigative agents in Washington.

Today was no exception. Bob Capone entered his boss's office on the sixth floor of the Hoover Building and waited for a cue. His superior, J.R. Connelly, looked up from his neatly arranged desk. "Please, Bob, have a seat. I've got something I want you to work on."

"But J.R.," Capone protested as he eased into the chair, "I'm making progress with the Davis thing. Maybe another few days and we can start working on depositions. I don't think I can juggle a new project."

This was a small white lie, as the Davis case had run out of steam. Capone was fishing for a reason to stall a few more days, hoping that something would break, and he wouldn't have to admit defeat on a two-year-old kidnapping case.

"I just want you to help Dave Blake out in Minneapolis. He called in this morning with something interesting. I need someone good."

"Oh no, J. R., I'm not going to help him find a bunch of sardines."

Connelly smiled, "No ..."

"Hell, send out a few of our custom's dogs.

They'll be able to sniff out those fish before I could pack my bags."

"Bob, it's not the fish thing. This is something else."

"Okay, I'll bite, what's up?"

"Bob, Dave called this morning. Apparently one of his moles, as he put it, informed him about a missing Empire Airlines captain. He thinks it's foul play. I called Empire about twenty minutes ago. They know about the disappearance but are totally in the dark otherwise."

"The guy just vanished? Just up and disappeared?"

"No one's seen or heard from him. They haven't found any close family yet who might know something. The county sheriff is looking into it. I want you to contact him, then call Blake in Minnesota. He's on his way to the captain's house north of Minneapolis. A small town called Sauk Centre. I've made you a copy of my notes."

"Hmm."

He handed Capone the sheet of paper. "Here."

Capone took a minute to review the known information Connelly had gathered. "Wild."

Connelly said, "By the way, all these times are Central. Dave should be halfway to the captain's house by now. He may find nothing. He may find a wife or girlfriend. He may find a suicide note, or he may find the place burnt to the ground, I've no idea. But Dave felt he should get started on something, and I agree. When this breaks, the locals will be all over it."

"You left out the possibility he might be sitting in a bar drunk."

Connelly said, "I hope that's not it. Dave Blake is good man. I'm hoping he'll have some answers after visiting the captain's house."

"Couldn't find a better investigator. Let's hope he doesn't find anything disturbing."

"We'll know soon," Connelly said, "Airline pilots, they're a bunch of goofballs anyway. I've got one for a son-in-law."

Capone smiled, "Yeah?"

Connelly replied, "Grab someone to help. I would like as much information as possible right away. Can we meet after lunch?"

Capone responded while standing to leave. "Better get started then."

He passed through the double door into the outer office. Marion looked up and said, "He keeping you busy?"

"Looks that way. Nice Flowers."

"It's my birthday."

"Happy birthday."

Entering the long hallway to the west wing, Capone began mentally compiling a list that he planned to jot down as soon as he reached his desk. His first task was to contact the sheriff in Midland. Several questions immediately came to mind. Were there motel guests who might have witnessed anything unusual last night or might even be involved somehow? The room would have to be sealed immediately and a team would have to wring it out as soon as Dave Blake made sure there was nothing at the Kiley place to explain the disappearance. That would be the trigger to start the clock. Background checks of all crewmembers and flight attendants would have to be made. Personal records, such as bank accounts and credit reports, would be combed. Car rental records in Midland should also be checked immediately and rental agents inter- viewed. They would have to get Kiley's photo. Motels in town would be queried along with relatives and friends. Dave Blake was already nearing the first priority—Kiley's house.

Capone was thinking, we don't want to jump the gun, but every minute that passes can mean lost opportunity.

He was just getting started but he'd been through this drill a hundred times and got better progressively. Not only did he know the Bureau's guidelines by heart, but he had taught them at the training center in Quantico.

Capone occupied one of the larger offices in the new headquarters building on Pennsylvania Avenue in the heart of the nation's capitol. Lo- cated on the sixth floor at the far west end of the building, his office was one of the few with a decent view. The south exposure allowed short sections of the Potomac to periodically peek from behind buildings and monuments as it snaked through the city. He could monitor tourist activities from the West Potomac Park to the Capitol Building. Near the door, his tan Burberry coat hung neatly on a wood coat tree along with his Dobbs, Black Anton hat. There was a large L-shaped desk, certificates on the wall, bookcase, and metal file cabinet. Nothing fancy.

Capone had slid into the computer age with ease. During the last eight years. His already exceptional work was bolstered by the electronic speed and accuracy germane to new software tools, providing instant access to information about any subject and nearly any individual. But he continued to take meticulous notes during meetings and telephone conversations, using a yellow legal pad and a #2 wood pencil.

Capone reached for the legal pad in the center of his desk while snatching a pencil from the collection in the coffee cup next to the phone. He scribbled on the pad and pressed the speed dial button on his phone labeled, JIM.

"What's up, Bob?"

"Connelly just put the Davis case on hold temporarily. He wants me to help Dave Blake with some problems back in Minnesota."

Jim responded under his breath, "Oh oh."

"Blake has run into something that Connelly wants us to help him with. If this turns out to be what it appears, Connelly will probably assign someone permanently. I would like it to be us.

Can you come right up?"

"Bob, this isn't that tuna fish deal, is it?"

"That's funny. I asked Connelly the same thing, but it's not tuna, it's sardines. No, slightly more interesting. Grab a pot of coffee on the way in, will ya?"

"On my way."

Within minutes, a tall FBI agent, á la Cosmo Kramer, lumbered into Capone's office. He held a pot of coffee and an FBI souvenir mug in one hand and a notepad in the other. Size thirteen loafers advertised his entrance.

Capone looked up from his desk. "Great, Jim, that was quick. Thanks for the coffee. Let's move next door to the conference room."

Capone grabbed his notes and an empty FBI mug. The two moved to the adjacent office.

"I'm actually glad you called. I've been about ready to toss in the towel on the Davis thing. I hope this one involves people who can fog a mirror," Jim said.

"Everyone's still alive, as far as I know. Got a pen? We'll be moving fast."

"Let 'er rip."

Capone started at the top of the bulleted list that Connelly had given him only minutes earlier, then turned to the items he had detailed since leaving the Director's office. He continued to add to the list as he talked. Capone had long ago tossed out any thought of using standard procedures. He was drawing from the hip and improvising his plan as he spoke. When he finished, he asked for Jim's input. In fifteen minutes they had compiled a list of concerns to be addressed. They prioritized the list into three groups:

1) Immediate needs to be initiated as soon as they finished their meeting.

2) Urgent needs that would require accountability assignments by the end of the day, with deadlines established.

3) Items that would need attention and would be discussed later in the day.

"Jim, I think we need to talk to the sheriff in Midland first off."

"Uh uh."

"He may have some new information, maybe something he already knows that we don't. Maybe he can get started on some of these other items for us before our men get there from Corpus. I want you to work on that. Find him and make sure he tapes off the rooms. Someone down there knows where Kiley is."

"We need a photo of Kiley."

"Right. Empire should have one on file. Put someone on the crewmembers. I want to know where each one had their wisdom teeth pulled."

"What do we budget this to, Bob?"

"I'll get an account set up. Talk to Betty on your way out. She'll give you some numbers to use in the meantime. I'll work with Blake out in Minnesota. He should be at the house any

minute. What he finds there may change everything. I'll get our guys in Corpus Christi headed
toward Midland. I want you to keep your phone
on. Check back here if you find out anything
interesting. Otherwise we meet at one o'clock."

"Ouch."

"Connelly wanted information by the time
his lunch digests."

"Quit talking then, there's not much time.
I'll be back at one."

As Jim stood to leave, Bob's mind shifted
into overdrive. His instincts finally kicked in to
allow him to realize what it was that had been
bothering him since his talk with Connelly.

"Hang on, Jim," he said, checking his tall
partner at the doorway. He paused to consider
what to say.

A few moments of silence passed.

"Listen, Jim, when you find that sheriff, make
sure he puts tape across all the flight crew doors.
But also find out where Nicholson, the new captain, spent the night. Get a picture of him to pass
around. Ten to one he was in the same motel,
maybe even using a different name. I could be
wrong on this one, but when you find the room
he stayed in, even if it was somewhere else in
Midland, don't let anyone in it but our boys.
Then give it the full treatment, just like Kiley's
room."

Jim was aware that not only were the rumors
of his friend's uncanny intuition well-founded,

but they might also be underestimated. Jim knew his partner was on to something and he would just have to wait it out.

"You got it, see you at one," Jim said as he left the room.

Bob Capone flipped his notepad to a new page and wrote down several questions, leaving empty spaces in between. Referring to Connelly's notes, he wrote down the phone numbers for the Kiley farm and Dave Blake's cellular.

He decided to try Blake's number first.

CHAPTER 9

Minnesota-Wisconsin Border
11:15 Central Standard Time
February 1, 2007

"We've been driving for almost three hours, Mick. There's bound to be a McDonald's on the other side of the river. What say we make a pit stop?" Jack whined.

Mick was driving the Town Car and had calmed down considerably since the episode back at the farmhouse. He was beginning to warm up to Jack and regretted being bothered by Jack's remarks. The ACU was in the back seat, packed like a vial of nitroglycerine. Tony had demanded that Mick use a soft-sided Coleman cooler to place it in. Foam rubber was packed between the box and the inside of the cooler to mitigate damage if the unit were dropped or, God forbid, there was a car accident. In a few more hours, he would be paid generously for successfully carrying out his assignment. Mick wasn't about to let Jack ruin it for him.

"Sure, Jack. We can stop over in Wisconsin. We'll fill up, grab a coupla Egg McMuffins. You can drive for a while."

"Thanks. I'll buy."

The two had worked together previously but had never been friendly. Mick believed that Jack wasn't smart enough for the type of work Tony required. He disagreed with Tony's decision to include Jack on this assignment.

Jack, on the other hand, had been around New York for years. He had come to know most of the established crime figures, as well as many law enforcement officials. He was more capable than his looks and actions suggested. He had worked his way up the ranks the hard way performing virtually every type of crime specialty. He was, however, uneducated and clumsy.

His saving grace lay in two areas. First, he was unquestionably loyal. At one point, a pawnbroker involved in a money-laundering scheme with a well-established smuggling gang had been picked up by the NYPD. To avoid jail time, the man provided names to the authorities. One was Jack Esposito's, the young delivery man. Jack was pulled in and questioned at length. The police and FBI weren't interested in Jack, but they wanted the suppliers. They pressed Jack for names. Jack refused to talk. Rather than rat on his associates, he opted for a five-year sentence, getting out in two for good behavior. The story of Jack's loyalty to his employer, even to the point of going to prison, spread through the streets. The prison leadership council had heard of his commendable performance and waived the normal period of bullying and harassment that most new inmates were subjected to. He was immediately accepted into the lower level of prison hierarchy. He went on to reinforce the impressive reputation that had preceded him. He provided unyielding devotion to the governing crime figures within the prison population. It was then that the Bennetti organization first contacted him.

Second, odd as it seemed, he was consistently reliable. Despite his mental slowness, he was determined and cautious. He was aware of his own deficiencies and was relentless in avoiding screw-ups. He double and triple checked everything. Simply put, he was dependable.

Mick was aware of all this but nonetheless found it difficult to accept Jack. Although he was rough around the edges and had a face that belonged on a jungle beast, Mick was intelligent and charismatic. Tony Bennetti and the other associates held him in high regard.

Mick had the connections and the cunning to set himself up in business, but he was content working for the Bennettis and had no desire to break away. Even though he disagreed with the decision to send Jack along, he had decided to make it work. He even had begun to see some potential in the clumsy felon sitting next to him. The Town Car's close quarters during the last few days may have been what was needed. Jack was starting to feel better about Mick, too.

Mick drove the speed limit and was alert to the other traffic on the highway as they traveled eastward out of St. Paul. The high-rises were behind them in the distance and the view out the side windows revealed snow-covered fields, and northern pines and hardwoods. Small shopping centers and isolated businesses periodically peppered service roads where only ten or fifteen years prior, cornfields and silos dominated.

Far ahead, a structure appeared to sprout from the flat Minnesota landscape where the road met the sky. It gradually grew taller as the distance closed. The huge galvanized structure swallowed the vehicle as it traveled between tall vertical supports, which held back two-inch thick tethering cables. The supports rose skyward as they passed the window, and shrank incrementally to the size of a pencil at the Wisconsin side of the river.

Jack craned his neck looking upward in awe. To him, it looked like framework made by Goliath using a king-size erector set. He wondered what had kept the structure from dropping into the deep canyon below as it had been assembled. He experienced the same thoughts when driving across the St. Croix bridge in the opposite direction two days earlier.

Jack's mind was full of questions about the bridge. Had the builders started at each end and met in the middle? If so, how were the ends supported until they were joined together? Or, had they started on one side and worked their way across to the other? Again, he wondered, *what held it up until they got to the other side?* Each of these visualizations involved large helicopters with long cables holding up the unsupported pieces. He wished he had been born with, "more of a better brain." Maybe he would have been a bridge builder.

He had to know how it had been done and said, "Mick, how do you suppose they got this bridge across this wide river? You think maybe they put it together down there at the bottom? Maybe they used floats where it crossed the river to hold it up? Then maybe jacked it up onto the posts?"

He peered hopefully at Mick, looking for re-assurance.

Mick knew Jack didn't have a clue. "Jack, they don't use floats and they don't use jacks. These things are built by civil engineers who've studied the strengthening properties of geometric relationships, combined with steel alloys that provide the right combinations for the design and for the climate. They use techniques that were refined by the Romans, Greeks, and Egyptians. Understand?"

Like Jack, Mick didn't know how the bridge was built across the wide ravine, but he didn't want Jack to know he didn't know. He knew that his response would provoke no more questions about bridge building. *Why doesn't he ask me about muzzle velocities or bullet speed verses size regarding knock-down power?* Mick thought.

"I guess so," Jack said, becoming mesmerized by a sprinkling of tiny, feathery flakes that had started to assault the windshield but never quite made contact before being swept off to one side or the other by the seventy-mile an hour wind.

He scanned the edges of the highway for a tall pole supporting the familiar golden arches.

CHAPTER 10

The Kiley Farm
Sauk Centre, Minnesota
11:20 Central Standard Time
February 1, 2007

The forest-green and beige Toyota 4Runner pulled to a stop just behind where Mick and Jack's black Town Car had parked three hours earlier. Dave Blake was already making mental notes as he unbuckled his seat belt. The front seat of the car looked a lot like the office he occupied in Minneapolis. Two days' worth of mail rested on the dashboard behind the steering wheel. Unanswered letters were stuck behind the passenger visor, and sunglasses occupied the same space on the driver's side. Next to him on the seat lay the St. Cloud Yellow Pages, a cell-phone powerpack, an empty Wendy's bag, and a bag of Doritos. On the passenger side floorboard sat a white Jack Daniel's liquor box that provided storage for his office supplies. The back seat was similarly organized.

Dave reached into the box and fished for a new composition book from a stack of ten or twelve, and a mechanical pencil from an assortment loosely strewn about the bottom. He used the pencil to fill in the letters K-I-L-E-Y in the white rectangle title area on the composition book. He opened booklet and wrote the time, the address of the Kiley farm, and a short summary of what had caused him to be here. He skipped two lines and started to record the visual he surveyed through the car glass.

Dave took photos of two well-preserved sets of footprints leading to the front porch and of the vehicle's solidly packed tire tracks. The front door to the house was ajar. Notwithstanding the evidence of recent activity, there was no indication the house was occupied, at least not since the last heavy snow, which Dave recalled had been three days prior. He mentally calculated the exact day and date and recorded them in the composition book. There were no car tracks in the driveway or other disturbed snow around the house, except the tracks leading across the front yard to where the intruders had parked their vehicle. All the curtains were pulled. Dave surmised that the heavy accumulation of snow on the roof denoted the house hadn't been recently heated. Or perhaps, the old house was insulated better than most homes of the same vintage.

Dave surveyed the landscape, hoping to find a nearby farmhouse where someone might have observed the recent activity. The nearest residence was about three-quarters of a mile away to the west. It was unlikely there would be witnesses. The road had been traveled but not plowed since the light snow three days earlier. One wide lane showed where most of the vehicles, traveling in both directions, tended to stay in order to get the best traction. Near the shoulders, the snow was less disturbed, except where the car had pulled over and parked at the bottom of the drive. Two persons had exited the car and walked to the house. Similar groupings of tracks identified the return trip to the road.

His notes filled the first page. He numbered the second page and started with a date and reference just as he had on the first. He wrote quickly and scrawled with a shorthand that any physician would be proud of.

He didn't worry about the deep snow or the 4Runner's capabilities to cut through it, but he elected to walk. His years of experience taught him many lessons that were now part of his nature, even when off duty. He had pulled up short of where the others had parked so he could examine the area carefully, without disturbing things. He knew that when people enter or leave an automobile, they tend to discard items such as cigarette butts, chewing gum wrappers, receipts, or a legion of interesting items.

Once, near an area where a suspect's car had been reportedly parked, Dave had discovered a small chip of hard plastic. The investigation had become snarled when the accused couldn't be placed at the scene. Dave's piece of plastic had turned out to be a chip from inside the suspect's car. The perp had apparently been sitting in his vehicle, nervously picking at a loose piece of dashboard, and had pulled it apart, tossing it out the window with his fingerprints on it. Dave was already well-known for his fastidious searches and detailed reports, but the plastic dashboard chip anchored his investigative genius into the Bureau's short list of recognized specialists.

Dave removed his print kit from the box on the floor before opening the car door. He stepped out into the stiff northern wind, glancing toward the overcast sky, and recognized signs of a pending storm. The sky, which had been a blinding blue only three hours ago on his way to work, now was overcast and filled with puffy clouds of varying shades of gray. Dave watched the interesting way they swirled in one direction while traveling in another – faster moving dark ones overtaking the lighter ones above, and a few renegades that seemed to be moving against the flow. *Amazing how fast the weather can roll in up here,* he thought.

His experienced eye found nothing around the area where the car had been parked. He was aware of the fortunate timing because soon, everything outside would be covered with snow. Had that been the case before his arrival, Dave would have agonized over what clues might have been found.

He took measurements and several pictures of the car tracks, and then walked to the porch, inspecting the areas around the suspicious footprints on the way. The wooden planks, partially protected from the weather by the porch roof, were covered by a thinner layer of snow that enabled Dave to spot two pairs of shoe prints. They appeared to be large size dress shoes. One heel mark bore a distinctive design. He took measurements and photos.

He nudged the door open with the back of his hand and stepped cautiously into the entry. There was heat in the house, but the open door had allowed the frigid Minnesota air to subdue the deficient gas furnace that was silently groaning in the background. Dave bent down and placed his fingers on a scattering of water droplets on the oak flooring near the first step leading upstairs. He looked across the shiny wooden surface toward the living room and kitchen. He could see no additional evidence of the intruders. *They went straight upstairs*, he thought.

Dave followed the trail of the two trespassers into the upstairs bedroom, as though being pulled by a string. He stopped halfway through the door to assess the overall picture. His attention was drawn to the open safe inside the closet. Experience restrained him from rushing directly to the vault. Instead, he began a routine search of the room from the doorway to ensure he didn't overlook something.

Starting to his left, his eyes slowly moved, taking in every detail. His observations were only preliminary. The investigative team would dig deeper using extraordinary techniques that would uncover clues not discernable by human senses. Dave had to make sure there wasn't something missed that could help J.R. Connelly close the gap. A gap that was growing by the minute as the offenders fled the area.

Dave noted the safe and its contents, the disturbed bedspread, the position of the light switch, which was on, the position of the room and closet doors, the pulled drapes, and the fold in the oval braided rug. *There isn't much here*, he thought, *except for the safe*.

He stepped into the room and got down on his knees to take a closer look. There were a few drops of moisture similar to those downstairs. He found nothing unusual under the bed or behind the door. The braided rug looked dry but was moist to the touch where the two men had stood. After donning a pair of latex gloves and photographing the entire room and the vaults interior, he removed the contents and laid them out on the bed, keeping the order intact. He scrutinized every item and noted points of interest in his book. Then, just as tentatively as he removed them, he returned the papers to the shelves in the same order he found them.

A hole had been drilled at the bottom of

the safe. Sharp metal filings on the floor indicated that the modification had been done in the closet, probably by Kiley, and probably quite recently. An electric cord passed through the hole and was plugged into a nearby wall socket. The other end lay forlornly on the floor of the safe. It had an unusual female fitting of a type Dave didn't recognize.

He took two more photographs and dusted the safe and doorknob for prints. Finding a few excellent specimens, he was satisfied that time was of the essence and that the prints would have some significance. Dave Blake was proud of himself for reacting quickly to the sheriff's call. Another agent without Dave's concern for exacting methods might have waited and missed the opportunity that time could provide, or take away.

Dave was certain that the critical area was the bedroom, particularly the safe, but he nevertheless performed a thorough search of the entire house. He was careful to adhere to the rules of law. The open door with the splintered section of wood that left the deadbolt dangling provided unquestionable probable cause to proceed. The homeowner was officially reported missing, and there was positive evidence of criminal activity at the house. There might have been victims inside, maybe critically injured, or worse, dead. His justification for conducting the search was reasonable. He had sufficient probable cause to isolate the house as a crime scene and cordon the area to seal it off. Which he did.

He returned to the 4Runner and started the engine. While the engine warmed, Dave sat uncomfortably, his breath creating a fog on the glass. On a new page in the composition book he listed the items he would focus on during his report to Connelly. His mind was racing and he felt excited for the first time in months.

The 4Runner accelerated away from the Kiley farm. Dave Blake pulled his right glove off with his teeth, grabbed his cell phone, and located Capone's number.

CHAPTER 11

FBI Headquarters
Washington, D.C.
13:04 Eastern Standard Time
February 1, 2007

Bob Capone rotated his powerful neck as he had done during pre-game warm-ups forty years ago at high school football practice. Stretching out shoulder muscles cramped from long hours at the desk, he pushed away from the neatly stacked manila folders and groaned like a waking crocodile. Capone had worked nonstop since leaving J.R. Connelly two hours ago. His head was starting to throb from the lunch he hadn't eaten and from the frustration of not accomplishing anything worthwhile. He had the most complete and sophisticated network of investigative tools in the world at his fingertips, but so far, he was striking out.

"Need a break?" Jim asked. It had been nearly twenty minutes since Jim had brought the results of his research, and the two had just completed a cursory review of the sketchy files. There wasn't a whole lot of encouraging information. Dave Blake hadn't called back in from Minnesota with an update on what he had found in Sauk Centre.

"No, I think we should stay with it. I had hoped to find something here, but these Empire crewmembers are pretty boring folks. I believe you're right in that we should go back to each of their colleges. The fact that McIntyre and Kiley attended the same school is a little coincidental but separated by too many years to be of any significance. Check there anyway. Call Fresno State for Lawrence. Nicholson's school, MIT, isn't too far away up in Cambridge. Give them a call. Better yet, snatch someone from downstairs, call ahead to Boston, and see if we can get someone up there today. We should be able to use one of the helicopters.

"Already working on that Bob, but it's doubtful we'll find anything there," Jim said with obvious pessimism. "I sent Webster, you know, the young kid from California, to see what he could dig up. He's probably there by now.

"Webster's the only one you could find? He's pretty green."

"Yeah, I know. He was all I could dig up. But you know he's a bright kid, little geeky maybe, but they say he's a dynamo."

"I heard. Big degree from UCLA and did pretty good at Quantico. He's eager. If there's anything to find, he'll probably dig it up."

Jim hadn't been able to gather much infor-

mation in the short time since leaving Connelly's office. He had initiated military file
transfers on the three pilots and talked with
Sheriff Sergeant. The personnel manager at Empire was sending files out, and the Provost at MIT
had offered to help. Little significant information could be retrieved immediately from the
vast electronic research network at headquarters.

The review of Jim Everett's research was sur-
prisingly non-productive. There was little to go
on. The parties identified so far had no criminal records, and the FBI computer network
wasn't finding any histories. They had, however,
started a lot of wheels in motion.

The phone rang. Capone snapped up and
plucked the receiver from its cradle. "Bob Capone."

"Bob, this is Dave Blake, out in Minnesota."

"Dave, how are you making out?"

"We've got a situation, Bob. I'm in the car
headed to St. Cloud. I wanted to brief you on the
major points. I know you need to meet with Connelly."

"Right. I'm late now. Give me the meaty stuff.
I'll call you back when we get organized."

Dave Blake began his report, sticking to the
items he felt were important, but struggling to
not include every detail.

"I arrived at the Kiley farm in Sauk Center
at eleven-twenty, twelve-twenty your time. A

light snow was beginning to dust the area. There had been recent activity, probably a few hours before I arrived. A car had been parked at the street. Two sets of tracks led up to the house. The vehicle's wheelbase was about 117 inches. I'll send photos of the tread design. Try and get me some possibilities on the car. I'll have the boys check with the gas stations to see if anyone remembers two, large out-of-town boys. Probably nicely dressed. Maybe they stopped for gas up here or made a call. If you get me a car style, it'd help. I also found some shoe prints. Both pair look like dress shoes. They measured thirteen and a half inches. Someone solid kicked in the door. The side panel was ripped off and the lock-set busted clean away."

Dave Blake didn't come up for air as he continued his review of the crime scene. "Droplets of water in the entryway where they brought snow in. They went straight upstairs. Knew where they were going. They had the combination to a large safe in the bedroom. It was left wide open. Again, the floor was damp from the snow. Something curious, a hole had been drilled at the base of the safe, metal filings still on the floor. An extension cord, with a funny fitting on the end, was fed through the hole. The other end still plugged into the wall. I'm sending photos. The undisturbed snow tells me no one's been there during the last three days, except these two. Nothing else in the house."

"Jeez"

"Bob, we are right behind these guys. I've got some good fingerprints. I'll go into St. Cloud and get the local guys to let me use their equipment and work with our people on checking out the house. I'll produce negatives of the fingerprints, upload the photos, and type up a quick report. I'll e-mail everything out to you from St. Cloud. You'll have it in two or three hours. Get me something to work on from my end. I need the names and photos of these guys. Let me know what kind of car they're in. I have to interview the locals before the end of the day while this is fresh. What else?"

"Damn, Dave, you're good! Will you marry me?"

"Can you cook?"

"Sorry, that might be a problem."

" Listen, I'll run with this. Get me that e-mail. We'll ID these guys. I'm heading out to talk with Connelly. Thanks a lot."

"One more thing, Bob."

"What's that?"

"Ask your boys to ease up on the sardine thing. At first the fish jokes were funny, but the e-mail is tying up my mornings."

"Sorry, I'll work on it. By the way, are you about ready to reel that bunch in so we can put 'em in the can?"

"Thanks."

"Sorry. Couldn't resist. Phone in your St.

Cloud number to my secretary when you get there. Her name is Betty. I'll call you as soon as I can."

Bob Capone returned the receiver to its holder and looked up. "Jim, I believe we may be handing the Davis case to someone downstairs permanently."

"Really?"

"Dave has lived up to his reputation. Two guys broke into the captain's house in Sauk Centre and took something from a big safe in the closet. This thing is alive now and I believe Connelly will give it to us. The bad guys left us a few gifts to work with."

"All right. Tell me more."

"Whoever broke into the place has only about three or four hours on us, so there's a slim chance we can close the gap if we work fast. Let's get this stuff down to Connelly. I'll fill you in as we walk."

Still talking, they entered the large anteroom to Connelly's office and approached Marion's desk.

She looked up from her work as they approached. "It's the boys of the hour, must be something going on. Thanks for the flowers, Jim."

"My pleasure. Pretty things for a pretty thing."

"You're dangerous," She said coyly.

Jim winked.

"He's expecting you two. Go on in."

Going through the doorway, Capone uttered, "You're disgraceful."

J.R. Connelly was standing in the center of his large office as the two walked in. He acknowledged the junior agent first. "Come in. Hi, Jim." The two shook hands. Releasing Everett's vise-like grip, he turned to Capone and the three walked to a small conference table near the window.

"Let's get started," Connelly said, pointing to the chairs.

Capone opened the briefcase on his lap and removed the stack of files he had assembled with Jim's help. "J.R., Jim's been busy and so has Blake out in Minnesota. We've definitely got a problem unfolding."

"Afraid of that."

Capone continued, "I'd like to spend more time here and examine everything in detail, but there is some urgency, so if we can move along with that in mind, I think it would be prudent."

"Fine, Bob. You've got the ball. Hit the highlights and we'll sit down for a maneuvering session later today."

"You might want to tape this," Capone said, as he watched Connelly prepare to take notes. "We've got quite a bit already, and I think it may be wise to move through this as quickly as possible. If, after we've discussed what we have at this point, and if you agree, we may want to escalate and expedite our efforts. We'll provide you with a complete report as soon as we can squeeze it in".

Connelly set up a Sony recorder on the table and Capone started his report. "I enlisted Jim's help in the interest of time, not knowing what we were dealing with a few hours ago. I haven't begun an official investigation yet, but we have more than enough reason to start one. I presume that will happen immediately after this discussion. You'll have to let Jim and me know if you want us to stay on this or not."

"Keep going," Connelly said.

"First, let's go over the more significant findings that Dave relayed to me only a few minutes ago."

Capone related Dave Blake's entire phone report, stressing the importance of the ticking clock. "We have about two hours before Dave sends us something concrete that we can use."

"Good."

"I believe we can get a general idea of the car type, and with some luck, faces to go with the fingerprints. We'll get Tom Gerrard to match the tire treads and wheelbase to some possible models. I'd like to get all this back to Dave within a couple hours so he can interview as many people as he can in Sauk Centre. Today if possible. If the car's still on the road, we might be able to intercept it.

Connelly reclined in his high-back chair and

listened intently. With every word he became more intrigued.

Capone occasionally referred to his notes but maintained a seamless delivery as he summarized the morning's findings. His gravelly voice was low and even as he segued into the situation in Texas. "Jim finally contacted the sheriff in Midland who had only sealed off the captain's motel room and not bothered with the other crew members. The sheriff questioned a few of the people there and has his force canvassing the car rental places and motels."

Connelly leaned forward, "Go on."

"Jim called our men in Corpus and they're on the way with a complete team. He also had the sheriff go back and cordon off all the crew-member rooms. The sheriff's putting together the entire guest list for us. I talked with Empire and I'm getting the crewmember files, particularly a photo of Kiley for the sheriff to use. He should have it by now. He'll try to find someone in Midland who's seen him. Dave Blake is putting a team on the Kiley house. His men are heading up to the area to help canvass. If we match the prints and can get photos for Dave, we might get lucky."

Connelly asked, "What about the cord in the safe, and whatever it was they removed?"

"Don't have a clue right now."

"This is all much more than I expected. You, Jim, and Dave have done a great job. I want you two to work on this and give Dave whatever support he needs. Activate a file and set up an account. Dave knows what to do in Minnesota, and I know you and Jim can handle this end. Just keep me informed. I want to know immediately if you ID the prints. Treat this as high priority for now. Let's talk before I leave today. Five o'clock okay?"

"We'll be back at five."

CHAPTER 12

There was more weather than we anticipated coming into Kansas City, but it hadn't
yet turned into the real serious stuff. Strategic
vectoring brought us through the thick wall of
rain with a minimum of turbulence. This part
of the country can be a nightmare in the summer months, with colossal thunderstorms ex-
tending over forty thousand feet, developing
wind shears and updrafts that can easily rip a
large commercial airliner into twisted chunks
of sheet metal. Fortunately, the present conditions were not so severe. Nevertheless, the ride
was bumpy.

I've become accustomed to expecting the
perfectly synchronized maneuvering of inbound aircraft by the controllers guaranteeing
safe separation. The radar specialists accepted
the challenge as routine and calmly guided us
into position while providing pinpoint headings between the perilous balls of wind. Usually,

this fusion of skills between controller and pilot occurs without notice. Today, for some reason, the specialist working us had abnormally heavy traffic, and Captain Nicholson, who was working the radios this leg, delivered his requests and acknowledgements with exceptionally succinct, well-phrased transmissions. All the while, Ted executed flawless heading and altitude control. I had been busy figuring best-range cruise speed based on our current weight in case we had to enter holding to wait out the storm. During all this, we had been completing the lengthy landing checklist and reporting to operations our updated ETA and maintenance requests. This was great flying and was the payoff for years of difficult training and personal sacrifices.

Ted piloted the jet expertly throughout the ILS approach, breaking out of a three-hundred-foot ceiling, dead perfect on the runway's extended centerline. As we glided over the numbers, Ted eased back on the throttles and flared smoothly to slow the descent. Moments later, the main gear squeaked timidly and accepted the weight of the plane with little indication that we had transitioned from air to ground travel. None of the passengers in the back were aware of the remarkable synergy of man and machine that had taken place during the approach. The complexity of the aircraft, the air traffic control system, and the piloting skills that must mesh during every second of every flight continues to amaze me. I still marvel that air travel remains the safest way to get around.

Several hundred feet farther down the runway, after the nose wheel joined the others on the deck, Ted applied the reversers, making it immediately apparent to everyone we had reached Kansas City. Ground Control accepted us as their responsibility, and we were directed to the gate without delay. The Jetway was in position immediately, and I reached up and turned the seat belt and no-smoking sign off. Unfortunately, the FAA hadn't passed a law to fine passengers that get up early, and the race had started several minutes prior. By this time, half the passengers were jammed into the first-class section, inducing a new-found closeness as they pressed uncomfortably against one another, waiting for the front exit to be opened.

We had a forty-five-minute break this leg before heading back out with the same aircraft to St. Louis. I decided to stay with the plane and get things ready for departure. I had second thoughts about offering the young boy at the window seat a tour of the cockpit. Not that I don't like kids, but another day would be better. This would have been a good time to build on the promising start with Claire. There wouldn't be much time in St. Louis with the quick turnaround, and she said she had a date tonight in Chicago. I wondered who she knew there.

"Halfway home, guys," Nicholson said to Ted

and me as we unbuckled.

Ted looked back in my direction. "Those bag meals are getting pretty lame, Mac. Want something from the deli?"

"No, thanks, I'm fine," I replied, as I stood and tucked my shirt in. I had gotten the St. Louis and Chicago weather from our operations people while taxiing to the gate. Knowing the other two hadn't had an opportunity to check the forecast, I filled them in. "Looks like we have more of this stuff ahead. Heavy rain and some thunderstorms around St. Louis. They're reporting three miles and twelve-hundred-foot ceilings; it's snowing in Chicago, two miles and overcast at three-thousand, gusting to forty-five."

"Thanks, Mac. We'll have to keep an eye on that. My brother is picking me up at O'Hare tonight. Hope he doesn't get snowed in," Nicholson said.

"This trip should work out nicely for you then, Mike. I mean, having a last-minute layover in the same town where your brother lives. Been long since you've seen him?"

"We don't get together much," he said flatly.

We exited the plane as a group. I was anxious to hear what they had found out about Kiley and imagined all sorts of ridiculous things, but nothing came to mind that seemed plausible. I completed the exterior inspection and went back to the cockpit to try and get ahead with the checklists before inviting the young pilot "wanna be" up front.

As I monitored the Air Terminal Information Service through my earpiece and recorded the weather conditions, the cockpit door opened behind me.

"Hey, Mac. Got time for some training?"

I recognized Claire's cheerful voice immediately and turned to see her and the young boy from the window seat. "Well, hello, Michael. I see you've managed to pick up the prettiest girl on the plane. You'll have to teach me some of your secrets later. Come on in."

Claire said, "Sure you've got time?"

"Sure."

I got up from my seat, allowing the boy to advance farther into the tight space. "Go ahead and sit up here in one of the pilots' seats," I said, pointing to Ted's seat on the right side. I moved the armrest so he could climb in.

"Hi, Claire, I see you've met Michael."

"Erin introduced us. She was going to bring him up herself but got tied up. So, since the poor guy is obviously suffering from some sort of common-sense deficiency and thinks he wants to be a pilot—terribly sad thing—I felt I should act as his guardian. I'm afraid you might feed him some line about the sacrifices you pilots have to make, and the long years of high-octane training you must endure on the road to aviation greatness in the big leagues."

"Claire, your mind has obviously been contaminated by someone impersonating an aviator. Most of us are humble, hard-working, decent guys, whose only purpose is to please our passengers and fellow crewmembers. In fact, it is so arduous we seldom have time to eat."

"Sure, Mac, sounds terrible. There's nothing worse than a whining pilot, so please spare us."

She turned to Michael with a devious grin and said, "Michael, do you know the difference between a pilot and a jet engine?"

Michael perked up, "No, tell me."

"Well, a jet engine usually stops whining soon after touchdown."

Michael laughed. "That was pretty good. Do you have another?"

Claire glanced my way, enjoying her momentary victory. I wanted to tell a joke I had heard about flight attendants but couldn't in front of the kid. I wouldn't have anyway because I felt I still had a chance with his escort.

"Sorry, Mac, we should be a team. You make a good straight man."

"Thanks. I'm not sure my ego can handle it."

Turning to Mike, I could see he was intrigued by all the gauges and switches. "How long have you wanted to be a pilot, Michael?"

"Ever since I was a little kid."

I had estimated the boy to be about twelve and wondered what age qualified as being a little kid. He seemed to be a well-adjusted and intelligent boy. I was thinking that someday, I would like to have a son. Maybe he'd want to be an aviator too.

"Well, you have to do well in school, and even then, there's a lot more work to it than you might think." I ignored a strategically timed snort from Claire. "What type of flying do you think you might want to do?"

"My uncle is an Air Force pilot. I want to fly F-16s."

Not wanting to demean his uncle or offend the young man, I refrained from educating him regarding the differences between people who wear the blue Air Force uniforms and fly planes, and highly skilled and professional naval aviators. He would surely receive this valuable instruction later in life.

"Excellent," I lied. "I'll bet you'll make a fine Air Force officer. Why don't you hold onto the yoke here, and I'll show you what happens if the plane experiences a stall."

Michael put both hands on the yoke, and I reached overhead and held back the stall warning test switch that caused the yoke to vibrate and a computerized voice to announce, "Stall, stall, stall, stall, stall."

"Neat. That's what happens if the plane stalls?"

"It's supposed to. I've never tested it in the air though." I added a few interesting facts about the Boeing 727. "This plane weighs about 200,000 pounds, is over half as long as a football field, and cruises at right around six hundred miles an hour. This was the first three-engine jet to fly as a commercial airliner."

Michael seemed interested in the statistics and asked me a few questions about the various panels. I allowed him to play with some of the switches and listen to the tower on Ted's head-set for a couple minutes. Turning to Claire, I noticed she seemed to be enjoying Michael's enthusiasm.

"Do you have any brothers?" I asked her.

"No, just me. But I have lots of cousins, a couple about Michael's age. He's having a lot of fun. Thanks for showing him around."

Claire's love of children was obvious. She'd make a great mother someday. I was about to take this opportunity while she was serious and seemingly relaxed, to ask her out. Then she reached out to touch Michael on the shoulder.

"We should get you back to your seat, fly-boy, and let Buck Rogers here wind up the springs on this flying machine."

She looked at me with the same wide smile. It was working pretty well. *Maybe in St. Louis*, I thought.

CHAPTER 13

The Tomlinson Financial Building
Chicago, Illinois
13:15 Central Standard Time
February 1, 2007

Nearly four hours had passed since Robert Bennetti discussed the most recent developments with his brother, Tony. Robert had completed all the preparations for leaving the country with his brothers. All that was left was to try and not allow any mistakes during the next twenty-four hours. *This will be a busy night*, he thought, as he reached for the phone and dialed John's New York number.

"Hi John, got a few minutes?"

"Sure. I guess you've met with Tony. Sorry I couldn't make it. Tying up loose ends. Everything on track at your end?"

Robert said, "Yeah, pretty much. Tony said the payment to Kiley went well. He's probably in Mexico by now. Nicholson was assigned to Kiley's flight."

John asked, "Those two goons get the ACU?"

"Yeah, they should be well on their way to

Madison."

"You mean Chicago."

"No, remember, they're stopping in Madison to charge the ACU."

"That's right, six hours, then on into Chicago. Do you have rooms for us?"

Robert said, "Yeah. Everything is set up. Seven rooms at the Hyatt. You, me, Tony, Short Eddie, Nicholson, Mick and Jack. Have you talked with Arbari?

"Long talk this morning."

Robert continued, "Did you confirm that he has the initial twenty-five million? Is there any question that we will be able to move it once the first ten planes go down?

John said, "I've done all I can to lock that in. Arbari gave me access to look at the account. It's there. All I can do is look at it right now."

"How about the rest?"

"I'm reasonably sure we'll get that too. The money isn't that much to him. He wants total devastation. He'll pay. I think we'll end up with a number of additional planes. He'll like that."

Robert said, "Did you tell him that Kiley was able to install 27 more units?"

John said, "That really helped. Arbari was definitely excited about those extra PSDs. He's more than happy to pay an extra hundred grand for every plane after the first twenty."

Robert said, "I think that could be on the low end."

"Right, but as soon as that number twenty hits terra firma, we should be able to confirm the final payment. If we don't have it right away, we can stop Nicholson until we do have it.

"No problem with that"

Robert added, "I bought three tickets. One in your name, one in Tony's, and one in mine. Three of my men will use them to impersonate us."

John asked, "They've got IDs and suitcases with our stuff."

"Yeah. They think we're using them as a red herring while we flee the county."

"They'll be on 867, departing right behind Nicholson?"

"Right, should be the first plane to crash."

"That was genius on your part. We should be able to assume new identities in Rio without worrying about the Feds."

CHAPTER 14

Black River Falls, Wisconsin
13:20 Central Standard Time
February 1, 2007

The black Town Car was now mostly white as it traveled through heavy snow during the last two hours. Nickel-sized flakes smacked relentlessly against the windshield and the wipers beat monotonously, maintaining just enough visibility between strokes to provide Mick with an adequate view of the Nissan Quest three-hundred yards ahead.

"Mick, do you want me to drive for a while?"

"No, Jack, I'm doing fine. The road isn't too slick. Fortunately, we made good time up until about a half-hour ago. If this gets any worse it might take us the rest of the night to get to Chicago. How far away is Madison from here?

"What was that last town we just passed?"

"Black River Falls."

Jack studied the map for over a minute. Looks like about a hundred and ten, a hundred twenty miles, Mick."

"Well, we should be able to hold forty miles-an-hour in this stuff. That would put us there in about three hours, I guess."

"Not bad."

Mick glanced at his watch. "Around four-twenty. Six hours of charging the ACU gets us back on the road by eleven this evening. We're only an hour behind schedule. No sweat."

"Hope we're not too late getting there."

"Tony said not to worry if we get behind, the main thing is to get the box to Nicholson before his flight in the morning."

Jack asked, "Should we call Tony to give him an update?"

"I'll call Tony when we get to the motel."

"One good thing," Jack observed, "there's not much traffic in this stuff."

"Right, but that doesn't make the driving much better. Every time one of those damn semis goes whizzing by, I'm blinded for about thirty seconds. When we get to Tomah, we'll pull over and get a snack. You can drive."

"Sure, Mick, I could use something to eat," Jack responded as he stared at the windshield, mesmerized by the swirling flakes jitterbugging on the glass. He was wondering if every single one of them were actually entirely different. *Surely, out of the billions of snowflakes out there, a few would be the same*, he thought, *or at least damn close. What would qualify them as being different anyway, some almost undetectable difference in the diameter or width, even though maybe the pattern was exactly the same? On the other hand, if the guidelines weren't so strict, then certainly there had to be a few of those flakes that were close enough alike to be considered the same.*

Jack believed he had discovered a flaw in the age-old phenomenon regarding the uniqueness of snowflakes. He thought it noteworthy enough to bounce off Mick for some input.

He turned away from the view outside to look at Mick, who was concentrating on the road, alternating his focus between the Nissan Quest in front of him and the road behind. For the last two or three minutes he had closely tracked a truck that was closing the gap from the fast lane. The white Quest, still a few hundred yards ahead, helped maintain a nice set of tracks for Mick to follow.

Jack studied Mick's face. He had a huge head, but then not only his head was huge, everything about him was big—big ears, big hands, big lips, and big, long, bushy eyebrows. Biggest of all was Mick's off-centered, bulbous nose, which had been broken numerous times. Jack wondered if, with all the money they would make on this assignment, Mick might get some plastic surgery. He briefly considered suggesting the idea to his new pal, then reconsidered. In fact, having spent the last thirty seconds or so studying the gangster's grotesque face, Jack decided not to ask about the snowflakes either.

The semi was advancing faster now, and the

turbulent sheets of blowing snow exploding from the base of its wheels made Mick nervous. He hadn't noticed that the driver of the Quest had slowed in preparation for the pending blast of wind, shrinking the distance between the two vehicles.

The driver of the 150,000-pound truck, filled with produce, was unaware of the developing combination of circumstances that were about to unfold. The accumulation of heavy snow in the left lane had not affected the handling of the eighteen-wheeler. In fact, the reduced traffic on I-94 this time of day was even a little relaxing to the fatigued driver. The truck's right front fender was now adjacent to the rear bumper of the Town Car. The road ahead was clear, and the trucker would soon be able to slide over in front of the Quest into the well-packed right-hand lane.

The young lady driving the minivan had her small child strapped into a car seat behind her. She continued to slow to better control the surge she knew the semi would generate as it passed. The distance between her and Mick became uncomfortably close, prompting him to tap his brakes just as the rear of the semi passed his front bumper. Mick's rising anxiety, combined with the loss of vision from the swirling snow, caused him to apply too much pressure to the car's hydraulics, momentarily locking the brakes. The Town Car swung quickly to the left, just missing the rear of the passing truck. Mick stayed calm and maintained control but over-corrected, bringing his vehicle too far to the right.

The young mother watched him in both her mirrors and began to panic. The huge wall of riveted sheet metal was now directly out her side window and the blowing snow was attacking from all directions. Wind from the fast-moving truck exaggerated the crisis, raising her level of stress.

The Town Car looked farther away in her rear-view mirror then it was, but it was rapidly approaching the back of her van. She hit the brakes hard, instinctively trying to slow the van's speed before the crash, which she was certain would occur. Her only concern at this instant was for her two-year-old boy nestled in his car seat in back. Her attempt to slow the van was well-meant but only aggravated the situation.

The van began to slide and rotate simultaneously sending its rear end sharply left toward the truck. The trucker wisely decelerated to avoid losing control of the big rig and continued to track straight ahead. The back of the van swung around fast into the side of the semi, momentarily hanging in the ripped sheet metal. The front continued around clockwise, picking up momentum.

The two autos were now only feet apart and closing uncontrollably. The final seconds were a blur. Mick saw the young woman's face as her vehicle twisted around toward him. Their eyes met, and Mick became aware of her torment.

Mick could hear her scream from the shape of her mouth, but there was no sound. There was no sound at all, even as the two cars spun out of control, first crashing into each other and then sandwiching the van between the Town Car and the truck. The young woman and the Town Car occupants were in shock. Their senses dulled— the assault on their flesh annulled by adrenaline. They felt no pain nor heard sounds as they entered a semi-conscious state that obscured the effects of the crash, and the agony that would have otherwise been unbearable.

The truck's huge mass served as a shield, limiting the damage to the large rig. The young driver continued to decelerate and ease toward the shoulder of the road. In his passenger side mirror, he watched the separation grow between his truck and the dancing autos behind. The Town Car spun ahead of the van, which was tumbling violently end over end, and hurling powdery clouds of snow in all directions.

Pulling to a stop off the right shoulder, the trucker took a final look in the mirror. The long black Lincoln was resting in the ditch, front end pointed back toward the highway. A spray of clumps and white mist exploded forty feet into the air and fell, forming a moonscape texture of mounds and craters where moments ago had been an unsoiled blanket of snow. The finer particles continued to drift earthward, even as the trucker looked back in disbelief.

The van wasn't as fortunate as the Town Car. It had rolled several times before coming to rest on its top, sixty feet behind. Everything became still.

The truck driver had begun reporting the accident on his CB while coasting to a stop. His transmission was acknowledged by a driver in the opposite lane, who had witnessed the accident and made a report to 911.

The trucker brought his rig to a stop and set the brake. He grabbed his jacket from the passenger seat and jumped out onto the road, near the shoulder. He searched the highway in both directions, hoping to find an approaching vehicle that might stop and offer help. Only one car was in sight on the other side of the median. The Quest rested inverted on its top several hundred yards beyond the back end of the truck, its rear wheels still turning.

The Town Car was hidden behind the large aluminum trailer but came into view as he jogged closer. His breathing quickened and the cold dry air burned deep into his lungs. Finally, he stopped where Mick and Jack had ridden out the last forty feet off the road, the burning in his chest becoming too painful to continue. Crouched, with his hands on his knees, he tried to catch his breath.

The car faced back toward the edge of the road where the trucker stood and studied the scene. He could see the driver inside, slumped over the wheel, motionless, but the passenger was moving. The pain in his chest subsided somewhat but his heart continued to pound unabated. Forcing himself to move ahead, he stepped off into the deep snow and crunched forward. He trudged awkwardly through the drift, slipped, and fell near the right headlight. He crawled the last few feet to the passenger side where Jack was trying to force open the damaged door.

The smell of gas fumes filled the air but neither Jack nor the trucker took notice. Without speaking, they timed their efforts to force open the door. They managed to enlarge the opening with each attempt—Jack pushing from the inside with his back propped against Mick's limp body, and the trucker using his left leg against the car. The heavy door finally snapped as the two forced the tightly crimped pieces apart, then a loud pop. It fell open.

Jack eased out through the tight opening. "I'm okay," he announced loudly. He had been involved in accidents before and knew that for several hours the shock would prevent his body from relaying the signals from bruised or broken bones. Fortunately, he had been wearing a seat belt. Although dazed, he was uninjured. Mick was unconscious with a severely lacerated face.

Jack thought that perhaps Mick would have a good plastic surgeon at the hospital who could put him back together better than he had been before the crash.

The truck driver continued to breathe hard and leaned against the open door while evaluating Jack's condition. He peered inside at Mick and quickly looked away. "Are you sure you're okay?" he asked Jack between breaths.

"Yeah," Jack replied. "My friend's hurt bad and needs an ambulance. Can you call one?"

"There's one on the way," the trucker said, bending down to take a second look at Mick. The skin was torn away from below Mick's right eye to his upper lip. Bone and cartilage were exposed, and blood dripped off his chin onto the steering wheel and seat. The trucker felt nauseous and turned away, unable to look at Mick's face for more than a few seconds. He remembered the other car and looked over the top of the Lincoln toward the wrecked Nissan.

"Could you check on those people?" Jack asked.

The trucker nodded, not wanting to deal with Mick's face. He turned quickly and worked his way back onto the highway where he started into a slow jog toward the up-ended Quest.

Jack managed to get the back door of the Town Car open. He reached inside and removed the Coleman cooler. Without turning back, he ran as fast as he could through the snow to the gravel road paralleling the highway.

The trucker found the occupants of the van alive. He spent the next ten minutes carefully extracting them from their seats. When he returned to the black Lincoln, he was surprised to find Jack gone. Strangely, there where footprints leading toward the tree line several hundred feet away.

The sound of sirens echoed off the snow-covered landscape, and within minutes the Tacomah fire-and-rescue team arrived on the scene.

A quarter mile in the distance, Jack stood alongside the one lane road just off I-94. There were no buildings or cars in sight, except for a white truck coming toward him. With no winter jacket or gloves, he looked strangely out of place to the young couple in the Ford F-150. He also looked harmless and cold. They pulled to a stop after passing him and backed up to offer him a lift.

Jack set the cooler in the bed of the truck and climbed in front next to the young girl.

CHAPTER 15

Bob Capone looked up at the government-issue clock above the door to his office, he wondered where the day had gone. He hadn't stopped to eat lunch. In fact, he hadn't even thought about it. Picking up the phone, he glanced at his notes one last time before dialing.

Connelly picked up at his end. "Connelly."

"J.R., you said if we ID'd the prints from Minnesota you wanted to hear about it. We have two solid matches and a bit more, if you've got some time."

Connelly said, "If you think it's important, I'll make time. The door's open."

"On my way."

Capone returned the receiver to the cradle, grabbed his notebook, and started to reach for a worn yellow pencil in the center of the desk, paused, then opted instead for a new one from the full cup next to the phone. The carefully sharpened #2 pencils had become a tradition over the years to the extent that Betty kept boxes of them on hand. She routinely replaced any dull ones in the cup with fresh replacements each morning.

There was something permanent and dependable about the yellow pencils that Capone liked. They were a perfect design for their intended purpose. Capone had heard the story about the son of a ship captain who created the first "Dixon" pencil over two hundred years ago. He knew there were very few things that survived that long without falling to a better design. Capone tried hard to emulate the wood pencils. They were dependable, functional, and had lasting power. He wanted people to see those qualities in him. The yellow pencils reminded him to stay focused on things that mattered. Betty knew the yellow pencil story.

He carried one in his free hand and walked through the open doorway to Betty's vestibule. She looked up attentively as he entered. She expected the usual short briefing of where he could be reached, but instead he continued toward the outer hallway, gave her a quick glance, and said, "Be right back."

He walked hurriedly down the dimly lit corridor and wondered if maybe he had overreacted to the new information assimilated during the previous hour. He'd been right about his feelings so many times, but it was those rare errors in judgment that kept him awake at night, agonizing over a mistake.

Marion looked up from her desk and smiled as he circumvented the normal protocol and continued directly through the wide double door to J.R. Connelly's office.

"Have a seat, Bob. I'm anxious to hear this."

Capone was aware that he was slightly out of breath from the walk. "J.R., things are moving fast. I've never seen the ducks line up so quickly. I'm nervous just the same. There are a few things that don't add up and I'm afraid this may be bigger than we thought."

Capone continued without pausing, making it difficult for Connelly to interrupt.

He spoke without reference to his notes, and said, "At first I was sure we were dealing with the theft of the item in the safe and that Kiley was probably dead. Then I thought Kiley had gotten hold of something valuable that he wasn't supposed to have, sold it, and skipped to Mexico. Then I thought maybe he was blackmailing someone, the deal went sour, and he's at the bottom of a river with a pocket full of rocks.

J.R. found a break, "You don't believe any of that."

"No, I've got a funny feeling, and even though we've got oil all over the canvas, I'm not sure there's a clear picture yet."

"What kind of feeling, Bob? I trust your instincts on these things. Lay it out."

"Let me tell you about some of the things we've discovered so far. Blake sent us some phenomenal stuff and performed some magic to get it here as fast as he did. Forty-five minutes ago, I received two sets of prints from Kiley's safe, and some from the interior locksets in the house. We matched them quickly. Both men have been guests of the good state of New York, one at Oneida and one at Elmira. We've identified them as Mick Mallory and Jack Esposito. I believe you know them both."

"I know Mallory. Don't recall the other."

"Well, they both work for Tony Bennetti. I'll fill you in later. As I said, this thing is growing like bamboo in Taipei. I've got Jim sending photos back to Blake on these two gangsters, as well as our best guess on the car. Looks like maybe a Crown Royal or Lincoln Continental frame. If Bennetti is involved, we can conclude it's a Lincoln. We've also put a net over a five-state area using the usual agencies. As you know, Mallory isn't our worry. Tony Bennetti and his brothers are behind this. Tony and John still operate out of New York, but brother Robert is a big-shot racketeer in Chicago. I think that's where our two safe crackers are headed. If they're using I-94, we can place them within a hundred-mile section of blacktop in Wisconsin. We stand a good chance of picking them up within the hour."

Capone took a breath and continued, "I saved

137

the best for last. Blake sent a copy of an invoice that he lifted from the safe. It looked curious to him, and it does to me too."

"An invoice?"

Pulling a folded sheet from his notepad, Capone handed it across the desk to Connelly. "This invoice is from a sheet metal company in Minneapolis called Sanderson Fabrication. It shows an order for one hundred items. The specifications in the top section are interesting, particularly the color which calls for a match to the 'Aviontrics Day-Glow Orange - sample provided.' J.R., I ran a check on Sanderson Fabrication and didn't find anything yet. We're sending someone out to Minneapolis. I looked for a company called Aviontrics and found out they make specialized electronic equipment for military and commercial aircraft.

Connelly interrupted, "What makes you think there's any reason to connect this invoice for... what are they, orange boxes...to Kiley's disappearance, Bob?"

"I'm getting to that. In the photographs that Blake sent of Kiley's safe, there was an unusual electrical cord fed through a hole at the bottom and plugged into the wall. The photograph clearly shows the cord's end piece inside the safe. Blake thinks that whatever was removed from the safe was connected to it. Why else was it there, and why was the cord still plugged into the wall outlet? Also, why would Kiley keep the invoice to the boxes in the safe? I passed the photo around downstairs and it seems the fitting is called a cannon plug. It's commonly used to connect electrical components together on airplanes to power up the plane's electronics. I agree with Blake. There's a link here between what was taken from the safe, the Sanderson invoice, and Aviontrics."

"Good, Bob. Continue."

Bob said, "Now we have the Bennetti gang involved through Esposito and Mallory. Maybe. The Bennettis don't do small-time stuff, so this is something significant. I don't know about the orange boxes yet, but I'll lay odds they're the key. The connection to large aircraft manufacturers and one hundred aircraft avionics boxes worries me. Kiley could be selling sophisticated military components to some overseas whacko through the Bennettis. He's vanished now, and whatever it is he sold is in the wrong hands. We've got to find out what it is, and our best hope right now is grabbing Mallory. I really believe we have a tight window."

Silence stretched between the two old friends before Connelly responded, "I agree. There seems to be much more here than was indicated earlier. I see on the invoice, the order is only for what looks like a sheet metal container or some sort of housing. I assume that our big concern is what's inside. Do we have a lead on that?"

"Not yet. Of course, you're right, it's the guts of the thing that's important. We're working on that. I'm hoping that we might find something helpful in the rest of the papers in the safe. Maybe the dimensions of the box and the type of electrical connection can help identify what's inside and what it does. The color may be significant. Kiley could sure help if we can find him, but by now he's probably in Mexico. We'll keep trying."

Connelly was beginning to show concern. His face was expressionless, and his eyes narrowed as he evaluated the new information. "I'm calling home to tell Janice I'll be staying tonight. You and Jim will stay tight on this through the evening and at least for the next day or two. You can have whatever you need for support. If we find out tomorrow that Kiley is wondering around the Texas desert with Alzheimer's and the boxes were Christmas presents for his grandkids, then we'll both probably get an early retirement. That wouldn't be all bad. Now, tell me who's where quickly. I've got some calls to make"

Capone flipped the pages of his notebook for reference. He tapped the sheet with the sharp point of the yellow pencil and made a check by each item as he went through his list. "Jim's working on the background checks. He has someone assigned to each crewmember, including Nicholson. I've already mentioned the state troopers working on rounding up Mallory and Esposito. Blake and his guys are handling the Kiley house and should be working on getting someone who can recognize the photographs. Maybe someone will recall exactly what kind of car they're driving, at least the color. One of our teams should be arriving in Midland any minute. Standard procedure there, and at the Kiley farm as well. I'm going to work on the orange box thing and re-visit Sanderson and Aviontrics. I'll have to dig up a military aviation expert somewhere."

Connelly jumped in, "I'll take care of that one, Bob. I'll get back to you with a name within the hour."

"Thanks," Capone said, cutting the director off. "I'm also talking with the Empire people and getting what they have on the crewmembers, especially Kiley. Once Dave has jumped through all the hoops, he'll be sending out the contents of the safe and anything else he uncovers. That's about it. Will you be in the building?"

"I'll let you know if I leave the office. You do the same."

Capone rose and turned to leave, not waiting for an indication from Connelly.

"Bob, keep me posted."

Capone continued through the door, raised the hand holding the yellow pencil, and replied, "Yes sir."

CHAPTER 16

Empire Flight 808
1,100 Feet Over Illinois
15:35 Central Standard Time
February 1, 2007

The conditions continued to worsen during our approach into St. Louis. Climbing north toward Chicago, the rain turned to snow, and the clouds were evenly spread into a solid line that stretched from Minneapolis to Chattanooga. The whole system slowly crept eastward, blanketing the northern states with a thick coat of wet snow. South of St. Louis, the warmer temperatures created slightly unstable pockets of weather consisting of rain showers interfused with isolated thunderstorms. The thick, low cloud cover sealed the troposphere, holding the warmer air near the ground, resulting in more mild temperatures and wetter snow. Climbing toward the first of three reported overcast layers, the Doppler radar on the front console was devoid of the bright red and yellow areas that indicated dangerous turbulence. Instead, it depicted larger areas of green that meant less moisture and smoother air. The forecast predicted we would enter the base of the first layer around fourteen hundred feet and break out on top of the last layer at twenty-two thousand.

We were busy during the climb, completing the after-take-off checklist and cleaning up the plane—raising the gear and retracting the flaps. During this phase of flight, we performed our individual tasks while looking for traffic in the congested St. Louis departure area. The visibility was about three miles, barely legal to allow pilots to fly under FAA Visual Flight Rules (VFR) below the cloud layer.

The radar controller broke the silence. "Empire 808, traffic at twelve o'clock, two miles, heading two eight zero, squawking VFR, turn hard right thirty degrees. Now!" Conveying to us that he had received a blip on his screen from a plane, flying without an instrument flight plan and at an unknown altitude, but pretty much directly in front of us. The controller directed us to make a sharp evasive turn to the right.

This wasn't a good situation in bad weather. The poor visibility limited reaction time, and we would be unable to avoid a collision if one became imminent.

As we received the traffic report, I looked up at the fourteen-hundred-foot cloud base above, then at the altimeter passing through eleven hundred feet. Nicholson rolled the plane over to a new heading, thirty degrees to the east. We both strained to find the small plane in front of us, even though we were about to disappear into the soup. *Surely, he wouldn't be flying in the clouds without an instrument flight plan*, I thought, *but it happens*.

The first thud was loud and got our attention quickly. The next came within seconds and by then we were in the clouds. Instinctively, each of us scanned the instruments for any telltale sign of engine problems.

Ted spoke first, and calmly. "Any ideas?"

Everything appeared normal. We climbed smoothly through the overcast. Mike Nicholson continued to fly the plane as though nothing had happened. "Your panel okay, Mac? Any breakers out?"

With just a hint of apprehension, I asked, "Everything's great back here. What the hell was that?"

"Not sure," Mike offered. "Any ideas, Ted?"

"Bird strike maybe? Any geese moving this time of year?"

Mike's hand lifted from the throttles, as if to say, of course, and then stated, "That must be it, I haven't had a bird strike in years. I believe you've got it, Ted. They must have hit the nose cone. Would you take a good look outside when we get on the ground, Mac?

"I'll check it out," I said.

Nicholson said, "From the sound of it, we should have a couple good dents in the skin."

"I'll take a look and make a note in the logbook," I replied, wondering if Mike and Ted had correctly diagnosed the noise. Fortunately, one of the large birds hadn't aimed for the windshield. I visualized fourteen pounds of Canadian goose parts hurtling through the cockpit at three hundred plus miles an hour. Realistically, that probably wouldn't happen because the windows are designed to withstand such an event. They're provided with a heating system that makes them more flexible and able to withstand that type of impact without shattering.

Thinking of the bird going through the windshield reminded me of a story I heard years ago. The story involved a large aircraft manufacturer that fired live chickens out of a cannon to test the strength of their windshields. According to the account, the animal-rights people got involved and pressured the company to discontinue the use of live chickens. In response, the plane manufacturer stopped using live chickens and started using thawed processed chickens purchased at a local grocery store. Later, a new cannon man was conducting the tests and no one told him to thaw the chickens. The frozen butterball not only exploded through the glass, but continued on through the back wall of the building and into a manager's car in the parking lot.

I never found out if the story was based on actual events or not.

Karen entered the cockpit with a squeamish look on her face. I could tell she was troubled, "What's wrong, feeling a little airsick?"

"Not funny, Mac," she replied, "you have to come back here."

"What's wrong?" I asked again, wondering what the problem might be that would contort her face in such a way. My first thought was that they had found a dead rat or something in one of the galleys. Maybe one of the passengers was drunk and acting up.

"Just come back here. You'll see."

"Mind if I go check it out, Mike?"

"Go ahead, we're fine."

I unbuckled and released the lever to slide my seat back. I was glad for the excuse to get up and walk around, but I hoped this wasn't going to be anything messy. As Karen left the cockpit, she moved toward the front exit and allowed me to enter the cabin first. I didn't notice right off, but after three or four steps the mystery almost knocked me down. The smell was abominable. I recognized it immediately but couldn't place it.

"Is the whole plane like this?" I asked.

"It's everywhere. What is it?"

A past memory was rekindled. I knew the smell. *What is it?* I'd smelled this before. Then it came to me. My father would hunt duck and clean them in the kitchen sink when I was younger. This smell was unquestionably that of dead waterfowl.

"It's a goose," I stated with certainty.

"A goose?"

"We thought we heard some of them hit the nose just a few minutes ago. This confirms it. It's definitely the smell of a disemboweled duck."

"Really?" she responded.

"We pressurize and condition the cabin with air pulled off the engines. When the bird went through the turbine blades, it was mulched into tiny pieces. The smell came in with the second-stage air we use for pressurizing the cabin."

"Can you make it better?"

"Unfortunately, no. Nothing we can do about it."

"Ooh," Karen groaned.

"I'll tell Mike in case he wants to make an announcement. I'd suggest, though, that you go ahead and talk to the people and let them know what it is."

"Okay."

"I have no idea how long before it clears up," I said.

Karen cupped her hand over her nose and mouth to keep the smell out.

"Thanks, Mac, I'll do that. Could you go back and explain it to Erin and Claire?"

Perfect, I thought. "Be glad to."

Heading back, I took a quick look at the first-class passengers. Occasionally, one liked to ask a question of the flight-deck crew. I thought that if anyone looked particularly distressed from the smell, I should try to help. One elderly lady in Seat 5A looked pale. She seemed about to puke. The smell got worse the further back I went.

"Ma'am," I started out, "I apologize for the unpleasant odor. We apparently flew through a flock of geese, and one of them entered an engine."

"Oh, no," she said, looking nervous.

"Don't worry, no harm to the plane. We use compressed air from the engine to pressurize the cabin. That's why the odor."

"Thank you, Captain, I'm sure it wasn't your fault."

I accepted the promotion without correcting her.

She continued, "It makes me feel better that nothing's wrong with the plane. Will it clear up pretty soon?"

"I really don't know how long it'll take for the odor to dissipate. I haven't had this happen before. Are you feeling okay?"

She nodded, and said, "Oh, yes, I'm fine. I hope it doesn't last long."

She was looking a little better already. Her husband was reading a paper. His lip curled, giving me the impression that he was somewhat irritated. I thought it prudent not to ask him how he was. She offered a weak smile. I started to the back.

As I entered the coach section, I felt as if I were on display. The passengers in the back were a bit embroiled and I guessed were discussing the plane's environmental problem when I appeared through the curtain. Most of them looked up in my direction. I realized immediately that regardless of what had happened or who caused it, I was the one wearing a uniform that inferred I held a position of responsibility. I felt as if the stares were saying, "What the hell did you do?" from some and "When the hell are you going to fix this problem?" from the others.

I wished that I had left well enough alone and gone back up front after talking with Karen. I avoided making eye contact and skipped the wing inspection. Instead, I looked to the back to find Claire. Maybe I could address the odor issue and promote myself at the same time.

The same sailor who'd been with us since Dallas was back in his usual spot. He appeared to be interested in Claire. I hoped he wasn't the big mystery date she had in Chicago. He found a comfortable position, through experience no doubt, standing just behind the last row of seats across from the galley. The seat belt sign was still on, but passengers often get up to use the restrooms. He was probably on his way back to his seat.

I wasn't going to take any chances. As I approached, our eyes met. "We've had some reported turbulence up ahead," I lied for the second time today. "You should probably buckle in."

"What's that smell?" he asked without moving.

"The flight attendants will be explaining that shortly. Now, I really have to insist that you be seated."

He moved faster. I could smell alcohol on his breath. He was going home on leave from boot camp and was entitled to a little fun. I felt somewhat sorry that I wasn't a little nicer to him, but on the other hand, I was glad he was leaving.

"Hi, ladies," I said to the two attendants huddled together in the galley, probably attempting to hide from the gut-wrenching smell.

Erin held her nose. "What is it?" she asked, using her hand like a fan.

"We've been attacked by aliens. We've just been informed over the radio. They've released a toxin into our atmosphere, and there's no hope. We're the fortunate ones. It's much worse at ground level. The world is gone. We're the only survivors and will have to repopulate the planet. The president wants us to start immediately."

"Well," Claire came back without hesitation, "I thought you said we were the fortunate ones. I guess I'll have to use this escape door after all. Where's the key?"

I should have known better than to give her an opportunity. Not wanting to spend valuable time exchanging friendly digs, I shifted the topic to the odor issue.

"We apparently flew through a flock of geese. One or more were digested by the engines. The cabin is pressurized using air pulled from where the birds were emulsified, therefore the repugnant stench." I thought this was succinct but clearly stated the dilemma.

"Emulsified? Repugnant stench?" Erin said, looking disgusted and making a face I hadn't seen since grade school. "Yeechhhh."

"Well, sorry. It's unfortunate, but that's what happened. One of you should probably go through the back section and check on our guests. It might be a good idea to make an announcement. I'll explain the situation to Mike when I go back up front. He'll probably want to make his own announcement.

"I'll volunteer before you make me sick, Mac," Erin said somewhat coldly.

She moved quickly to scoot between Claire and the galley countertop on her way forward.

"She wasn't upset with what I said, was she?" I asked innocently.

"No, Mac. She was kidding. We appreciate your coming back to help out. I hope they weren't snow geese. They're so beautiful."

"I didn't get a good look. They smell like Canadian geese."

"Ha, ha. Do you want a cola or anything?"

"Thanks, that would be nice. Got a Seven Up?"

"Sure."

She reached into the hopper to find the green can of pop. I caught myself admiring her slim frame as she turned. I realized that what had been just a curious interest earlier was becoming more intense. I hadn't had this feeling about a girl in a long time.

She used a church key to pop the top and bend it back before asking, "Would you like a glass and some ice?"

It was evident she was a really nice person and that her feet were planted on firm ground. I hoped she wasn't involved with someone. Even though she'd been giving me some encouraging signals, I wasn't sure if it was just her friendly nature, or if there was something more. Maybe she treats everyone like this.

"No, thanks, the can is fine. Karen said you've been with Empire a few years. How do you like it so far?" I asked.

Now that was pretty lame. Maybe I should just head back up front now before I say something even dumber.

"Mac, I'm flattered. You've been asking Karen about me."

Now what? I'd like to say I'd been inquiring about her and admit I was interested, but then I didn't want to sound desperate. I also didn't want to make some joke about it because I was hoping to head into a more serious direction. I took a shot in the dark.

"Well," I started out, "we haven't worked together before and, okay, I admit it, I asked her a few questions about you."

"Really?"

"Let's see, you've been flying about three years. You're from Minnesota, some small town near St. Cloud, can't remember..."

"Big Lake," she volunteered.

"Oh yeah, Big Lake. I went to school in St. Cloud," I added, knowing Big Lake was only about twenty minutes down the road.

"Party school. I should have known," she said with feigned disapproval.

"Well, St. Cloud has come a long way. It's ranked pretty high academically now."

She was right about my alma mater's reputation. Usually I was sort of proud of my college years, but now I wanted her to see my more mature side. I was uneasy finding myself in untested territory.

"Okay, since you learned so much at that highly-acclaimed institution of learning, spell chordate."

"That's easy," I lied, now for the third time today.

I pronounced it out loud, CORPS DATE, provided my spelling, C-O-R-P-S-D-A-T-E, and then offered my definition as a bonus. "It's when a young woman has an agreement to go to the movies with a marine." I figured that if I guessed wrong on the spelling, I could dazzle her with my improvisation.

"Wrong on both counts, Einstein. It's spelled C-H-O-R-D-A-T-E, and it's relevant to a marine species of vertebrates that include lancelets and tunicates."

"Well, of course," I retorted, hoping to finesse my way along. "That's the other chordate."

"Mmm, hmm."

"You should have been more specific," I said.

"You did well on evading the question though. You must have gotten an A+ in BS 101. You might want to consider politics."

"No, thanks. Flying gives me all the thrills I need. But not to make excuses, marine biology wasn't an elective in my program. Maybe I could get you to give me some tutoring sometime."

"I think I'd like that," she said, becoming serious now.

I felt I had made a little progress and thought it might be wise to head back to the cockpit on a high note. I paused long enough to allow the moment to sink in, and said, "I better get back up front. Thanks for the Seven Up. See you in Chicago."

"See ya, Mac." She began to turn, but then paused and started to say something. "Oh... "

"What?"

"Try not to kill any more geese."

CHAPTER 17

After meeting with Connelly, Bob Capone spent over an hour on the phone trying to identify the boxes that had been assembled at Sanderson Fabrication in Minneapolis. His suspicion about the critical nature of the unusual avionics' housings had become more of a certainty. There was nothing definite to prove his theory, but down deep he knew he had to find where this piece of the puzzle fit.

Ten minutes earlier, his conversation with Dave Blake in Minneapolis revealed that photographs of Mick and Jack had been electronically delivered to all the law enforcement offices around Sauk Centre. The process to find a country store, or gas station, where someone might remember the two odd characters, had already begun. More information about the make, color, or style of the vehicle would help the Wisconsin Highway Patrol in their search along I-94.

The St. Cloud police were providing excellent assistance to the local sheriff in Sauk Centre by sealing off the Kiley property, canvassing the entire area, and researching local bank and police records.

Kiley had attended college a few miles down the road in St. Cloud, so some attention was directed there in the hopes of finding something in his past that would expand his profile. His ex-wife at the lake home in Minneapolis would be questioned, as well as his son, Bob Junior. Jim Everett worked on obtaining Kiley's military records through normal FBI channels back at headquarters.

From his office in Minneapolis, Blake provided coordination among the various local law enforcement agencies, especially the Wisconsin State Patrol. Wisconsin officials had entered information of the search into the Mobile Data Communications Network (MDCN). Highway patrol units along Mick and Jack's projected route had been contacted personally by the Eau Claire district chief.

Dave had been working with the St. Cloud District Attorney to initiate the legal procedures that would allow full access to the contents of the safe. The process was slow, but he needed access to the documents in order to perform a complete inspection. During all the activity, Blake had been transcribing his meticulous notes into a formal preliminary report for Director Connelly.

Capone's partner, Jim Everett, had also been busy. Four agents were thoroughly briefed and assigned to investigate Kiley, Nicholson, Lawrence, and McIntyre. No reports were forthcoming as yet. Jim talked with Sheriff Sergeant who had received and disseminated photos of Kiley. Midland and the entire state of Texas were being combed for the missing Empire captain. The FBI team from Corpus had not yet arrived, but were expected in Midland soon.

Capone received a call twenty minutes earlier from Major Edward Samson, a military aviation systems expert. He was unable to provide meaningful information about the boxes, using the description Capone gave him over the phone, however, he requested a faxed copy of the invoice and photos of the electrical cable in Kiley's safe, which he felt would help.

Empire Airlines Vice President, Roger James, told Capone he would willingly share the personnel jackets of the Empire crewmembers. He immediately placed the files on a plane to DC and an FBI currier was dispatched to pick them up.

Capone's telephone conference with a Mr. Briscoe, Vice President of Research and Development for Aviontrics, was encouraging. Briscoe suggested that Capone fax him the Sanderson invoice with the box specifications, and he would match the dimensions to everything their com-

157

pany had fabricated during the last ten years. Perhaps an exact, or near exact match, might open a door. If the metal housings made by Sanderson could be matched to specifications on file at Aviontrics, then they might be able to find out more about what had been taken from the safe. If Aviontrics had previously manufactured an electronic unit with a matching casing, then this might be a clue as to where in the aircraft the boxes might be installed, and even possibly what type of function they serve.

Capone knew he was working long shots and grasping for anything that would add a piece to the puzzle. He didn't know exactly what he was looking for, but he did know that the more information he could gather the better chance he would have to find it.

He looked up at the clock over the door. The hour hand was not cooperating. *Four-forty*, he thought. *Damn. I just don't have enough time.*

He sat back in his chair for the first time in hours and tried to relax and let his mind clear. Things were becoming jumbled and his thoughts were drifting. Too much was happening at once. He needed to get away from it for a few minutes to clear his thoughts.

He realized he hadn't eaten. He was mentally exhausted, but the hunger won out. He decided to ask his secretary to find some food and reached for the intercom button, but she got there first.

"Call for you, Bob. It's a Lieutenant Dodd with the Wisconsin Highway Patrol. He says it's urgent."

"Please, Betty, put it through. Thanks."

"Mr. Capone? How should I address you?"

"Bob's fine. And your name again, lieutenant?"

"Dodd, sir, Larry Dodd. I have some information for you on Mallory and Esposito."

"That's great, Dodd, go ahead."

"Well, we would've had this to you much earlier but rather unfortunate timing aggravated things a bit.

"How's that?"

"Well, our department received the information on your two boys about an hour-and-a-half ago, about three o'clock your time. A half-hour before that, there was a pretty nasty accident about fifty miles south of Eau Claire involving the subjects, a bit before we started the search. Only one of the suspects was still at the scene. He was banged up pretty bad. He's unconscious in the La Crosse Hospital."

"How bad?"

"He's not doing well. Won't be telling us anything for a while."

"Which one is that?"

"That's Mallory."

"How about Esposito?"

"He apparently bolted."

"Shoot."

Detective Dodd continued, "We didn't make the connection until about ten minutes ago. You know, we really didn't have much of a description for the car. Our officer on the scene was busy for almost an hour and didn't receive the word on the search."

"That's okay, what else?"

"As soon as he found out about your investigation, he immediately made the connection and called me. That was ten, maybe fifteen minutes ago."

"Okay, Dodd, you guys did great. You say Mallory isn't talking?"

"Not now. Probably not anytime soon. Do you want us to book him?"

"Yeah. Start with breaking and entering. We'll build on that later. I want a man at his door twenty-four hours. Let me know immediately if he comes around. I'll be sending one of our agents to the hospital."

"Anything else?"

"Did you search the car yet?"

"We did. Nothing in it, but we haven't torn it down."

"No need at this point. Any other information on Esposito?"

"We've got a new APB with a more accurate description of his probable location. Got a car working specifically on him. There was a truck driver involved who's been helpful."

"Good, Dodd. Keep him handy."

"We'll be talking to him soon, if we haven't already. I'll keep you posted."

"Great. You should call Dave Blake in Minneapolis. He can provide you with details for charging Mallory. I'll give you his number."

"Got it already."

"Okay. Esposito is dangerous, but I don't want him killed. He's got information we need. He'll steal a car and get back on the road. He'll then probably drive for thirty minutes or so and dump the first car and get a new one."

"Expected that. We're combing the area for a missing vehicle."

"You'll have to work fast. Good luck."

"You too. I'll be in touch."

Capone replaced the phone and looked at the Wisconsin map on his desk. Glancing at his notes he searched for the time the accident occurred. He was thinking—*two thirty in Black River Falls, two hours ago, minus thirty minutes to steal a car and get back on the road. Minus another twenty minutes to dump the first car and pick up a second. This means he's had a little over an hour of travel time through bad weather.*

He checked the mileage key and mentally calculated how far Jack could have driven in a little over an hour at fifty miles an hour. He estimated the distance to be about sixty miles, about two and a half inches on the map. He made a circle around the town of Mauston and penciled the time Jack should arrive there. 16:40

He grabbed the phone and located the number to the St. Cloud police headquarters scrawled on the bottom of his notepad. A female voice answered and offered to locate Blake. A good minute passed in silence. Capone used the time to organize his thoughts. Other than sending out the remaining documents from the captain's safe, Blake was pretty much done in Minnesota. The Wisconsin Highway Patrol would have to work fast.

"Dave Blake."

"Dave, this is Bob."

"Didn't expect to be hearing from you. What's up?"

"Just got a call from a Lieutenant Dodd, over in Wisconsin. They found your safecrackers."

"That's great. Where?"

"Don't get carried away, it's not as good as it sounds. They got in a wreck halfway across the state."

"A wreck?"

"Yeah. Sounds like they bounced around pretty good. I didn't get all the details, but Mallory is unconscious. Alive, but he won't be helping us for a while. Esposito had time to get away. I figure right about now he's near a small town called Mauston, about sixty miles southeast of Black River Falls."

"I'm familiar with that area. Unbelievable. Got in a wreck, huh? Anyone else hurt?"

"A lady and her kid. Don't know how bad."

"Ohh."

"Look, Dave, I just wanted to let you know we got the car they were in and we'll have to pick up the pieces over in Wisconsin. You've got us a good start. Lieutenant Dodd, highway patrol over there, will be calling you."

"Dodd?"

"Yeah, he's been working with me. Doing a good job."

"Okay."

"Any luck with getting us the stuff in the safe? I need something here to work with."

"Just finishing up with that. Will be sending everything out within the hour. I don't think I can do much more at this end. I'm going to find a quiet hole and study copies of the documents I'm sending you. I'll swing by Kiley's farm one last time before I head back to the cities tonight. Anything else?"

"No. I'll keep you posted. Thanks, Dave."

"Good luck."

Capone knew it was imperative to intercept Esposito before he got to Chicago. He tilted his neck back and said out loud, "I hope Dodd gets his man." *Every time I start to gain some momentum, the rug gets yanked out*, he thought to himself.

He stared at the phone, hoping it would ring. The Sanderson invoice lay on the desk, the dimensions specified at the top, next to the requested color of day-glow orange. He tried to picture the object in his head with the actual dimensions and coloring. The bright orange rectangle took shape in his mind against a black background. It slowly revolved in space like a 3-D rotating computer model, showing views from different angles. He could see it clearly and wanted to capture the picture. With one of the yellow pencils from the cup, he transferred the image to the pad on his desk.

The completed illustration would have impressed Mr. Nickel, his high school drafting teacher. The perspective presented an image that looked three-dimensional. Every detail was accurately placed according to the specs provided on the invoice: a large hole on the side, a smaller one on what would be the top, and folds resembling those on a business envelope where the metal was bent around each side. He dug through an assortment of highlighters in his lower desk drawer until he found an orange one. He colored the box and made small circles for the two holes. *What goes in the holes?* he wondered.

"Betty?"

"I'm here, Colombo," the box on his desk answered.

"If you could get me something to eat, anything, I'd be eternally grateful."

"You haven't eaten yet?" Betty said, astonished.

"Not yet. It's been a rather busy day."

"Don't pass out. I'll be right back."

Capone stood and stared out across the city, taking a moment to reflect on the many hard years filled with different occupations and assignments he had held within the law enforcement community. He remembered the early days fresh out of the Marine Corps when he first checked in for training. His first big case carried him across twelve states during a six-month manhunt, terminating in a Wild West shoot-out in Oklahoma. One agent had lost his life in a botched attempt to rush the trapped killer.

Capone met Janet shortly afterward while attending college part-time in Delaware. She had remained loyal and supportive after twenty-five years of marriage. He remembered the awards, commendations, and degrees, displayed proudly on the wall near the coat rack. The friends he had lost in the line of duty. The years had flashed by. For a skinny, unpopular kid from a small town in Iowa, he had achieved a great deal. *What have I learned?* he wondered.

Just getting his mind off the case helped. He was beginning to feel rejuvenated. Turning away from the window, he leaned back in his desk chair, allowing his eyes to fall on the drawing of the orange box. *What is it? What does it do? And, most importantly, who'll be hurt by these things?*

Several minutes passed as he sat transfixed, trying to come up with the answer. The door opened and Betty entered with a Styrofoam take-out food container, napkins, plastic utensils, and a matching white Styrofoam cup.

"You're staying late tonight, aren't you?" she asked as she set the items on his desk.

"I think so, this is going to be a marathon I'm afraid. We've stumbled onto something filled with bad elements. Lucky so far, but we may be running out of time. It's going to be a long night."

"Did you call your wife yet?"

"Damn! Thanks, I knew there was something I'd forgotten. I'll call her while I eat. What'd you buy?" he asked, as he reached for the drink with one hand and tried to pry the lid off the container with the other.

"Chinese," she replied. "You looked troubled. I thought this might help."

Capone smiled. Betty functioned as a combination second wife and mother, and she knew her boss as well as anyone. The small Chinese restaurant across the street was his favorite. He seldom had time to eat there and either brown-bagged or went to the cafeteria downstairs if he could find the time. Today he hadn't.

"Do you need me to stay late," she offered.

"Thanks. That won't be necessary. We've got a group set up in the war room. We'll mostly be winging this tonight. I doubt we'll be able to accomplish much this evening. Might get lucky, though."

"I hope you're successful," she said.

"Me too. Why don't you go ahead and leave a

little early?"

"If you're sure. If you change your mind let me know."

"I will. Thanks."

"Don't forget to call Janet," she said while leaving.

Capone used both hands to open the covered container. He was pleased to find his favorite, chicken egg foo yong. Pulling the notepad closer, he began to eat while studying the drawing. The clock on the wall read four forty-eight.

He thumbed through the pile of notes with his left hand while finishing the last of the rice. The phone rang loudly. He sat up startled, forgetting that Betty had left early and transferred the calls. In one fluid motion he placed the food container to the side, captured the receiver, and cradled it between his ear and shoulder.

"Bob Capone," he said, hoping the voice on the other end would be the bearer of new information about Kiley, Esposito, or the orange boxes. His wish was granted.

"Bob, this is Major Samson. Got a minute to talk about your avionics package?"

"You bet, major. Have you identified it?"

"No, sorry Bob. Didn't mean to get your hopes up. But I've looked at it closely and passed it around the building here. I'm afraid there really isn't enough to go on."

Capone sat back and said, "I was hoping that wouldn't be the case."

"I can sling a few things in the air for you to bounce around, though."

Capone didn't have time to chew his first large bite of the egg foo yong. He had to encourage the major to continue, with his mouth full. "Please, major, I'm willing to listen to anything. Go ahead."

The major spoke with an authoritative, low even tone. "First, it looks like someone's building the casing for some type of avionics gear. The color may be significant. Usually this bright orange is reserved for avionics packages that are critical to crash investigations. You may be looking at something like a voice recorder or possibly a flight data recorder, but I've seen other housings this color and some painted other colors for no particular reason. Traditionally, of course, most of our electronic casings have been black."

"Black boxes."

"Exactly. Through the involvement of the FAA and other regulatory agencies, we've grown a little wiser. One change was to paint the more critical components with a color that can help investigators locate specific items at a crash scene. The day-glow orange, more commonly international orange, is one used for this purpose. We also use various fluorescents. But then, the designer of your box may just happen to like orange."

Capone was captivated by the major's knowledge and by the detailed information he was receiving based solely on the orange color, and by the confidence in his delivery. "This is good information, major, please continue."

"We recognize the trade name 'Aviontrics' as a manufacturer of a number of different electronic components that we use in the aviation industry, from low-voltage power supplies to very high-tech global positioning interface couplers for automatic tracking of ground transports, and a plethora of avionics systems in between."

"Interesting."

"Now, the holes located in the top and side may indicate a couple of things. First, they're obviously access points to the interior components. My guess is that one hole, the larger one, is where the power source is connected."

"Major," Capone interrupted, "would that normally be connected using a cannon plug like the one in the picture I sent with the invoice?"

"You're a quick study," the major offered. "In fact, the picture you sent appears to be the right size plug to match a male counterpart that could be mounted in that larger hole."

"Hmm."

"The other hole could accommodate a few things, but due to its small size, I can make an educated guess."

"Okay."

"Well, if it were a bigger hole, I'd say it would

be for a switch or a dial, but since the specs called for it to be only three-sixteenth of an inch in diameter...one or two things come to mind.

"For instance?"

"First, I think the canon plug should allow all the wiring that would be needed. The one connector would allow easy removal for maintenance. This is a typical configuration."

"I see. You're telling me the small hole probably isn't for an additional wire. And you don't believe a switch or a dial is mounted there either?"

"Exactly."

"Okay, major. What does that leave then for the smaller hole?"

"This won't be any great revelation, but for what it's worth, I believe it's to accommodate a control power light."

"A power availability light?"

"Correct. Or, if it has a self-diagnostic system, it could also serve to show functionality. Good working order or not. A diagnostic light."

"Very good, major."

"Well, Bob, either way, my best guess is a light."

"I'm impressed, major. I didn't expect you to tell me exactly what it was with just the dimensions to go on, even though I was hoping. But I think you've managed to help describe the thing a little better. Sounds like we've placed the odds pretty high that the larger hole on the side accepts the cannon plug and the smaller hole on top may be the location of a small power or diagnostic light. The orange color probably means it's something that someone wants to recover following a crash. This information may come in handy. One more thing, major."

"Go ahead."

"Why do you suppose the cord was left in the safe? I figure, if it was necessary to have it plugged in while inside the safe, it probably should stay energized after being removed. Do you think that whoever removed it brought their own power source along?"

"I can see you've given this some thought, Bob."

"Some, but still not there yet."

"Well, obviously, the cord was necessary for the unit to remain functional. I doubt if the unit was being used for its intended purpose while in the safe. More probably, it was plugged in because it has internal circuits that require a constant voltage source. Some electronic chips loose memory or change configuration when unpowered."

"So, are you saying that when they unplugged the thing, it may have been damaged? Or possibly lost its memory or internal settings?"

"That's possible, but I believe it's more likely that if this thing is important enough to steal and catch the attention of the FBI, then it was probably removed in a more innocuous way. It's difficult to say at this point. Again, you're getting a lot of conjecture from me, but I could make another guess if you like."

"You've got a good track record so far. Give it a shot."

"Well, you're the detective, but here's the way I see it playing out. The unit was plugged in to keep it energized. That's easy. If it's necessary to keep it powered up, then it follows that the power should remain on when it's being transported, or if the main power source fails."

"Like a power outage at the house?"

"Exactly. If a storm caused a power failure to the house, there would have to be a contingency feature that takes over."

"It would need an internal battery," I said.

"Now you've got it. I would guess the thing was plugged in to keep the battery from wearing down. In order for this to work, the unit would have an internal charger to maintain the battery voltage."

"Right...right. I see."

The major added, "Also, integral to the unit would be a transformer which would step down the one hundred ten volt house voltage to a lower value used by the electronics inside. This setup is really very common and easy to configure."

"I think I'm beginning to understand. It would be safe for the box to be unplugged and removed because there's likely an internal power supply keeping the circuits powered up. The cord's not absolutely necessary until the battery runs down."

"Right. You can assume that it will be installed wherever they intend to use it sometime soon before the battery becomes depleted. Otherwise, it will need to be plugged into a one hundred ten volt source for recharging. If that's the case, whoever took it probably came prepared. They knew what they were coming for and most likely brought their own cord."

I said, "That would eliminate the need to detach the cannon plug, remove the cord, and then reassemble the pieces. Big waste of time when you're in the middle of breaking-and-entering. Especially when another cord could be prepared in advance."

"Excellent, major. This all makes a great deal of sense. I think you've very logically explained a number of things that had me a bit confused."

"Glad I could help. Will you let me know when you find out what it is?"

"You'll be the first to know. Thanks for your help, major."

Capone hung up his phone, reached into the left side drawer of his desk and found a red pen. Then he pulled the notepad with the drawing of the orange box close and colored the small circle in the center of the box red. He used a black pen to draw the cannon plug and cord on the side of the unit.

Somebody, somewhere, can recognize this drawing, he thought to himself.

CHAPTER 18

Looking out the living room picture window toward the southeast, Norma Neumiller watched the storm and wondered at her God's majesty. She stared, entranced, through the huge blue spruce and black walnut trees that lined the drive, at the thick coating gracing the trees and fields with a dazzling new white jacket. Although seventy-eight years had passed since she was born to first-generation German parents, not four miles from this house, she still marveled at the beauty of the Wisconsin winters. Turning toward a huge overstuffed chair, covered with a tattered hand knit throw, she surveyed the white-haired, overweight farmer who had been her husband for fifty-six years. He slumped into the deep cushion, comfortably watching his wife move about the room.

"We better bring in a load of wood, Grandpa," she said. "We may be snowed in for a day or two this time."

The old man didn't look up but instead closed his eyes, hoping the sound waves that carried the suggestion would continue on into the kitchen and dissipate out in the mudroom.

"Thomas," she said firmly, and more loudly. "Don't close those eyes and pretend you didn't hear me. We need to bring in some wood. Now pick up that withered old butt of yours and move it out to the wood pile."

The old man began to move, but ever so slowly. First, he caressed the pipe that had been smokeless for twenty minutes, then tapped it on the glass ashtray. The stub of a forefinger that years ago had been picked clean from the blades of a thrashing machine clenched the bowl tight as he dug at the hardened tobacco with a worn Old Timer. He studied it for several seconds, then he began to scrape again using the small blade of the knife. Dark pieces of tobacco fell in the ashtray, and a final inspection of the pipe brought a faint smile to his face.

Norma's stern expression resembled that of an angry mother who had just caught her small child with chocolate on her face from stolen fudge brownies. "You might just find yourself locked out in the cold if you keep this up, Mr. Andretti."

The old couple had few friends left in the small farming community and seldom left the house. Their activities consisted of daytime television, romance novels, kitchen chores, and idle conversation. About once a week, one of the relatives would drop in with a small gift or baked goods. Sometimes the visit would be announced, but more often not. Regardless of who decided to stop by or whether or not the visit was expected, these occasions had become the greatest source of excitement for the couple.

Outside the farmhouse, a quarter mile down the lightly traveled road to Mauston, a white Ford F-150 pickup plowed slowly along, keeping centered in the single set of tracks that widened as each vehicle passed. In the driver's seat was a big man dressed in expensive clothes. A Coleman cooler rested next to him on the seat.

I've got to get rid of this pickup, Jack thought, as his eyes searched the edge of the road for a likely place to make a swap. He was anxious. During the last two hours, his mood had gone from confident and almost childlike to what was now the nervousness of a trapped animal. Jack Esposito was beginning to worry. Things had gone terribly wrong, and now he was alone and unsure of what to do. He knew that he must ditch the stolen pickup before it was reported missing. He had to replace it with a new vehicle. One that wouldn't be missed for at least a day. His plan was to find a secluded house just off I-94 where he could pull up and feign car trouble, or a health emergency. *That's what I'll do,* he thought, *I'll pretend to be having heart trouble. Once in the house, I'll grab the first person that answers the door, shove the forty-five to her head, and get everyone else together. I'll tie them up, take their car, and be on my way to Madison. They'll have to be tied up good, though. They can't get loose until morning. I have to make sure the car isn't reported stolen until tomorrow.*

He suddenly spotted a driveway leading to a cluster of trees, and a farmhouse hidden from the road. Slowing as he approached the drive, Jack reached under his arm and pulled the pistol from its holster with a right hand that could palm a watermelon.

Back in the farmhouse, the elderly couple continued to squabble. "Look, you senile old farmer," Norma insisted, "turning that hearing aid off isn't going to work with me this time. Now move out. I'll throw a couple more logs on the fire and make some room for you." The willowy old woman moved with assurance to the soot-stained rock fireplace and effortlessly hefted a large birch log onto the dying embers. Her husband edged toward the kitchen to the back door as the white Ford pickup slowed at the side of the building.

Jack held on tight to the pistol grip and placed the weapon inside his coat. Stepping from the pickup, he began acting in case someone had seen him drive up. He maneuvered around the tailgate and lumbered to the front door, squalling unconvincingly. "Help. Someone help me."

Norma's husband was just reaching the mud-room and slipping into a pair of black rubber overshoes. The woodpile was outside the door against the back of the house, close to where Jack had parked the pickup. After fastening the hooks on his boots, he reached for the plaid wool hunting jacket and heavy cap that hung next to the Remington twelve-gauge on the wall. He slipped his gloves on and started out, not hearing the knock at the front door.

Jack didn't notice the cold. His only thought was not to mess things up more than they already where. He had to do this right and get back on the road in a car that was safe to drive. He knocked louder and clutched the gun under his left lapel.

"Just a minute," Norma yelled as she headed toward front door. She had grown trustful in the community of her childhood where so many close friends and relatives had lived. She would never consider that a visitor could bring anything other than friendship and company. Her eyes searched through the square opening in the door. She saw a huge man who was clutching his chest and whose face was twisted in agony.

She had to try to help him and bring him into the warmth of the house. "Come in, young man." She opened the door wide, reaching out to grab his thick arm. "Are you all right?"

Jack wasn't a good actor, but because Norma Neumiller was unsuspecting, his poor performance went by undetected. He passed as being injured or sick. He walked into the house, using the old lady as a crutch and moaning, "I think it's a heart attack." Norma tried to assist him and wrapped her arms around his waist while he draped his free hand over her shoulder. She guided him into the parlor.

In the back of the house, Norma's husband walked to the end of the woodpile just around the corner from where Jack had parked. He stopped to adjust his gloves and looked up at the dark gray premature dusk. The wind had picked up and the tall northern pines and blue spruce swayed in different directions, as though each individual tree had its own source of wind.

He stepped from the walk into the snow, selected a nice piece of birch near the end of the pile, and pulled hard to free it. The ice and snow holding the pieces together loosened and several logs tumbled to the ground. Undaunted, he sidestepped closer to the corner of the house to where he could stoop and gather them up. Jack's pickup was only a few feet away around the corner. When he stood with the logs and stepped back, the bumper came into view.

He set the logs back on the stack and walked around to take a closer look. He wondered who might have come by unannounced and in the middle of a developing storm just before dark. He looked inside and noticed the Coleman cooler. *Maybe*, he thought, *someone had brought a home cooked meal.* He turned to follow the visitor's trail to the house and saw that the front door was slightly ajar.

The old man didn't suspect anything unusual and looked forward to visiting with whoever the stranger might be. He started across the shoveled front walk, careful not to move too fast and slip on the ice-coated path. The natural instinct to look into the big picture window drew his eyes up to a clear view of the small living room. The sight of a mountainous stranger wearing a dark gray suit, with one elephantlike hand clenching his wife's neck and the other holding a weapon to her temple, seemed like a surreal dream.

He absorbed the scene in an instant and froze. Jack was looking through the glass directly at him. Thomas was confused and frightened. He thought of his twelve-gauge shotgun mounted on the kitchen wall but knew it wasn't loaded. The long trip to the back of the house and around the woodpile would be impossible with the younger man chasing him.

He turned to run. He remembered the white pickup and with only a split second to react, he decided to try to reach the stranger's car, hoping the keys would be inside. When he turned, his old tired legs failed, and he slipped and stumbled. Jack was moving toward the front door, dragging the old woman by the neck. He continued to squeeze unconsciously, and her legs moved only in reflex as he towed her through the doorway into the blasting cold.

The old man stumbled toward the car, his legs not responding. He gasped for breath and reached out for the car's door handle. There was no time to go around to the driver's side. He had to get the door open and start the car before the stranger reached him. He must get help and come back for her.

Jack's right arm was extended parallel with the ground, the pistol steady, aimed at the old man's back. Norma's limp body supported by Jack's unconscious grasp was motionless.

Two loud blasts from the forty-five jolted the stillness and cracked like a bolt of lightning. The shots echoed off the snow-covered trees and then it became eerily quiet. Jack watched the old man's momentum propel him against the pickup door. He dropped lifelessly to the frozen earth. Deep red splotches painted the side of the pickup and a crimson smear marked the trail of the body as it slid down the door. Blood oozed from under the old man's torso and pooled in the sparkling snow. The boot covered foot twitched, performing the last official body function.

Jack returned the gun to its holster and remembered the old woman dangling from his shaking left hand. He realized the bodies should be moved out of sight. Moving fast, he pulled them both inside the house and locked the door.

He searched the living room and the kitchen, until he located the old woman's purse, then dumped the contents on the table. A small leather strap hid within a pile of objects and attached to it were the keys he hoped to find. He knew one would fit the ignition of the car inside the garage out back.

He left the house through the kitchen and mudroom, out the back door, and around to the pickup. The gore was worse than he expected. There was more than blood on the side of the vehicle. The large-caliber handgun had removed sections of Mr. Neumiller's neck and slung them against the window where the bullet entered the passenger side. Snowflakes landed in the pool of blood, instantly melting. Soon the blood would freeze, and the snow would begin to cover the carnage. He had seen similar messes before. It wasn't all that shocking to him. He wondered for a few seconds about what to do with the disturbed walkway but dismissed the problem and moved the pickup around the back of the house. He then opened the garage door and found a snow shovel to cover the blood in the front of the house, hoping that if someone came over, the corrupted snow would not immediately cause alarm. *Maybe*, he thought, *the new snow will cover things before anyone drops by.*

He retrieved the Coleman cooler and opened the garage door. Inside was a blue Buick Riviera that responded immediately to the keys from the women's purse. Jack backed cautiously from the group of trees, hoping to avoid notice, until reaching the edge of the road leading back to Mauston. With his right arm resting comfortably on the Coleman cooler, he noted the time on the dashboard clock. Five-ten. *I'll find a McDonald's and take a break. Wonder how Mick is doing?* he thought.

Jack had already forgotten about the two old people who had donated the blue Buick. He figured he'd be getting into Madison about six o'clock.

The radio was tuned to a swing station. Dean Martin was singing—*When the marimba rhythms start to play, dance with me, make me sway...*

CHAPTER 19

O'Hare Airfield
Chicago, Illinois
17:05 Central Standard Time
February 1, 2007

The weather in Chicago required the three of us in the cockpit to test our piloting skills, bringing the Boeing 727 through heavy blowing snow that decreased visibility to landing minimums. The world-famous O'Hare congestion was expected, but today the air was like a beehive that had been kicked by a horse. Our controller rattled directions to the inbound planes like an auctioneer. Ted worked hard to extract the instructions from a continuous broadcast of directions, responding with calm precision while dialing in new headings, altimeter settings, and frequencies on the radios—all while looking for traffic, reviewing the approach plates, and monitoring Mike's corrections for deviations. I enjoyed watching them work as a team and found myself wishing I were up front where all the action was.

Mike glanced down for a quick review of the

approach as he rolled out of the teardrop turn. We intercepted the inbound course, perfectly aligned with the runway heading and approaching the glide slope. Mike made the necessary corrections with the throttle, holding a rock-solid track toward the end of the runway. We broke out at two hundred feet, splitting the large runway numbers that lept out of the clouds just in front of the nose. Moments later, Mike gently squeaked the main gear down just beyond the painted "32" runway numbers. Ground control gave Ted instructions to the gate, and Mike guided the plane around the maze of turns with the same familiarity I enjoy when driving around my hometown. We reached the gate on time, and the long day that had begun with Kiley's mysterious disappearance was officially over.

"Nice work, guys." I said to the two up front.

"I enjoyed it, Mac." Mike began to unbuckle. "This crap will hopefully blow over by morning and we should have a clear day tomorrow. I'm gonna check in and try to get more information about Kiley. I'll fill you both in tomorrow."

Ted finished buttoning up his side of the cockpit in preparation for leaving the plane. He looked in my direction and asked if I had any special plans for the evening.

I had always been a loner and normally preferred to spend my layovers either working out in the motel's weight room, jogging, or visiting one of the better restaurants in the area. Tonight, I was hoping to get a moment alone with Claire to see if she actually was meeting someone. Maybe she'd been leading me along about her date, and I could still work something out for tonight. If not, there seemed to be some hope that something might develop later.

"I'm not sure yet, Ted," I answered. "I think I'm gonna hide out somewhere, maybe turn in early. How about you two?"

"Guess I'll do the same," Ted said.

Mike was equally short in his response. "My brother's meeting me here. I'll hook up tomorrow with you two at the plane."

About that time, the cockpit door opened, Karen poked her head in. "Nice job, boys. It's almost cleared out back here. We're leaving this stinky thing and heading up to see if we can catch the limo."

"Okay, Karen. Thanks for the help. I've got to stay and take a look outside, see if there's any damage from the bird strikes. Mike's going to be visiting his brother. I guess Ted will meet you up there. See ya later." *Shoot,* I thought, *it'll take me a while to inspect the plane, and the girls will be gone by the time I get up to the street.*

I turned to Mike and said, "I'll do a good inspection and get someone to check out the damage from the geese. I've detailed the bird strikes in the book and informed Ops. Are you coming outside to take a look?"

"No, I guess not, Mac. Sounds like you've got it under control. I'll be curious to hear more about what you found out in the morning."

The passengers were out of the plane. Mike and Ted were behind me at the door, waiting for the flight attendants to file out. They said their good-byes as I watched from my seat, waiting for the small room to clear. Past Mike, and through the door, I could see Claire bounding up the aisle, pulling her bag. When she got to the front, she poked her head into the cockpit.

"Thanks for getting us through that nasty weather, guys. Let me know when you're ready for your first marine biology lesson, Mac." Then she turned and raced up the Jetway to catch up with the other girls.

Ted turned around. "Well, I guess I know why you're so tied up tonight, hotshot. You and Claire got something going?"

"Nah, we just met this trip. Seems like a nice girl, though. I wouldn't mind getting to know her."

"Do you want me to check the plane out so you can catch up with her?" Ted gallantly offered. That idea seemed a little too aggressive.

"Thanks, Ted. I'll wait until later. She's apparently meeting someone here in Chicago anyway."

Ted and Mike turned and left, leaving me room to stand and gather my things. A mechanic was at the door waiting to get in to check the logbook and investigate my report of the goose incident. He was a stocky fellow wearing tan Empire work bibs. The name Brandon was stitched in red Italics inside a white oval patch on his chest. Cocked at an angle on his head was a well-seasoned Chicago White Sox ball cap. He held a clipboard. A stuffed tool belt in similar condition to the ball cap, hung loosely from his right hip.

"Heard you hit some ducks," he said casually, looking for me to offer a little more to go on.

"Departing St. Louis," I started, "at about a thousand feet. We heard two loud thumps, and then a few minutes later the smell started in the cabin. Nothing else I can add. The engines didn't even blink."

"Well, we'll take a good look inside to make sure. You've got a couple good dents on the nose cone. One on each side." He reported his preliminary findings while recording my comments on his clipboard.

"Interesting. I'll have to go out and take a look. Think there might be some damage to the engines?" I asked.

"Doubtful. I've seen this a few times, and we've never had it affect the turbines. You never know, though. We'll have to inspect all three and keep the plane for a few hours. Fortunately, we've managed to juggle a couple of ships and it won't affect the schedules. Anything else?"

"No. Other than the smell, this was a good

plane."

The mechanic reached over and picked up the cockpit logbook to review the last few entries before continuing with his investigation. I slipped into my jacket, grabbed my hat and flight bag, went back to the front closet, found my suitcase, and placed everything in the Jetway so I could go below and check the exterior of the plane. I mostly wanted to satisfy my curiosity. Getting ready to open the door to the stairs that led to the ramp, I noticed a familiar flight attendant bouncing down from the ticketing area. She seemed to float effortlessly, despite her mid-sized heels.

"I got tired of waiting for you up there, so I thought I'd come down and see if you were having trouble getting your seat belt undone."

"Claire, what are you doing back here?" I said in a tone that advertised I was glad to see her. "I thought you were meeting someone?"

"I just called him. He lives close by and is on his way. I've got fifteen minutes or so to kill, so I thought I'd see if you'd walk me to the street."

I didn't know what to think. Here she was meeting her boyfriend in fifteen minutes but going out of her way to come and talk to me. Even asking me to walk her up to where this guy was meeting her. If I were him, I probably wouldn't appreciate her doing this, but then again, I didn't know the whole story. It could be that this was their last meeting, or maybe it was a platonic relationship.

I didn't want to pry, so I just said, "Love to," trying not to show my disappointment that I would be walking her up to the terminal, only to hand her over to someone else. "I need to take a quick check outside to inspect the nose. I told Mike I would let him know what kind of damage there was from those geese we hit. You got a minute? Want to go down and take a look?"

"Sure," she said eagerly, and deposited her things off to the side of the walkway next to mine.

I opened the door and let her through, unable to help myself from staring at her back side as she descended. She seemed so confident and in control. I was a little nervous and hoped it didn't show.

"I don't want to make you late."

"You won't, Mac. If I'm a little late, he's very understanding. He'll wait. Take your time. This is interesting. Anyway, I was curious about the geese. Does that happen often?"

"This is the first time for me." I thought about telling her the story of the company that tested aircraft windshield glass by firing chickens from a cannon, but was more interested in listening to her talk.

It was cold outside, and the ground was patched with areas of snow where the plows hadn't completely scraped it clear. I hadn't brought gloves on this trip, and the round metal railing was ice cold. She reached the bottom and looked back at me with both arms folded across her chest. She beamed with enthusiasm while waiting for me to catch up and seemed oblivious to the frigid weather. Without thinking, I grasped her elbow to steady her on the icy pavement. I felt that a small hurtle was cleared when she accepted my gesture naturally and seemed to shift toward me a bit. We walked together under the Jetway to the front of the plane. The strong smell of exhaust from the busy jet activity filled the air and the roaring, high-pitched whine of a starting engine nearby, made our conversation difficult. Occasional gusts of wind caused her to constantly rake long strands of hair away from her face.

Standing directly in front of our plane, we both looked up simultaneously at the small crater on the right side of the nose cone, just below the horizontal centerline. There was a small streak of blood that settled any doubt about whether or not we had hit a bird.

"Well, I'm pleased to tell you that from the angle of impact, the altitude of the encounter, and the coloring of the body fluid, the evidence doesn't appear to indicate that the unfortunate victim was a snow goose."

"Really," she played along.

"It appears to be the common Canadian Fenwick goose, known to be extremely aggressive toward larger, stronger enemies. He undoubtedly attacked the plane and tried to bring it down. They've been known to team up in these raids and have caused many air disasters. The FAA is afraid to release the truth. They know the public would panic and refuse to fly. It'd kill the industry."

"You know so much Mac! You just continue to impress me."

"Well, thanks. I do a lot of reading."

Her eyes lit, and she moved closer. I couldn't help but feel she was as interested in me as I was in her. We walked around to the other side and found another small dent, higher up and farther back on the fuselage.

There really wasn't much else to see. The maintenance crew would do a thorough inspection and put the plane back in service. The repair to the skin would wait until the next major overhaul. "I've seen enough. Ready to go?" I said.

"Sure." She had to talk loudly over the noise of a jet that was pushing back from the adjacent gate.

I used the opportunity to hold her tighter before I spoke, and leaned over so she could hear better. "You must be freezing," I said.

She wore only a tan, lightweight uniform coat. With the gusting wind, the twenty-degree temperature seemed more like ten. I saw a few snowflakes hit her face and melt on impact.

She looked up and replied to my remark about the cold. "I'm used to this. Big Lake kid, you know.

We walked together back to our things with her arms wrapped tightly around my biceps, brushed off our jackets, and kicked the snow from our shoes. Then we started up the mobile Jetway to the concourse.

"Have you heard anything new about Kiley, Mac?"

She sounded caring and concerned, even considering who she was talking about.

"Nothing. This has been an unusual day. I just can't imagine what could have happened to him."

"Do you know him well? Does he have any problems in his life or anything?"

"I really don't know him well at all. You know what he's like. He doesn't give people much of a chance. I know he's divorced and has a son."

"Well, I just hope he's okay."

"You know, he lives not too far from you. He grew up in Sauk Centre and went to St. Cloud."

"Where are you from, Mac? Were you raised in Minnesota?" she asked, leading the conversation to a more comfortable area.

"My dad was in the service. We moved around a lot, but most of my relatives live in Minnesota. I graduated from high school in Bloomington, so it's pretty much home for me now. How about you? Have you always lived in Big Lake?"

"Well, I don't live in Big Lake anymore. In fact, I haven't lived there since Mom died three years ago. We moved to Edina right afterword, and Dad started working for a big insurance company. He moved out of state last year."

While we walked, I was thinking of a way to ask her out. We were getting close to the baggage area where she was supposed to meet her date. Curiosity was killing me and I had to ask, "Is this a serious thing you have with this guy who's picking you up, Claire?"

She turned and looked at me curiously. "Well, I guess I'd say it's pretty serious, Mac. How about you? Are you involved with anyone right now?"

This was a blow. I really had gotten the impression that she was available and was setting things up for me to ask her out. Now it seems she was seeing someone and not only that, it was serious. Just my luck. I finally meet someone with all the right qualities, and she's taken. Well, no wonder, what was I thinking? Someone like her wouldn't be sitting around the house, just waiting for the phone to ring.

I decided that I had made a tactical mistake in reading signals and resigned myself to the fact that I would be facing a long evening alone in the motel, with no promise for a brighter future when I got back to Minneapolis.

Upon hearing her discouraging words, I drifted off momentarily and realized that thirty seconds or so had passed since she had told me about her involvement with the mystery man. I felt I should say something but I was thrown off guard and my planned attack was obliterated by the news.

Claire broke the silence. "There he is, Mac. Come on, you have to meet him. You two will like each other."

Wonderful, I thought, *just what I need is to meet the guy. What does she mean, we'll like each other? Is she nuts? Women sometimes act in ways that defy common sense.*

I couldn't get out of this. She pulled my arm toward a group of people near the baggage conveyor over which read "Empire Flight 808" in yellow lights. I tried to discern to which man I was about to be introduced. None of them looked the part. She dragged me toward an unlikely suspect, handsome, but old enough to be her father. Certainly not her type.

"Dad," she said spiritedly as we neared the man. Her excitement in seeing her father was evident.

They hugged, and there was no doubt that the tall, exuberant flight attendant was still her daddy's little girl. "I want you to meet Mac."

Then she smiled wickedly, knowing I had expected to meet my competition, but instead had been fooled by the surprise introduction. Her faint smirk let me know she was proud of her deception. "Mac, this is my father, Richard."

"It's a pleasure to meet you, Mr. Elliott," I managed, trying to recover from my surprise and hoping that my face didn't betray me. I glanced at Claire momentarily with an expression that told her I wasn't overly happy about being tricked. On the other hand, I was relieved she didn't have the kind of date I imagined.

"Hi, Mac," he shot back with the same enthusiasm that I found so appealing in his daughter. He looked at Claire, a little perplexed but cheerful, and asked, "Do we have a change of plans?"

Now I was feeling awkward because her dad didn't expect me and wasn't sure if Claire and I were together for the evening, or if I just happened to be with her. "I was just walking Claire up from the plane, Mr. Elliott. I'll be leaving you two for your visit and catch my ride to the motel."

Claire jumped in, barely allowing me time to finish the sentence. "Dad," she said, "can we bring Mac along with us to dinner tonight?"

"Oh, no," I said, not wanting to intrude. "You two want to visit, and you don't need me tagging along."

Claire's dad was adamant. "You have to join us, Mac. Claire makes it out here to see me quite often. It's a short trip from Minneapolis, and I only live a few minutes away. We were planning on having dinner at Les Deux Autres. I insist you come along."

"I didn't bring anything to wear," I argued. I

thought I would enjoy it, but I really would have preferred that my first date with Claire included just the two of us.

"You're about my size. We'll drop you off at the motel so you can take time to regroup. Then we'll come back and pick you up. You can wear the slacks you have on and I'll bring a shirt and jacket back when we pick you up. Claire can run them up."

"Sure, Mac," Claire chimed in, "don't be such a bore. You look fine."

I could tell they both were sincere. I had a good feeling about Claire's father. "Okay," I said, "sounds like fun."

CHAPTER 20

Bob Capone had always believed the war room was a misnomer. *Who coined it and under what conditions?* he wondered. Capone preferred to call it a command center, although many times over the years the room had in fact resembled a war zone, or at least a room from which war activities were directed. Large detailed maps hanging under Plexiglas covers were used for event tracking. A podium was squarely positioned at the front of the room. A full complement of modern audio-visual equipment was neatly arranged on a desk to the side of the podium and file cabinets nearby contained copies of everything connected to the current event. Eleven desks were aligned across the back portion of the room, each equipped with computers, telephones, tape recorders, notepads, pencils, and blank CDs.

Capone had just moved his files and some

personal effects to this room and was standing at the doorway watching the activity. This wasn't what he would consider a fully involved situation. The degree of energy was mild. This bothered him.

Jim Everett had not yet moved down from his office. There were three agents in the room. One was engaged in a telephone conversation, another, a woman, doodled on a piece of scratch paper, and the third was paging through a personnel file. The remaining eight desks sat empty. A female clerk was at a small table typing on a computer keyboard. The woman agent looked up from her pencil drawings. She raised a hand, acknowledging the senior member's presence.

Capone knew why the room was so passive, and he also knew that if he was unable to close in and solve this case soon, more sinister elements would begin to turn the place into turmoil. The fact that the media had not yet aired the news of the missing captain kept the priority of the case somewhat disguised. At the present time, a federal crime hadn't yet been committed, or at least declared. There was an airline captain who failed to show up for work and what seemed to be a breaking and entering, but no complaint from the property owner, or anyone else for that matter. Technically he shouldn't even be on the case. However, there was enough evidence to suspect foul play and take prudent measures. Capone figured that even if the captain wasn't being held somewhere against his will, then he might have committed an illegal act that had carried him across state lines. Maybe even into Mexico.

It was likely that he had used one of Empire Airline's jets to commit the crime. If none of these suppositions were true, Capone reasoned that the captain could be held accountable for wrongfully interrupting commercial air travel. If he had intentionally abandoned the flight, this may arguably be a federal offense in itself.

With the recent information about the orange boxes and the involvement of the likes of Mick Mallory and the Bennetti brothers, Capone was positive that when the actual crime was uncovered, it would be substantial. The war room would become a flurry of activity.

He announced his presence to those in the room while moving toward the large desk at the front. No clarification was necessary for the four individuals in attendance that this was where decisions would be made.

Capone leaned against the desk and spoke. "I know you've all been briefed and you each have assignments. We'll discuss those individually in a few minutes."

He proceeded to review all the important facts relating to the case, including the new information about the car accident in Wisconsin, and the interesting contents of the safe. He held up his drawing of the orange box and summarized his discussion with Major Samson.

"I think that you've all been around long enough to know that the information you've been given will very likely lead us into a sticky situation come sunrise. We have a gun to our heads. The clock is our enemy. I don't want this thing to consummate. If ever there was a case that was laid in our lap, allowing us a chance to save lives, this could be it. Don't let the current low-profile become a distraction."

He stood and began to pace. "I believe that people are going to be seriously hurt if we can't move fast on this. Please come up individually and fill me in on what you've found so far. Ladies first, Meg?"

Meg Gerrity was experienced and one of Capone's favorite associates. Her brunette hair was cropped short, a style easy to maintain during the long, hectic hours in the headquarters building. She's thirty-one, single, more attractive than not, and wore a skirt emphasizing a figure often used to gain advantage. Meg was aware that even though all the men in the department were professionals and would never admit to seeing her as anything other than a fellow member of the force, they were still men. Meg worked this, but not so it was noticeable, or to an extent she could be accused of inappropriate behavior. She knew better than to think Bob Capone would be influenced by a tight skirt.

She pulled her hem down and eased into a

chair next to Capone's desk.

"Bob, I've been working on McIntyre. There just isn't much here right now. His father was a naval aviator, career man, twenty-three years. He later worked for the FAA. McIntyre's brother, George, graduated from the Naval Academy. He ended up a Marine aviator. Interesting, he holds the record on the rifle range at Quantico. He retired after twenty as a major. We may want look deeper into brother George."

"Maybe."

She paused and took a deep breath. "He now works for Lockheed as a maintenance officer. Mac, the younger brother, went to college at St. Cloud State University in Minnesota, same as Kiley. I believe that's a bizarre coincidence. Not a very impressive GPA. Two point oh one. Before becoming a naval aviator, he was enlisted for about a year and received training in avionics. We have a man at St. Cloud trying to find more on both Kiley and McIntyre. I'm hoping for information any time now."

She stopped again, this time to allow Capone a moment to analyze her short report.

Capone continued to complete his notes. "Good, Meg."

She had worked hard to gather this much in only about three hours and was proud of herself. Particularly the information about Mac's brother working for a major aircraft manufacturer and that Mac himself was trained in avionics, a vocation focusing on the repair and maintenance of aircraft electrical systems.

"Meg, you're doing good work. I'm glad I talked Ed into letting you go for a few days. How've you been?"

"I've been well, Bob. Been working long days on the Florida drug situation. Our pilots down there are remarkable. I'd like to get into that action someday."

"I'll see what I can do. Are you a pilot?"

"Not that I would brag about. I've been taking lessons. Working on an instrument rating."

"Excellent. Well, you're on the right track with what you done so far with this. I know you can't control what's going on in St. Cloud, but when you hear back from whoever we have up there, let me know. And obviously, what you found about McIntyre's brother is interesting. I'm adding him to your list. Check him out."

"Okay."

Capone said, "I've been thinking about Nicholson. He was apparently a whiz at MIT, electrical engineering degree. Maybe there's something from his studies that's tied to this avionics mystery. Now you throw McIntyre into the equation with his Navy training, and his brother working for Lockheed. We have a lot to work with here. Concentrate on what we talked about and let me know if you turn over a suspicious rock. Anything else?"

She looked away, hesitating. Capone noticed

the pause. "What is it, Meg?"

"Well, you told us where you thought we should focus. At least what seems to be the main concern, the orange boxes. You believe the problem might be grave."

She seemed to be stalling, not wanting to get to what was troubling her. Capone sensed this. "Yes, I'm certain that the boxes manufactured by Sanderson are important. I also think there may be serious consequences. What's your concern?"

"Well, I know we think that the devices are related to the aviation industry and are probably some type of avionics equipment, but what do you think they'll be used for? I get the impression you have an idea of what we're up against."

"Meg, there are many possibilities. Could be a copy or new design of some military equipment that the Bennettis are selling to a Third World air force. The boxes may have been planted in our planes to be used later. They may have a date chip inside that could expire at a certain time, maybe affecting our own Air Force at a critical time. Or they may be simply a black-market copy of something that isn't so ominous but being sold as original hardware."

"You don't believe any of that, do you Bob?"

"No, but it's only a feeling. I'm afraid, considering all the elements, it looks to me more like a ransom of a large number of commercial jets. I'm concerned there may be hundreds of innocent passengers in play."

"Doesn't that seem like an awfully huge undertaking considering our government is known for not giving in to hostage demands? This seems like a terribly complex conspiracy for an unlikely ransom recovery."

"I know, it doesn't quite fit."

Meg agreed, "It doesn't."

Capone said, "Where would the one hundred boxes go? And how would they be triggered? Also, it takes time to come up with the kind of money they would be asking for. The planes would have to land, and then what?"

Meg offered, "They might as well put a bomb in a mall or a large building."

Capone said, "It doesn't make sense to me either. I'm convinced, though, that the boxes are the key and they're related to aviation. Kiley ties it to commercial aviation. Besides, the passenger factor fits in well. I just don't know, Meg. I agree that it doesn't seem like a well-laid plan for hijacking commercial airliners. I don't have all the answers yet, but I have a strong feeling that if we don't stop this quickly, there'll be a threat of massive destruction to passenger-laden aircraft on tomorrow's news. I could be wrong."

Meg knew he could be wrong, but she also knew his reputation for being right about things long before anyone else had a clue. Her face was somber as she sat back in her chair. She wrote some notes on her pad, stood, and said, "I'll get something for you Bob."

Capone's eyes momentarily fixed on her tightly wrapped hips while she rounded each desk on the way to her seat. He mentally rebuked himself for the transgression. Then he titled a new page in his notebook before calling the next team member.

"Dusty, you got anything at all for me?" Capone asked hopefully, while motioning for the youngest member of the group to come forward.

"Not much," Dusty said, "but there's a few things."

"Let's have it."

Dusty Howard should have been known around the building for his quick mind, but unfortunately, he had been born from a set of diminutive parents. His stature became his trademark. He had fibbed slightly about his height when applying to the Bureau and spent a month strapped to a homemade stretching machine before taking the comprehensive FBI physical. Although he was short, he was built like a tank. He grabbed the back of the chair next to Capone's desk and slid it away as if it were balsa wood. He was eager, but took his time opening the manila folder cradled in his lap. "I've been looking into Nicholson, Bob."

"Tell me you found something interesting."

Dusty shook his head. "I don't know about this Nicholson guy. Webster's been over at MIT and is on his way back now."

"That was quick."

"I'll let you know when he returns. He did discover that Nicholson is somewhat of an electronics genius. Graduated with a 4.0 GPA peppered with honors and awards I've never heard of. The provost at MIT sent Webster to the school library to look for research papers, or other works by Nicholson."

"The school library?"

"Yeah, I wouldn't have thought of it, but apparently the very brightest graduate students submit original manuscripts relating to their field of study. Nicholson would be in this category."

"He was that smart?"

"Oh, yeah. There could be something there. Never know."

"Dusty, that's very interesting. This is a good start. Has Webster been to the library yet?"

"He called me fifteen minutes ago. I hope I did the right thing. I told him to bring back everything he found. He could have faxed it, but there were almost two hundred pages. He's using the helicopter, so I told him to just bring it all back."

"That's okay, that's what I would have wanted."

"I figured you'd want it checked out by engineering. I called Thermond Redmond. He was still in the lab and is going to stay late. I briefed him as fully as I could. He said he'd go over the material quickly and come straight up."

"That's outstanding, Dusty. We're bound to get lucky soon. What else?"

The muscular little man spoke rapidly. He was one of the Bureau's young stars with an impressive academic file. He had degrees in criminology and computer science, and was quickly building a reputation for detailed and logical thinking. Capone had high expectations for the young agent and was glad to have his help.

Jim Everett entered the room carrying a cardboard box that he used to mark claim on one of the remaining desks. Without emptying the box, he began typing information into his computer.

Capone decided to place another call to Mr. Briscoe in California. The Aviontrics plant would still be open, and he hoped to get information on the orange boxes before their business day was over.

Briscoe picked up on the first ring.

"Al, this is Bob Capone in Washington. I hope I'm not pushing too hard, but I wanted to catch you before you left. Have you had any luck finding a match for the specs I sent out."

"I'm afraid we haven't found anything yet. I have two of my people going through the files. Unfortunately, we have no way to cross-reference dimensions or paint colors electronically. We're going through everything by hand. It's extremely labor intensive. I do realize the importance of identifying the device, and we'll work overtime this evening. If this can help prevent a troublesome situation, I want to do what I can."

Bob Capone was disappointed but relieved at the same time. There was still hope Briscoe would find something.

"I appreciate your help, Al. This is an important thing you're doing for us tonight. Please let me know if you come up with anything. Anything at all. Do you have a feel as to how long it may take to complete the search?"

"I'm afraid to make a guess, but I'd say maybe two hours, give or take."

"I won't hold you to that, but it helps. Thanks again. If I don't hear from you in about two hours, I'll check back."

CHAPTER 21

Wisconsin Dells, Wisconsin
18:00 Central Standard Time
February 1, 2007

The red numbers on the Buick Riviera's electronic dashboard clock clicked over to precisely 6:00 as Jack Esposito carefully guided the stolen car through the icy lot of the Dells Day's Inn, toward an open spot near the main entrance. The hard-packed snow made crunching noises as the car slowed to a stop. Jack turned the ignition off and placed his head on the steering wheel, resting. Considering the tragic incident on the highway back at Black River Falls, and then the unfortunate ending to the car swap in Mauston, he figured he had done quite well to get this far with the Coleman cooler. During the last half hour on I-94, the weather continued to clear. Jack was torn between moving on to the original stopping point in Madison or pulling over now to check in with Tony Bennetti. Unlike Mick, Jack had not received training on the ACU and wasn't sure how important it was to get the unit plugged in.

He raised his head, leaned back in the seat, and let his head relax on the headrest. He began to calculate what time he would leave if he charged the ACU for six hours. He figured he would be pulling out of the lot around midnight. If he drove straight to the Chicago Regency where Tony Bennetti was staying, he might be able to get the box delivered by four o'clock in the morning. He knew Tony would have high praise for him if he finished this assignment successfully.

After checking in at the front desk using a George Smith alias, he went directly to his room and peeled off the duct tape from the Coleman cooler. Wisely, he decided to wait the few minutes that it would take to call Tony before doing anything that might harm the box. He gently removed the foam packing and then the unit, placing everything on the bed. Using the business card Tony had given him with the Chicago Hyatt number penciled on the back, he read the instructions on the motel phone, dialed eight to get an outside line, and then Tony's number.

"Hello." Tony's familiar voice answered.

"Mr. Bennetti, this is Jack, I'm in Wisconsin Dells, about an hour from Madison."

Immediately, Tony Bennetti suspected something was wrong. It wasn't normal for Jack Esposito to be calling. He should be farther down the road than Wisconsin Dells. "Where's

Mick?" he asked immediately.

"We had a problem. . ." Jack started, hoping to explain before being interrupted. "Don't worry, Mr. Bennetti."

"What kind of problem?"

"I've got the box and it's okay. But we had an accident and Mick's in the hospital."

"Okay, Jack," Tony calmly said, trying to settle Jack's nervousness. He was experienced at dealing with fouled operations and was aware that panic would only aggravate an already bad situation. "Jack, start at the beginning and tell me what happened. We'll work it out."

"Well, we got in an accident a few hours back. Mick was hurt pretty bad. A semi was involved, and the driver called for an ambulance." Jack voice was shaky.

"Okay, calm down Jack."

After a pause, Jack started again. "He went to help the people in the other car, and I grabbed the ACU and left. I ran across a field to a side road and waved down a pickup truck. A coupla kids were in it. They gave me a lift. I didn't hurt them, but I had to keep them quiet until I could get a different set of wheels, so I tied them up down a back road."

"Shit, Jack."

"It's okay, Tony. I drove for about twenty minutes and found a farmhouse hidden behind some trees. I got a new car. I had a little problem, but everything's okay now." Jack was hoping he wouldn't have to explain the murder of the two old people.

"What do you mean a little problem, Jack?"

"Well, the old man that lived on the farm tried to run. He would have gotten the police. I had to kill him."

"Jack."

"The old lady was an accident."

"Shit, Jack. Did you get rid of their car yet?"

"No, Mr. Bennetti, I covered everything up pretty good. You can't see their place from the road, and unless someone happens to stop by..."

"Unless...happens?" Tony was starting to get angry but tried not to alarm Jack. He didn't need a second-rate muscle man panicking while controlling the fate of the ACU. "Damn it, Jack, if the cops find the bodies, that car will be as hot as a peperocino sandwich. We'll have to take care of it. Did you plug the charger in yet?"

"No, Mr. Bennetti, I thought I should call you first. I wasn't with Mick when you explained how to charge it."

"Okay, that's good. We need to plug it in. There's not much to it, Jack. Do you have it out of the cooler?"

"It's on the bed."

"Good. Take the key and open the box. You'll need to make sure the black toggle switch is in the BATT position before plugging it into the wall."

All the good feelings that Jack had experienced about his masterful recovery from the accident vanished. He realized Mick still had the brass key that opened the box in his pants pocket, and Mick was at the La Crosse hospital at least two hours away.

"Mr. Bennetti, Mick has the key for the box."

There was a long silence on the phone. Jack realized the mistake he had made. The magnitude of his oversight seemed overwhelming. Tony amazingly remained calm but was becoming increasingly agitated. The silence seemed like an eternity to Jack.

"All right, Jack, stay calm. I might have done the same thing. There was a lot happening, and you did good to get away with the ACU. There are two switches inside the box. One is the main ON-OFF switch. It's chrome in color. Mick should have left it in the OFF position. The other switch is also a toggle switch, but it's black. The black switch is the power source selector. Once you've plugged the cord into a wall outlet, you'll need to place the power source selector to the AC position. Do you follow, Jack?"

"Tony, I'm really not very good with electricity."

"Okay, let me try to explain. Now pay attention. You can't get to the switches right now anyway with the box locked. Mick should have returned the switch to the DC position after removing it from the safe. To use the charger, we have to switch it back to the other position, the one that's labeled AC, after we plug it in. The AC position connects the internal battery charger to the AC power source. The internal wiring and the switch arrangement allow for a smooth transition. Can you follow that?"

"I think so Mr. Bennetti. You're saying that I'll have to change the position of the switch after I plug it into the wall?"

"Yes, Jack, exactly. We need to get the box open. This possibility didn't come up in our planning, but we'll take care of it even if I have to drive out with the other key. I'll find Nicholson. We'll figure this out. Are you with me Jack?"

Yes sir, Mr. Bennetti. You want me to wait until you talk to Nicholson. I'll stay right by the phone."

"Don't hang up Jack."

"What, Mr. Bennetti?"

"Tell me what room you're in and give me your phone number so I don't have to look it up."

Jack did as he was told.

"Okay. Now Jack, while I'm getting Nicholson, you need to get rid of the car. Go out and drive it a block or so away and park it where it can't be seen from the road. You know, where the police won't see it cruising by. I want you back in that room in a half-hour."

"I'll get right on it, Mr. Bennetti. I'll be back here in a half-hour."

Tony Bennetti slammed the hotel phone down and studied the time on his watch. It read

six fifty-five. He knew that the ACU had been removed from the Kiley safe around eight o'clock
that morning, and twelve hours was pushing the
battery's charge. He could drive to Wisconsin
Dells, which was probably four hours away, but
that would extend the time on the battery beyond twelve hours. His options were to either
drive up to the Dells with the spare key or force
the box open. Having evaluated the situation,
Bennetti picked up the phone and dialed Nicholson's room.

Nicholson answered without emotion.

"Mike, this is Tony. We have a problem. Can
you come up to my room?"

"What kind of problem?"

"Jack just called from Wisconsin Dells. He's
about two hours behind schedule. Mick Mallory
is in the hospital and he has the key to the box.
We need to discuss this."

"Yeah, sure. I'll be right up."

When he arrived, Tony explained the recent
developments. "What do you suggest," he asked.

"Well, we really don't have much choice. If
we try to drive up with the key, we risk the battery running low and losing the PSD IDs that are
stored in memory. If that happens, the two devices won't be able to talk to each other when
I activate the system. We may or may not have
control of all the PSDs. The best thing to do is
to have Jack try and pry the lock open with a
knife or a small tool of some sort. It's a cheap

lock. Jack should be able to force it, even if he bends the lid a little, as long as he doesn't try and muscle it too much and accidentally allow the knife or whatever he uses to slip and damage the circuitry on the inside. I think we can talk him through it."

"Okay, you're the expert. We'll call him in about fifteen minutes and see if he's back. You can talk him through the process."

Nicholson nodded. "I can't believe those two idiots," he fumed. "All they had to do was drive a car across Wisconsin. How do we know that Mallory will keep his mouth shut in the hospital?"

"You don't have to worry about Mick. He's been with me for thirty-five years and won't say a word. I'll take care of him later. I'm concerned about Jack, though, I wouldn't have trusted him to do this without Mick."

Bennetti didn't tell Nicholson about Jack murdering the old couple in Mauston. It would serve no purpose.

"As soon as we get the box open and the charger hooked up, I'll drive out myself, while it's charging, and bring it back. We have plenty of time before your plane leaves tomorrow," Tony said.

"Let's hope Jack doesn't destroy it trying to pry it open."

The two waited a few more minutes before dialing Room 303 at the Dells Days Inn. Jack answered eagerly on the first ring. "Hello."

"Jack, did you ditch the car?"

"Yes sir, I drove it behind an apartment building. It won't be noticed for days."

"Good job. I've got Nicholson here. We want you to try to pry the lock open. He says it's a cheap latch and it won't be a problem if you bend the lid a little or break the lock. But Jack, don't touch anything on the inside with your knife or screwdriver, or whatever you use. Do you have a pocketknife?"

"Sure, Mr. Bennetti. I think I can get the lock open, if it's okay to bend it some. Do you want me to get started?"

"Hold on. Talk to Mike here and make sure you do what he says."

"Sure, boss."

"Jack," Nicholson began, "what are you going to use to jimmy the lock?"

"Well, I've got a pocketknife that I think will work."

"Go ahead and try that. But you must be careful not to let the knife slip. If it touches any of the circuits inside, you stand an excellent chance of shorting something and rendering it useless. The battery and charging unit are on the right-hand side as you're looking at the lock. That's the safest place to work. You're fairly safe to the right of the latch. Just behind the lock, and about a quarter inch below the seam is the top circuit board. It doesn't quite touch the edge of the box, but it's close. What I'm saying is, if the knife slips while you're prying the lock and it goes inside the unit, don't bother bringing it back. Do you understand?"

Jack was starting to get nervous. A few minutes ago, before receiving all the information about how sensitive the damn thing was, he would have easily pried the latching lever away from its catch and lifted the lid. Now, with the protracted lectures about how he could ruin the thing if his hand slipped, he wasn't so sure.

He held the box up and tried using the blade like a key, not expecting the lock to turn. It didn't. He was nervous and his hands were shaking. This wasn't the type of work he was normally asked to do. He wasn't good at fixing things, particularly small mechanisms. Having hands the size of a baseball mitt slowed his progress. *Why had Mick gotten into the accident? It was all Mick's fault.*

"Can't I just drive it back and charge it in Chicago tonight? Won't the battery last four more hours?"

"No, Jack," Nicholson said sharply, "you have to open it and be careful in the process. It's not dangerous, and you won't mess it up. It's just a simple metal box. The inside is the sensitive stuff. Just don't go inside."

"All right. I'm working on it."

Jack worked the knife blade into the lock, attempting to turn the simple mechanism with the pointed tip of the blade. Trying several different angles, even rolling the knife over, he couldn't get the lock to turn. He tried harder, which only resulted in snapping off the end of the blade.

"Now I broke it," Jack exclaimed angrily."

"What do you mean you broke it?" Nicholson blurted in disbelief.

"He broke it? What do you mean he broke it?" Tony shot back.

Jack came back on the line. "No, I broke the knife tip. Don't worry, I'm being careful. I'm going to try and pry the lid apart a little and release the catch."

Nicholson relaxed and eased back in his chair. "Don't worry," Nicholson said to Tony, "he just broke the knife blade off in the keyhole. He's going to try and pry the lid."

Bennetti rolled his eyes upward and shook his head.

Nicholson said, "If you're prying the lid, Jack, don't let the knife slip into the box."

"Don't worry. I'm being careful." Jack felt more at ease as he worked the remaining portion of the blade under the lid and around the lock. He bent the edge of the top outward and could see a little of the latch piece inside the box. He forced it wider apart trying to release the catch.

"Shit!" Jack yelled into the telephone, and again but much louder, "SHIT!".

Nicholson feared that Jack had allowed the knife to slip through to the circuit board. He pulled the receiver away from his ear, cringing, and looked at Tony.

"What?" Tony asked, both hands rolled with palms up in a questioning gesture.

"He let the knife slip. Sounds like we're out of business."

"Give me that phone," Tony demanded. He snatched the receiver from Nicholson's hand. Tony Bennettis dark Italian face reflected his fury, and his facial muscles tightened from the pressure of his clenched jaw. "Jack, damn it, what happened?"

Back in the Dells Days Inn, Jack set the ACU on the bed, and the phone on the desktop. He was wrapping a face cloth around his hand, near the sink. Tony continued to bellow into his end of the line, but Jack wasn't listening. "Jack, answer me." Now Tony was screaming into the phone. Nicholson sat on the edge of the bed with his face buried in his hands.

Tony looked over to Nicholson. "He's not there. What the hell?"

Jack returned to the phone and said, "Mr. Bennetti. . . Mr. Bennetti." He wasn't getting a response because Tony was trying to get an explanation from Nicholson. Tony returned to the phone in his hand.

"Jack, are you there?"

"Mr. Bennetti, I'm sorry. I had to leave for a few seconds. I was getting blood all over everything."

"Blood? What are you talking about?"

"I was trying to bend the cover out with my knife, and it slipped. I nearly cut the end of my finger off."

"Did the knife go inside the box? Did you touch any of the circuit boards?"

"No, boss, I was being very careful. If you hang on a minute, I think I've almost got this thing open."

"Go ahead Jack, but no more excitement."

Nicholson looked at Tony in anticipation and asked, "What's he doing? What happened?"

"It's okay. The knife slipped and he cut his finger. We're okay."

"Mr. Bennetti, you there?"

"Go ahead Jack."

"I got it open. Everything's okay."

"Good job, Jack. I'm handing the phone over to Nicholson. He'll tell you what to do to get the thing safely connected to the charger.

Tony quickly described the situation to Nicholson while handing over the phone.

"Jack, this is Mike again. Do you have the lid open now?"

"It's sitting on the bed with the lid open. Some of the lights are on steady, a couple of them are blinking."

"That's normal. Did the knife touch anything on the inside of the unit?"

"No, I said I was being careful. Everything is fine. I just bent the lid back a little so I could get to the latch and pry it."

"Great. Very good. Now you need to make sure the silver switch is in the OFF position."

"The silver switch is OFF."

"Okay, now check the black toggle switch on the right side. The black switch should be in the position labeled DC."

"That's the position it's in."

"Good. So far everything sounds normal. Now see if you can find a steady red light next to the black switch that is labeled READY. Is it lit and not blinking?"

"Yes, I see a single light next to the black switch. It's not blinking."

"Good, Jack. That's a circuit diagnostic light. It's telling us the unit is working normally. Now all we have to do is plug the charger in. Do you have the cord with the cannon fitting with you?"

"Mick packed your cord in with the cooler. We left the one that was on it behind, because the fitting wouldn't fit through the hole in the side of the safe."

"I knew that would be the case, Jack. Now listen closely. This is a very simple process, but you have to do a couple of things in the proper order, so I'll explain it first, and then we'll do it. Okay?"

"Okay. Go ahead."

"All right. The first thing to do is screw the cannon plug onto the fitting located on the right side of the box. There are six holes on the plug that must line up with the prongs on the box. A small slit or keyway will prevent you from putting it on wrong. Do you see how those two pieces fit together?"

"Yeah, I get it."

"Great, Jack. Go ahead and screw that cannon plug onto the box. When you're done, plug it into the wall."

"Okay."

After a minute, Jack said, "It's plugged in."

"Good, Jack, now flip the black switch over to the AC position. This'll provide a bumpless connection to the charger."

"The black switch is in the AC position."

"Okay, good job, that's it."

Nicholson handed the receiver over to Bennetti.

"Jack, how are you doing? Is everything okay?"

"I'm fine boss. The ACU is plugged in and everything is fine now."

"You've done a great job and earned a bonus. We'll talk about it later. I want you to baby-sit the box. I'll be out there before it's done charging. If you need to call me, call on my car phone. Have you got my number?"

"Yes, sir."

"Good. I'll contact you before I leave. We'll unplug the charger when I get there and drive it back together. We still have plenty of time before Mike takes off in the morning."

"Okay, boss, I'll stay put but my finger is nearly cut off. Can I leave the room long enough to go down and see if the guy at the desk has something for it?"

"No, Jack. You'll live. We don't want to draw any more attention to this than necessary. I'll bring something out for you to wrap it with. You can see the doc in the morning."

"Right, I'll be fine. Thanks Mr. Bennetti."

CHAPTER 22

Empire Crew Motel
Chicago, Illinois
19:40 Central Standard Time
February 1, 2007

It had been about forty-five minutes since Claire and her father dropped me off at my motel. He seemed like a great guy, the kind of person that immediately makes you feel like you've known him for years. We told him about the goose incident, which he found entertaining. I told the story of the aircraft manufacturer that used live chickens to test cockpit glass. Both found it believable and thought it could have happened. Someday, I'll have to do some research and find out.

Mr. Elliott lived less than fifteen minutes west on I-90. Claire has kept a sort of second home there, with her own room and many of her personal belongings. She said they'd return to pick me up just as soon as she could get changed so we could get an early start and have some time to visit. I hurried to get cleaned up, took a quick shower, shaved, and turned on the news. I found it hard to concentrate on what the reporter was saying, thinking how much I was looking forward to going out and getting to know Claire better. I was at ease with her father, but still wished that she and I were going out alone.

There was a knock on the door. "Mac, are you decent?"

I had on a white V-neck tee shirt and felt a little silly with her bringing me clothes to wear. I opened the door and saw her out of the tan Empire uniform for the first time. She was wearing a sleek, black, below-the-knee dress with spaghetti straps and a scoop front. The three-inch heels and hair piled on top of her head made her an inch taller than me, at five eleven in my socks. Pearls graced her slender neck, and matching earrings dangled an inch below each lobe. Even though her dress was sophisticated and a bit formal, she wore very little make up and looked fresh and innocent. I was entranced. She was gorgeous.

Reaching out to accept the clothes her father had sent, I said, "You look great, I don't think these uniform slacks really compliment your outfit. Are you sure you and your dad weren't looking forward to a nice father-daughter dinner alone?"

"No. Now, you're not getting out of this that easy. Try this shirt on. It's probably a little big in the shoulders but the jacket will cover that."

"Thanks, you're making things much easier."

As I tried on the shirt and began to button it, Claire sat on the bed and waited.

"That wasn't very funny what you did back at the terminal," I said.

"What do you mean," she answered coyly.

"You know what I mean, the mysterious person that you had serious feelings about."

"I can't help it if you read something into what I said that wasn't what I meant. I never said I was meeting a boyfriend. Besides, I wasn't sure you were interested in me until we got to Chicago. You need to open up more."

"Too dangerous," I said. "Rejection is something I try to avoid. Besides, when did I say I was interested?"

"Oh, you're not?"

"Actually, I must admit you have potential. But I don't think I actually said anything to that effect. Yet."

"Yet? Does that mean you soon intend to tell me how attracted you are to me?"

"Maybe; depends on how the jacket fits."

She handed me a tie. "Try this on. You're beginning to clean up pretty good."

I accepted the necktie and lucked out with putting the half-Windsor in just the right place on the first try. She held out the jacket for me to slip into. With one hand on my shoulder she turned me toward her, straightened the front of the coat, and fastened the middle button. Claire was beginning to really get to me and at this moment, as I watched her finish with the button, I became aware of that special feeling that only comes along every once in a while between two people. "What do you think?" I asked.

She adjusted the shoulders of the jacket. "Well, it doesn't look quite as good on you as it does on Dad, but you look right smart big guy. Then she grabbed my elbow and gave it a gentle tug. "Dad's waiting in the lobby, let's get going."

We stood close together near the elevator door with her arms entwined around mine. "You know," I said, "I've really enjoyed this month. I mean working with you, even though Kiley has taken the fun away a bit. I've wanted to ask you out since that first trip to Seattle."

"You remember our first trip together? How romantic, I'm flattered. I remember it too, and I was wondering what I would have to do to get your attention. Are you always this slow?"

"Just a little shy, I guess." The elevator door opened, and we stepped in.

"Well, you got off to a good start with dad. He likes you, and that's a big accomplishment."

We met Mr. Elliott in the lobby. "Thanks for lending me the coat Mr. Elliott, you've got good taste. Not a bad fit either."

"Please, call me Dick. Looks better on you than it does on me. Claire gave me that jacket a few years ago for a birthday present. One of my favorites."

In the car, Mr. Elliot led the conversation. He got me talking about myself, where I had been in life and what I planned for the future. "Mac," he said, "what got you into the flying business?"

"Seems to run in the family, I guess. My dad was a career naval aviator, and my brother was an Annapolis graduate and ended up flying for the Marines."

"I've always understood the Navy flight program to be rather difficult to get into. Your father must be pretty proud of you and your brother."

Claire made sure that this positive statement about piloting didn't get by without rebuttal. "Dad, please, you have to be careful. You aren't supposed to open the door for a pilot to start talking about himself. You'll have to listen to stories about soaring through the clouds like an eagle, doing loop-de-loops, or maneuvering a flaming plane into a cornfield with a cockpit full of smoke."

"Don't mind her," Mr. Elliott said. "She's obviously interested in you or she wouldn't try so hard to make it look like she isn't."

"I know. She's tried every trick in the book to get me to notice her the last couple of days."

"Oh, Lord. This isn't fair. It's two against one. I give up," she said.

"So, Mac, where are you from?"

"Well, like I said, my dad was in the service, so we moved around a lot. It was interesting for me. We lived in Hawaii, Okinawa, Florida, Georgia, Rhode Island—I can't remember all the places. I always looked forward to the next move. I think it was a great experience. My dad retired in Minnesota where I finished high school in Bloomington and then college at St. Cloud."

"We were practically neighbors then. We lived in Big Lake for twenty-two years. Claire was born there."

"She told me. I would've loved that. Living right on the lake. I've been through Big Lake many times of course. Did you enjoy it there as a kid, Claire?" I asked.

"I wouldn't have wanted to live anywhere else. I have so many friends back there."

"She was quite popular in high school. She was an A student, played clarinet in the band, and was on the ski team and ran track," her father said proudly.

"Dad, he's not interested in my old high school days."

I was though. I wanted to hear more. "I didn't realize you were so athletic. What was your event in track?" I asked.

"I was a miler, and pretty fast too, third in state."

We talked about Claire's life on the lake well into dinner, and I was intrigued. She became more interesting by the minute, and her father loved to talk about her. The Elliot's life could have been taken from a storybook but unfortunately, there was a chapter that wasn't so pleasant.

She finished one year of college at the University of Minnesota with plans of becoming a marine biologist when her mother died of cancer. For a few years her life was upended. Her father was devastated and eventually sold the home she had grown up in, and they moved to Minneapolis to start a new life. His career carried him to Chicago. A fluke airline application that Claire had mailed in with a friend went straight through, and she soon found herself wearing the Empire uniform. The job seemed like fun and was a way of saving a little money for school while providing free travel for visits to Chicago to see her dad.

The evening flew by. I didn't want it to end but we had an eight o'clock departure in the morning. Claire and her dad drove me back to the motel and she spent the night at his home in Arlington Heights. I didn't make any plans with her for our days off in Minneapolis but knew we'd be seeing each other again at the first opportunity.

I laid my head on the pillow and couldn't help but think this trip would end up being one of the most memorable ones of my career.

CHAPTER 23

War Room, FBI Headquarters
Washington D.C.
20:50 Eastern Standard Time
February 1, 2007

Capone and Everett tried to make sense of the few facts they had accumulated.

Jim said, "It's imperative we find out more about the orange boxes. If we don't hear from him soon, we should give him a call."

"Let's give it a few more minutes. I'm hoping the stuff Webster brings back from MIT will help. Kiley's disappearance at basically the same time as his house was burglarized is meaningful."

Jim agreed, "That's obvious. There's a complex plan to all this. Nicholson has to be involved. It wasn't a mere coincidence that he was in Midland this morning and filled in for Kiley."

"That's been my thinking. Kiley, Nicholson, and the Bennettis are the key players."

Jim added, "No question. The fact that Mallory and Esposito had the combination to the safe, ties them and the Bennettis to Kiley."

"Right. Kiley gave them the location and combination to the safe. He was working with them."

Jim responded, "I think that's clear. But don't you think that they were a little sloppy? Fingerprints all over the place, kicking the door in, leaving the safe open with the cord still plugged in? The Bennettis are smarter than that."

Capone said, "No question, but I don't think they cared."

Jim asked, "What do you mean, didn't care?"

Capone explained, "It appears to me they're in a hurry. Whatever they're doing will be over by tomorrow. That's why covering up their tracks at Kiley's place wasn't important. Who would have ever stumbled on it right away? The only reason we did was because sheriff Sergeant called Dave, which was a total fluke."

Jim replied, "I think you're right. Even if someone had stopped by Kiley's and found the door kicked in, it would have only been reported to local authorities."

Capone added, "Right. A simple house burglary. Not a federal crime. The local police would have wanted to interview Kiley, but he wouldn't be around."

"And it would have taken at least a few days to find out that Kiley was missing."

Capone continued, "Exactly. The Bennettis just weren't worried about us because they knew they would be finished before we even got involved. They must be ready right now to carry this thing out, either tonight or first thing tomorrow. I'm sure of that."

Jim pressed Capone. "So then, you're the clairvoyant, what the shit are they up to?"

Capone was saved by the phone ringing. He picked up immediately. "Capone."

"Bob, this is Al Briscoe out in California. I think I have some information that might pick you up a little."

"Great, Al. Please go ahead."

"Well, we'd gone through a lot of files. In fact, we probably only had about ten percent left when Sherry, one of my clerks, found a perfect match to the measurements of your box. Not only were the dimensions an exact match, but so were the two holes that the Sanderson product specified on two of the sides. Our drawings called out the exact same holes right down to the size and location on the box. Even the assembly method was the same with tabs on the sides. Exactly the same details. The paint, of course, is noted on the Sanderson invoice as being our Day-Glow orange color."

"That's great, Al. What's the box for? What am I looking for?"

"Fortunately, this particular item isn't extremely sensitive. I'm surprised that out of all the things we make, the component we matched wasn't something requiring a higher level of protection. That's probably why it took us a lit-

NEWGATE'S KNOCKER

tle longer to find it. I started our search with more clandestine equipment and worked toward the less guarded files."

"I understand, Al. It is a little incongruous, but what's the thing used for?"

"The object you're dealing with is a flight data recorder. Our particular design is used on approximately forty percent of the larger commercial jets. There's not a whole lot of secrecy to these devices. I can't imagine that your concern could be that copies of these are in production. In fact, I can't imagine a market for such a thing. They aren't expensive and the technology is ancient compared to some of our other products."

"Well, there's something significant. I'm sure you've done much more than you realize at the moment. Do you have a number where I can reach you throughout the night if I need your help?"

The Aviontrics executive gladly provided Capone with several phone numbers and then asked, "Can I find out later what this is all about?"

"I'll phone you personally, Al. Thanks for your help."

Capone was thrilled. He had no more idea about what was going on than he had before the call, but through his many years of investigative service he learned that every new bit of information was often much more important than it initially appeared. One thing he was sure of

—this new knowledge would eventually lead to something he could use.

Capone detailed his conversation with Al Briscoe to his team, explaining the precise match to existing flight data recorders. He let it sink in, and asked the group, "If this means anything at all, or if it seems to connect with any information you already have, we need to know about it now. I don't care how stupid it sounds."

The room was silent. Capone looked at each person in turn, hoping to draw something out. He knew that invariably, even off-the-wall ideas or comments led others to open up or think of something that might prove helpful. Dusty had a look suggesting he wanted to say something but was hesitant, or didn't think it worthwhile.

"Dusty," Capone prompted, "you got something?"

"I don't know, Bob. Hell, you could probably toss out several wild-ass guesses here. Don't you think we should hold off until we have something more concrete?"

"Look, I'm not asking that we solve this case right now or even come up with an objective. I just want you all to start tossing possibilities at me. One of you might hit on something that somebody else can build on. Give it a try. No one's going anywhere tonight anyway."

"Okay. You know you have an order for one hundred boxes that appear to be an exact match to the flight data recorders in the airline jets. A flight data recorder isn't a dangerous thing. It's not the type of device that one would expect to bring huge sums of money on the black market. I'm trying to figure what benefit someone may obtain from tampering with a flight data recorder. Maybe insurance? If a jet crashed and the recorder proved the airline was at fault, well... maybe..."

Capone stopped him. "Not too good, but it's a start."

Meg held up a finger. "How about this? What if a hundred bogus flight data recorders, that didn't function properly, were placed in a competitor's airplanes. And then there's a crash and the investigation finds the entire fleet to have defective recorders. Could it make them look negligent and maybe be fined or shut down temporarily, giving an edge to the company that changed out the recorders?"

"I guess I asked for this," Capone replied in a tone that suggested Meg's idea was idiotic.

"Well, you wanted anything," she responded defensively.

"I know, you're right. You're doing good, keep it up."

Jim Everett was in the background listening in and searching for a hole in the reasoning. What weren't they thinking of? He liked brainteasers, and his high IQ provided him an edge when solving unusual problems.

Everett waited to make sure no one else was

about to speak and then said, "Maybe we aren't looking for a flight data recorder."

Meg was the first to find fault in his statement. "It seems pretty clear that Aviontrics had a perfect match to the specifications on the invoice. Don't you think it would be a stretch to think there is another product somewhere with exactly the same dimensions and design, right down to the paint color and size, and placement of the drilled holes?"

"That's not what I mean. Maybe we're looking for something that's put inside of a box that's supposed to look exactly like a flight data recorder but is something entirely different on the inside. All we know about what Aviontrics told us is that the housing and the color are the same as the flight data recorders they've previously manufactured. We don't know anything about what's inside the boxes Sanderson built."

Everyone sat back in their seats, quietly consuming their error. Even Bob Capone couldn't believe he had overlooked something this obvious. He had become so involved with all the other facts and in putting the pieces together, his thinking had become myopic.

"Jim, of course! We've all been making the most elemental mistake by assuming something to be but which hadn't yet been presented as fact. You've just managed to make the bunch of us look like first-year detectives."

He then looked at the rest of them as if to say,

"I told you so." Then, not wanting to lose momentum, he continued, "Now, I think we have something. We have one hundred boxes that are very likely meant to replace flight data recorders in one hundred airplanes. I'm still leaning toward passenger airplanes. And since we're talking airlines, why not use the one that's connected to everyone involved. Empire. Let's say, for the sake of argument, that there is, or will be, one hundred flight data recorders exchanged in their fleet of jets. Now what?"

Dusty spoke up, "That puts us back where we were before, Bob. That is, before we discovered that the boxes were modeled after flight data recorders, they could have been anything, including bombs. That's still the case, but now at least we know where to look for them. I say we get on the stick and start checking Empire's flight data recorders."

"Now we're cooking," Capone commented with enthusiasm.

"One more thing," Meg offered. "Wouldn't you say that a flight data recorder is strongly related to aircraft safety?"

"Yes, I would. Your point.?"

"Well, for the last three years your missing captain Kiley served as the chief safety manager for the company, representing the Airline Pilots Union."

"Meg, that may be extremely important. Kiley would have been in an ideal position to access Empire's recorders. He may possibly have been able to exchange the real ones with counterfeit units."

The room was becoming energized. Things were starting to come together. Capone was writing frantically, taking notes and writing down ideas as fast as they came to him. He knew subconsciously what needed to be done but couldn't write fast enough to keep up with his thoughts.

"We have two priorities that require attention immediately." Bob knew he needed to get his team organized and focused. "Dusty, I want you to go straight down to the engineering lab and bring Redmond up with the Nicholson papers from MIT. I don't care if he's done or not. Bring him up here now." Then he turned to Meg. "Meg, I want you to call Empire's president. What's his name?"

Everett helped out, "Brandon Sheffield."

"Thanks, Jim. Meg, call this Sheffield guy. When you get him on the line, and I don't care where he is, I want to talk with him. We need mechanics on his flight line tonight checking out his flight data recorders. Finish checking on McIntyre and Kiley. There may be something there that'll give us an idea of what these things are."

Meg turned and went straight to her desk to begin locating the Empire president. Dusty made a beeline for the door to seek out Thurmond Redmond, and Jim Everett returned to his keyboard to finish recording the day's events while things were fresh in his mind. Fifteen minutes had passed since receiving the information on the flight data recorders from Al Briscoe.

Meg was on the phone to Empire Airlines. It was after eight o'clock in the evening in Dallas, and the Empire World Headquarters was locked up tight for the night. Just as she suspected, Mr. Sheffield's home number wasn't listed. realizing the easy road was blocked, she tried one she hoped wouldn't be necessary. Using her FBI status, she called the Dallas Police Department and requested the senior officer on duty. After several minutes of holding, a man answered the phone.

"Detective Billings here."

"Detective, this is Special Agent Meg Gerrity, FBI, out in Washington. Can you give me a few minutes?

"You bet, Miss Gerrity."

"Listen, we have a rapidly developing situation out here. I'm afraid I just can't tell you much about it right now, but I need your help."

"Well, I'll do my best. What's up?"

"We have a situation that necessitates that I talk to Brandon Sheffield, President of Empire Airlines, as soon as possible. Immediately. His phone number isn't listed, and I don't have his address, but I know he lives in Dallas. I would be deeply grateful if one of your cars could locate his house and ask him to call me. He should be told that this is urgent and may involve possible danger to his fleet of aircraft. I'll work on getting more information from our system to help you out, but I had hoped to speed things up a little and get someone at your end started. I trust you'll keep this conversation between us, detective?"

"Rick"

"Sorry. Rick."

"Well, I'll be glad to help you out, Meg. I'll see what I can do."

The two exchanged phone numbers and the Dallas detective collected his hat and revolver from the rack and left the building. He hadn't had an opportunity to assist in a federal case for several years, and he welcomed the opportunity. It was unusual for the FBI to bring his people in on a government matter, especially in this fashion. His department had the resources to locate any resident in the greater Dallas area within minutes. He decided to handle this one himself.

Back in the war room, Meg told Capone about her conversation with the Dallas detective. He seemed pleased but bothered by the fact that Dusty hadn't returned with the engineer from the lab.

"Meg," he said with an edge of concern, "would you call Redmond's office and see what's keeping them? I believe Thermond was in the lab earlier and should've had time to complete his review. They should've been up here by now."

"Sure thing, I'll get right on it." Meg located a government directory on her desk and dialed Redmond's number.

The line was busy. Capone's phone began to ring. "Hello," he answered, "Capone."

"Bob, this is Dusty. Bad news."

"I can take it."

"Webster returned from MIT with the documents about two hours ago. There was some miscommunication when he handed them over to Thermond who understood him to say that you wanted them reviewed tonight but not immediately. He's been finishing up another matter and was just getting started when I walked in. He said it'll take him at least an hour to perform even a cursory overview."

"Shit. We'll figure out what we did wrong later. I hate communication breakdowns. Ask Redmond if he can do his work up here. If not, tell him to hurry and bring everything ASAP."

"Right, Bob. I'll be right up."

Capone looked at his watch. It was nearly 10:00 P.M. He had to locate Sheffield and get him to pull some flight data recorders immediately. If his suspicion that the recorders had been tampered with held true, the planes would have to be grounded. If no defective recorders were found, then he'd have to look elsewhere. *What*

*could possibly be the purpose of the boxes manufac-
tured by Sanderson?*

CHAPTER 24

Empire Crew Motel
Chicago, Illinois
22:15 Central Standard Time
February 1, 2007

I was lying awake staring at the ceiling when the phone rang. The bedside clock read 10:15.

"Did I wake you?"

I had been thinking about the evening in the restaurant with Claire and her dad, and imagining what we might be doing after tomorrow. I knew she would be flying a different schedule than me and the chance of our seeing much of each other next month was slim.

"Claire." I said, intentionally stressing my pleasure in hearing her voice. "No, as a matter of fact, I was lying here awake. I had a great time tonight. I enjoyed meeting your father."

"Thanks, I had a good time too. I wanted to tell you that, and that I hope we can do it again. Maybe without a chaperone next time."

I liked that about her. She wasn't afraid of coming right out and saying what she felt.

"I'm glad you called. I didn't get a chance to

ask you what your schedule looked like in the next couple of days," I said.

"Depends on what comes up."

"Okay, let me put it this way. How about a date?" I asked.

There was no hesitation. "I could be talked into that. I'm off Monday and Tuesday, then I have a three-day trip."

"Monday, then. I know an interesting place for lunch in North Minneapolis. You'll like it."

"Sounds like fun. You'll have to phone me and extend a proper invitation. I don't want to seem forward, calling you up like this."

"I don't have your number."

"It's in the book. Now I better get some sleep. Good night, Mac."

"Good night, Claire."

I was glad she had called but now it would be even more difficult getting to sleep. I started to think about the good fortune I'd had over the years.

Everything always seems to fall in place. This worries me at times, especially since landing the job with Empire, and now this good start with Claire. So far, karma had been good to me.

I had enlisted in the Navy not having any idea what I wanted to do with my life, but as luck would have it, I got my first choice of military training—avionics school in Memphis. I'd spent only six months as a "white hat" and just out of training my division officer recommended me as a candidate for naval flight training, which required I complete college. I finished up a four-year engineering program in three years.

It would have been hard to beat my years at St. Cloud, but after graduation my commitment to naval aviation began, and life as an aviator was equally accommodating. I made it through all the qualifying tests easily and entered the flight program in Pensacola in the heat of early summer. It was grueling but those of us that survived were bound as tight as the rubber wrapping on a golf ball. I had always been told that life was tough and that all I had to look forward to was getting up, going to work, and paying taxes. I wondered what kind of tragic life the person had who articulated that bit of philosophical wisdom.

As luck would have it, deregulation opened up the airline industry just as my military commitment expired and most of the major carriers were expanding. I was hired by Empire within weeks of getting out of the Navy and given Minneapolis as home base after training. Again, fate was my friend. Flying for Empire was everything I had ever imagined and more. I was back home in Minnesota and close to many of my old friends from college.

As time passed, I started to realize that maybe I might have exceeded my share of good luck. I became more and more nervous that at some point things might come crumbling down. The only big hurdle I hadn't yet completed was to meet the right girl and settle down. It appears maybe that too might come too easy.

Claire was the girl I had hoped would show up. As usual, the timing seems perfect.

CHAPTER 25

War Room, FBI Headquarters
Washington D.C.
23:22 Eastern Standard Time
February 1, 2007

Thermond Redmond is of average height and weight. He's forty-seven years old, has thinning gray hair, and an ivory-white handlebar mustache. He walked into the room carrying a tan leather briefcase matching an identically colored sport coat. A slight grin on his stubble-covered face revealed that he was pleased with the work he had performed on the Nicholson papers, once told of the urgency only an hour and a half ago. Thermond is the most experienced and knowledgeable engineering expert working for the FBI. He virtually lives in the large, well-equipped laboratory in the basement of the J. Edgar Hoover building. He had elected to remain there during his analysis of the material. He found the volumes of reference books and computer software in the lab helpful while researching Nicholson's writings.

Thermond had studied two lengthy papers

authored by the MIT graduate, each relating to a peculiar subject. One was titled, *A Warning for Modern Civilized Society - Prophesizing the Future of Invisible Weaponry*. It was Nicholson's prediction of how a new age of technologically advanced killing tools would be used against civilized nations, such as the United States, to weaken, and ultimately destroy, the infrastructure that had grown dangerously dependent on electronic processes. Thermond found Nicholson's evaluation of laser technology and electromagnetic wave disturbance relative to terrorist uses extremely well-documented and convincingly argued.

The second paper, the longer of the two, had been written during Nicholson's last year at MIT. It didn't seem to have any connection with his academic program but was apparently written as his way of expressing an unusually advanced understanding of the subject matter. Thermond would later explain Nicholson's manuscripts as an unconscious attempt to warn society of what he was considering, and what he was capable of. He even expressed his position in the title of one of the essays by using the word "warning". He had come right out and offered his intentions to the world, but no one had taken notice. The paper was accepted by the MIT library as a student-authored work recommended by the dean of the School of Engineering on the basis of advanced thinking and original scientific principles. This was titled, *Electromagnet Field Disturbance, an Evaluation of Ultra Low Frequency Pulsating Wave Energy and Consequential Effects on Electric and Electronic Machines*. Thermond found it to be a workbook for building a pulsating wave energy amplifier that could totally cripple a technology oriented society. The paper detailed the seemingly invisible nature of such a device and explained the disturbing consequences that could result if controlled by adversarial groups.

Redmond walked directly toward Capone's desk, and began to speak while still a few feet away. Capone looked up and acknowledged his presence.

"I think we need to talk," Redmond said, in an ominous tone.

"Sit down, Thermond. Thanks for going over this so quickly. I presume Dusty gave you an overview of what we're dealing with."

"I have a vague idea of the urgency now. I apologize for the earlier misunderstanding. It really wasn't Webster's fault. I think he was under the impression I was already aware of the situation."

"That's behind us. Let's press on. Is there anything in those papers that could be related to these mysterious avionics packages we're trying to identify?"

"If you think there's a possibility that the man who wrote this," he paused momentarily to hold up a thick set of papers, "has helped engineer the interior components to your black boxes, then you do indeed have a problem, black as Newgate's knocker."

Capone often found that Redmond's intellect could inhibit smooth communication, and now he had to backtrack for clarification. Capone sat up and leaned forward, "Who the hell is Newgate?"

Thermond shook his head, realizing he needlessly threw an unfamiliar idiom into the conversation. His photographic memory was often more disruptive then helpful. He frequently had to explain obscure expressions and uncommon concepts to others.

"Sorry, Bob, Newgate was a vile and merciless prison in England. Originally constructed in 1188, it was rebuilt several times and remained in use for over 700 years. For much of that time it primarily housed prisoners awaiting execution. Over the years, the door knocker became synonymous with dire expectations. I believe the implications of what I'm trying to explain are dire indeed."

Capone couldn't image what the bookish engineer had found. There was no doubt that Redmond's reference to Newgate's knocker had confirmed the fact that the Sanderson invoice was important. *What were these things designed to do? What has Thermond uncovered?*

"Give me your opinion of what Nicholson

may have built. Then we'll go over your reasoning and the supporting material you're holding."

"I hope I'm wrong about this, Bob. I don't know how much other information you have that points to Nicholson and the type of operation he's involved in. But if he's responsible for what's inside the boxes, I'm afraid the implications are very chilling. I say that because these two manuscripts first, contain very detailed and accurate descriptions of how to build an incredibly diabolical device and second, both were written by a young man over twenty years ago. Assuming the person who devised these ideas continued to develop and expand on the concepts, then advanced prototypes of these machines undoubtedly exist."

Capone listened intently, not wanting to interrupt the flow of Thermond's presentation. Capone tried to maintain eye contact with the engineer while feverishly scribbling on his notepad. He detected a growing seriousness in the man's face and feared the conclusion of his report.

Thermond bit his lower lip and considered what to say next. "Bob, these manuscripts are theoretically perfect. I'm not an expert in this field, but I've done some reading. In the last five years or so, there's been impressive testing of wave generators that work almost exactly as described by Nicholson's twenty-year-old work. He was light-years ahead in this field.

It's unthinkable that someone with this kind of insight would abandon his research, especially considering the impassioned tone of his discussions. I believe that Nicholson has perfected the equipment of which he had a clear understanding in college. The culmination of that work very likely lives in the one hundred boxes you're trying to identify."

Capone couldn't wait any longer. Thermond was a brilliant technical thinker, but he wasn't an investigator. So far, he was concentrating on the ideas he found important and interesting. He didn't understand the most important question that needed to be answered. Capone asked it. "Thermond, tell me what you think the boxes are for. What do they do exactly?"

"I thought you understood," the scientist said, sounding a little dumbfounded. "I'm sorry. I guess I didn't really explain it well. Having studied the transcripts for the last couple hours, I guess it's become clearer to me than it would be to someone who hasn't read this." He held the papers up and continued. "Let me explain. Nicholson's primary field of study was electronics. He minored in physics and was equally talented in electromagnets, wave generation, energy transfer, induction, and all that sort of stuff. He seemed obsessed with harnessing electromagnetic wave fields for the purpose of electronic interference." Thermond smiled. "The idea has been around for years but until recently, few

actual models have been successfully demon-
strated. However, a number of them have been
reported to be quite impressive. Russia has a
very advanced design. The models I'm aware
of are somewhat bulky and probably haven't
reached the stage of being practical for military
uses. The biggest concern that our government
has is what will happen if, or I should say when, a
terrorist entity has a unit with the bugs worked
out."

Capone was trying to be patient and allow
the engineer to explain the contraption in his
own way, but he needed to get to the point. "Listen, Thermond, if you don't tell me what the
damn thing does, I'm going to fling myself across
this desk and rip you tongue out."

Thermond finally understood what Capone
needed to hear. "The machine I'm talking about
has the capability to disable or stop almost anything that requires electricity or electrical components. That would include computers, television sets, radios, cars and even airplane engines."

"Jet engines?" Capone blurted.

"Very likely. Yes, jet engines."

The entire day had finally crystallized in Capone's mind. Immediately, all the unanswered
questions became clear.

"Bob, you should know that I only did a very
cursory review of this work. You were in a hurry.
I wanted to give you an idea of what these files
contained. There are two hundred and some odd

pages here. It would take me at least a full day to do even a basic review. I believe that I provided a close summation of the main points, but I really need a couple of days to do this justice. Do you want me to start on it first thing in the morning?"

"Thermond, I'm going to ask Jim Everett to provide you with a complete briefing of where we are with this thing. I believe there's extreme urgency to press on through the night. I want you to stay with us. We may need your expertise. Can you do that?"

"If you believe I'm needed, then I'll stay. Are you saying that these devices are implanted in airplanes now? All one hundred of them?"

"Yes, that's what I believe. We're going to find out tonight. I don't know this, but I have a feeling these instruments are set to be triggered sometime tomorrow. Unfortunately, I have absolutely nothing solid to base this on, and I can't hit the panic button yet."

Capone returned to his notes. He knew this new information was extremely important. There appeared to be a high probability that that some form of the wave generating device had been incorporated into the orange boxes. He was certain now that Nicholson was involved. He scribbled more notes on the pad, detailing new priorities. First on the list was to notify Brandon Sheffield and get someone out to inspect the planes on the ground in Dallas. Sev-

eral flight data recorders must be pulled immediately and checked for signs of tampering. He
looked over in the direction of the two younger
agents involved in a conference at Meg's desk.
"Meg," Capone said, just loud enough to attract
their attention.

Meg looked up and responded, "What, Bob?"

"Any word from Dallas yet?"

"Not yet. Do you want me to try another
angle?"

"No, I'm sure they're doing the best they can.
It's only been, what, about twenty minutes?"

"Thirty-five," she said.

She knew this was important and had hoped
the detective in Dallas would at least call with
an update.

Bob winced as he realized how long it had
been since Meg first called Dallas. "I need the
two of you to come over for a minute. We've got
some new information."

As the two approached, Capone began,
"Thermond just gave me a short synopsis of
some college papers Nicholson wrote some
twenty years ago while at MIT. Two particular
documents were enlightening, to say the least.
Turns out that Nicholson's something of a genius regarding how to shut down electronic
and electrical machines through magnetic field
disturbance. His college papers describe in detail how it would be possible for someone to
build a device that could silently and without

detection shut down the systems that keep our country alive. He describes how to shut down computers, and other electrical systems, by generating high-energy, electromagnetic waves. Imagine the chaos if bank computers and computers on Wall Street were suddenly disabled."

The statement was rhetorical, and Capone continued after a short pause to allow the others time to visualize the disruption that would occur. "Thermond explained that the equipment Nicholson describes in his manuscripts is capable of shutting down engines, specifically jet engines of the type found on large commercial aircraft."

Meg was horrified. "No. Oh no."

Capone reacted, "Right, it's bad. I don't think I have to go into a lot of detail. Thermond only briefly skimmed the papers and will go over them more thoroughly tonight. He'll be here for consultation if you have specific questions. Of course, our interest has been redirected. It's quite possible that Nicholson has constructed a sophisticated version of what he wrote about years ago. This is probably the guts of the orange boxes."

Dusty asked, "How certain can we be about the reality of all this?"

Capone said, "Of course, we're not certain of anything right now, but I can't think of anything worse that Thermond could have uncovered. I think we need to assume this answers our questions about the orange boxes."

Meg added, "I agree. Simple deduction and common sense suggest that the flight data recorder disguise is the vehicle for covertly hiding the devices in the planes. I think it's likely Kiley was involved and used his status as safety manager to install the boxes."

Capone said, "A reasonable assumption, Meg, good. I think that is a strong possibility."

Meg beamed.

"You're both doing an extraordinary job, but we can't slow down. The next few hours may mean the difference between innocent people living or dying."

Capone paused and looked at each of the two agents to ensure they understood the gravity of their assignments.

"Meg, I want Brandon Sheffield on the phone, now. Do whatever you have to do. Get together with Dusty in the interim and prepare an outline, nothing fancy, profiling the other crewmembers. We'll sit down in fifteen minutes to try and determine if we need to focus on any of them. I tend to think Nicholson and Kiley are the only two Empire employees who are connected."

Meg motioned slightly with her hand to get Capone's attention. "I don't think McIntyre, or his brother are part of this, Bob. Nothing showed up at McIntyre's college of any consequence. In fact, he was at the other extreme as Nicholson as far as academics. Although his degree was in engineering technology, this was really a program geared more toward management. He barely graduated.

"Okay, yeah, you're probably right."

She continued. "His grade point average was 2.01. What was he doing for four years? His avionics training in the military was also of little significance, since as soon as he finished training in Memphis, he managed to get accepted into the flight program and was released from his enlisted status to finish college. He never put the avionics training to use. He doesn't seem to have an interest in that field."

Capone looked up. "What makes you so sure?"

"Well, of course I haven't had much time, but there weren't any electronics or electricity classes on his transcript, other than the basic requirements of his program. He was involved in sports and was a member of a social fraternity. He just doesn't seem like the type to labor over circuit boards or to put in extra hours at the electronics lab. Seems more like the party type to me. I'm still looking though. Something unexpected might come up later."

Capone nodded. "Continue."

"That's really about all I've been able to dig up on McIntyre," she said. "His brother has been doing well since retirement from the Marine Corps and although he's involved in maintenance at Lockheed, I believe it's just a coincidence in career fields."

Capone was nodding his head in agreement. "Yes, I agree, Meg, but let's discuss all that one more time, and include Lawrence and the others when we get a chance. Tomorrow, when we have more help and offices open, we'll put someone to work on the rest of the crew. Anything else?"

The two indicated they had nothing further to add and retreated to their desks.

Earlier, Capone had asked his clerical assistant to find some food. She entered the room with two large pizza boxes when Megs phone rang. She answered and immediately waved Capone over to take the call.

"This is Bob Capone."

"Mr. Capone, this is Brandon Sheffield. What is it that requires a call in the middle of the night from the FBI?"

It really wasn't the middle of the night and, in fact, the time in Dallas was eleven-ten. Capone ignored the reference to the time. "Mr. Sheffield, can we use first names?"

"Of course. What can I help you with?"

"Brandon, are you aware that one of your captains failed to report for a flight out of Midland, Texas, this morning?"

"Actually, that was brought to my attention, but only because he failed to report from a layover location and the authorities had become involved. Apparently, there's some reason to believe that there may have been foul play?"

"Yes, a very good possibility. As a matter of fact, there is reason to believe that there's a much greater concern than just the missing captain. I need you to understand that we've been working on a rapidly developing case that started with the disappearance of your captain and has evolved into something with all the indications of a much more sinister plot involving your fleet of aircraft."

"You have my attention, Bob."

Capone explained the entire day's developments, knowing that this was pressing FBI policy to the edge, but also fully aware that the president of a major air carrier wouldn't consider holding one income-producing flight on the ground unless absolutely necessary.

Like any good negotiator, Capone concluded his report by making a request that he knew was beyond reasonable expectation. "Brandon, I really think you should prevent any of your aircraft from taking off until they're all thoroughly inspected."

The executive took no time to consider this suggestion. "Bob, I understand you're trying to do your job the best you can and that by holding my aircraft on the ground, you manage to buy time. I wish it were that easy, but I just can't hold back flights unless there's extremely convincing rationale. Air transportation allows the country to function. Shutting down just one carrier would create havoc. I can't even see where we have a reasonable indication that by grounding our aircraft we'd accomplish anything other than an inspection of the flight data recorders, none of which have failed to pass our predictive and preventative maintenance checks."

The airline executive paused and said in a more sympathetic voice, "You have an interesting theory Bob, but at this point that's all it is. I think that if your findings were carefully studied, one could come up with any number of possible scenarios, some which wouldn't even involve Empire Airlines. I appreciate the hard work you've put into this. You seem genuinely concerned about my company, and I appreciate that. In fact, first thing in the morning, I'll direct our maintenance people to examine every one of the flight data recorders as the planes rotate in for other checks. However, these units are sealed, and we don't perform maintenance on them. I believe we have a basic test of functionality and that's it. If one appears faulty, we merely exchange it out with a new one. I know you'll find out why captain Kiley's safe was broken into, and I hope you'll discover that it was a simple burglary and then go on to catch the culprits. In the meantime, I suspect you're directing the same effort toward finding my captain."

Capone couldn't believe his ears. There was every reason to believe that billions of dollars in aircraft could be in jeopardy, not to mention human lives, and this so-called executive wasn't even concerned enough to put things on hold for even half a day. Unbelievable.

He tried a different approach. "Look, Brandon, I understand you have a company to run. And I understand how crucial the flights are. But we need to exercise prudence. Let's at least do what we can tonight to protect your interests. You have to admit there's a strong possibility that your planes have been tampered with. Let's at least check a few of them out tonight. We're talking about lives here."

"I'll meet you halfway, Bob. But I'm not grounding any flights until I have reasonable cause. I have a twenty-four-hour maintenance operation in Dallas. We should be able to redirect a few people to pull some of the flight data recorders. But again, I'm not sure they could tell much by doing that. Like I said, we don't normally perform maintenance on them."

"I understand. That's a start though. Can you put this into action immediately? I'd appreciate it if you have your man in charge of that effort call me right away. I can put the manufacturer on the line with your people to help confirm the authenticity of the recorders. Would you do that much?"

"I'll make some calls. You can expect to hear from someone in twenty or thirty minutes. One more thing, if you find out anything new that I should know, will you wake me?"

"You've got my word. Thanks for the help."

Capone had gotten what he expected. He knew there would be no airplanes held on the ground until he was able to prove some of his claims. If it turned out he was wrong, then at least the worst-case theory would be eliminated. He thanked Sheffield and hung up. Meg and Dusty both sat nearby, intently absorbing the conversation on their phones. Jim Everett was listening from his desk not far away. They grouped again and exchanged ideas.

The time was twelve thirty-three.

CHAPTER 26

Empire Maintenance Hanger,
Dallas, Texas
01:55 Central Standard Time
February 2, 2007

Nighttime maintenance inside the mammoth Empire hanger was almost like life on another planet. Background noise was non-existent. Four workers huddled near a disassembled engine resting on a work stand near the wing of a Boeing 727, and lighting was reduced well below normal levels. Half of the large 480-volt mercury-vapor ceiling fixtures were shut off as a result of a cost-savings study. Special area lights illuminated the immediate vicinity of the engine overhaul. The men were dressed in identical tan jump suits, which made the scene reminiscent of astronauts working on the lunar module.

A loud ringing emanating from the hanger PA system announced an incoming phone call to the maintenance office located at the halfway point along the immense metal wall. Two men worked at a bench not far from the room where the phone was. The taller of the two, the shift foreman, set the armature of an aircraft alternator on the bench and went into the glassed-in office.

The heavyset man at the workbench also stopped working. He watched his supervisor through the glass. A phone call this early in the morning was unusual and generated some interest from the men working on the aircraft engine. Inside the glass office, the maintenance foreman stood over the cluttered desk, nodding and writing notes on a clipboard while conversing with Dan Murphy, the Empire Airlines maintenance manager.

"Ted," the manager started, as though they were old friends, "whatever you're working on, put it on hold. There is an urgent test we want you to make on some of the equipment. This involves the FBI, but don't be concerned, it should be fairly simple."

"I've never heard of any involvement with the FBI described as being simple."

"Let me put it this way, the tests are important or we wouldn't be doing them with no scheduling, but they are merely to help the FBI gather information regarding a sensitive investigation that does not involve you personally. I wasn't even advised of the specifics. This is a 'need-to-know' type of thing, and you don't need to know."

"Yes, sir. No problem here."

"Copy this down. When I hang up, I want you to phone agent Bob Capone at the FBI headquarters in Washington."

He provided the mechanic with two phone numbers having Washington, DC area codes.

The mechanic replied, "Got it."

"I will tell you what they told me. You'll be performing checks on flight data recorders. The agent, Bob Capone, will describe the tests to you. You will do the tests using reasonable judgment, as long as no morning departures are affected. You may have to remove several flight data recorders and perform diagnostic checks to determine their operational condition. That's it. That's all I know. If, at any time, you become uncomfortable or concerned about what you are asked to do, then stop and call me."

As the end of the conversation neared, the other worker entered the office, sat in a folding metal chair near the door, and listened intently.

"What's up, Theodore?" the junior mechanic asked.

The younger worker's name was William Terrell. Everyone just called him Billy. Billy was one of Moody's least motivated subordinates and was difficult to keep in check. Inevitably, whenever there was a phone call or any other excuse to become distracted, Billy would capitalize on the opportunity and wander away. Five minutes earlier, Billy seized the occasion to visit the candy machine. He gnawed a Babe Ruth.

"I'll tell you what's up," Moody said," it's not like we don't have enough work to keep us busy all night, now they want us to start pulling flight data recorders. When was the last time you had one of those out?"

"Can't say exactly. Took one out about a month ago as part of an annual. Don't think I've ever seen one written up. What's the deal?"

"Murphy wants us to work with a guy in Washington and pull a few for inspection. The FAA may have found a problem with 'em. Maybe they had a couple fail. Like it can't wait for day shift when there's more people out here. Shit, they could pay a little overtime for something like this. Maybe do a little planning and bring in some extra people. I can't pull anyone off the engine change. We're late as it is getting that one back on the line. You and I can handle this. Might as well plan on putting that alternator on hold for now. This wild-ass project has priority, and it'll take us the rest of the shift to get it done."

"You know we can't bench check those recorders tonight. They get sent back to that outfit in California when they roll around on preventive maintenance. As long as the power light's on, we usually leave 'em alone," the younger mechanic said, hoping to get the work postponed.

"I know all about how they work, Billy. I've only been doing this for thirty years. We're still gonna pull 'em. They may want us to open a couple up. The guy I'm calling knows what to look for. From the sound of it, I don't think we'll be doing anything substantial, probably check the power light and take a few readings with the ohmmeter. Look, it's not my damn idea."

"Okay, what do you want me to do?" Billy asked.

"I need you to grab some tools and get back here. I'll call the pro in Washington and find out what the hell's going on. Then we'll make 'em happy, yank a few, and do whatever is necessary to check 'em out. We'll have to get 'em back in time so no morning flights are delayed."

Billy opened the glass door and left the small office. The older man took a seat at the desk and wiped grease from his hands with an already oily rag. He checked the list of aircraft on his maintenance schedule and phoned operations to find out exactly which planes were parked at the gates waiting for morning departures. He had become accustomed to working around problems and knew that being prepared was the key to getting things done.

He checked his list of every plane on the ground in Dallas and divided them into three groups. The first were planes ready for take-off and parked either at the gates or at the on-deck area outside the hangar. This category included thirteen planes.

The second group included airworthy jets that required minor maintenance, or cleaning, but could be moved into position with little

effort. Two planes filled this list. It wasn't uncommon for there to be no back-up planes on
the ground ready to fly. Airplanes made money
only when in the air, and it was Ted Moody's
responsibility to keep them there. His job performance was based almost solely on aircraft
availability, and he wasn't pleased about this
sudden request in the middle of the night.

The last group included planes with more
serious mechanical problems and that wouldn't
be available for use in the near future. The two
jets in the hangar fell in this category. One of
them was undergoing an annual inspection and
the other was receiving a new engine.

Moody quickly pulled the computer files up
for the aircraft on his list and looked for previous write-ups relating to flight data recorders.
The swift review found no unusual notations
specific to that equipment, and he felt ready to
discuss the tests after only ten minutes of preparation. He picked up the phone and dialed the
Washington D.C. number.

"Bob Capone."

"Mr. Capone, this is Ted Moody, senior mechanic in charge for Empire Airlines in Dallas. I
have a message to call you."

"Ted. Can I call you Ted?"

"Ted's fine."

"Ted, I've been working all day on a very sensitive case. I talked to your superiors, as I'm sure
you're aware. First, I apologize because I know

you have questions, but I can't answer them now. I was told you'll provide full cooperation on performing some minor maintenance checks on some of your aircraft there in Dallas."

"Yes, sir, I've been directed to assist you in that effort. However, I hope you know that I was also told to have all our morning departures ready to leave on time."

"I'm aware of that. That's why time is critical. We wouldn't be doing this in the middle of the night if it weren't important. I trust that you and your men will keep this confidential, I don't want to unnecessarily panic anyone. We're doing some standard checks on flight data recorders due to a report of a possible problem. The defects that we suspect pose no threat to airworthiness. Now I'm sure your boss wouldn't be happy if he started getting calls from the public. Are we understanding each other?"

"Yes, sir. I have no reason to discuss this with anyone and I'll instruct my men to keep it under wraps. May I ask a question?"

"Go ahead.".

"Well, sir," Moody said, "I don't have the equipment or the procedures for wringing out a flight data recorder. I believe they're sealed and are normally only checked out by the manufacturer or from the FAA following an accident."

"I understand that, Ted. Let me quickly explain to you what we'll be doing. I want to check as many of the recorders as possible. I'll have an expert from Aviontrics, the recorders' manufacturer, contact you with what needs to be done. Now this next part is important. Some of your flights will be leaving early. I don't know your schedule, but I assume you have some very early flights headed for overseas and probably Mexico destinations. Forget the recorders in the planes that have those early departures because that'll shorten the time we have to inspect them. Can you use an intelligent selection process that'll give me a large sampling that can be checked in, say, an hour, and still leave time to have them re-installed so the flights won't be delayed? Do you understand what I'm asking?"

"Yes, I believe so. I'll not consider the early launch. There isn't a definite cutoff, but I'll do my best to get you maybe eight or ten boxes from the planes with later schedules. It may take me two hours, maybe a little less, to remove that many units. That means I'll be back in the hangar here around four. Add an hour for the checks, and we're at five o'clock. Two more hours to put everything back should allow me to finish around seven. I think that's a conservative estimate. We should have enough planes that are due out after seven o'clock to get you between six and ten tests. Sound okay to you?"

"It's a pleasure to talk with an organized man. Thank you, Ted. Please call me directly at this number or at the alternate one as soon as you've removed the boxes and are ready to take some readings. I'll line up the Aviontrics rep you'll be working with and set up a conference call with the three of us. I know you ball-parked the times, but I'll look for your call at about four o'clock your time."

"Well, if you don't have anything else, I'd better get busy. I'll call you in a couple hours, maybe less."

"Thanks, Ted."

Ted pulled the departure schedule up on his computer monitor. The breakdown was close to what he had described to Capone. Moody identified eight planes that could be used.

Billy was around the corner dropping coins in a beat-up red candy machine as if he were feeding tokens into the slots at Las Vegas. He wore a standard company jump suit that was badly soiled with grease. Even though he was only five ten, his overalls were a size extra-large, to allow for his protruding stomach. He had an elongated upper body, making his legs look too short for his height and the pant legs on the overalls were originally a good four inches too long. To keep from rolling up the cuffs, he had cut them off with scissors after his first day on the job two years ago. The washing cycles worked at the weave where the cut was made leaving an inch of grease-stained fraying, which swept the floor as he walked.

Billy did have some good qualities. He had a comprehensive background and generally did good work. Fortunately, the flight data recorders were located in the tail section of the plane, just to the right of the door at the top of the aft stairway. It was an unusually easy component to access and remove.

Ted startled Billy who was reaching for another Babe Ruth from the candy machine. "Billy, those things are gonna kill you. Why don't you bring in some decent food to snack on?"

"What do you mean? This is health food. Read the side here. We got peanuts, non-fat milk, corn syrup, sugar, cocoa butter, all kinds of good shit. Besides, this damn machine sits right here staring at us all night long, so what do you expect? You want one?" he asked, pointing the gooey bar at Ted.

"No. Grab a three-eighths nut driver. You might need a socket and a short extension, too. I've got eight side numbers we need to work on." He handed the junior mechanic a sheet with four plane numbers on it. "These are yours. Pull the flight recorders and do it quickly. Make sure you check the power light before you disconnect 'em. I don't want to be asked later if any of them had an abnormal indication and not have an answer. I'll tell the rest of the crew what we're doing. Don't get chocolate all over the cannon plugs when you unscrew them."

"Very funny. Do I get the rest of the night off if I get my four out before you finish yours, old man?"

"I'd make that wager, Great Bambino, if I didn't think you might go in with wire cutters and a crowbar. Do me a favor though, try and get this job done quickly. We'll be answering a lot of questions come morning. We're being watched closely."

An hour and forty minutes later, there were eight, six-by-ten-by-fourteen-inch day-glow orange flight data recorders lying side by side on a folding table near the office window. Ted Moody mentally noted the time. Three fifty-five. He was proud of his accurate estimate of how long the job would take. Billy had performed well and finished his four-plane assignment shortly after Ted.

"You did check each control power light prior to removing the supply wire, right?"

"Yep, they were all good."

Moody continued to emphasize the importance of the assignment by confirming everything he said to Billy and double checking each step. He kept operations appraised of the status of the planes at the gate. So far, everything had gone smoothly, and Ted was confident he could return the eight jets to an 'up' status well before departure time.

He picked up one orange box, some tools, and his clipboard, and carried them with him to the workbench. He located a yellow, hard plastic Fluke voltmeter with one black and one red test wire wrapped around it. Bringing all the items with him, he went into the office, cleared the desk, and dialed the Washington number.

"Bob Capone."

"Mr. Capone, Ted Moody here."

"Ted, you're right on time. How're you making out?"

"Well, so far so good. I've got eight of the boxes pulled. We've got about an hour, as I said earlier, and then I've got to return these to the aircraft. How do you want to do this?"

"I'll phone the Aviontrics representative in California who's expecting our call, then I'll put us on a conference line, and he'll tell you what you need to do. My understanding is that you'll need a voltmeter. Are you an electrical type or do you need to round someone up?"

"I'm trained in avionics, sir. This should be routine for me. I have a meter and the box in front of me. As we do the first test, I'll write down the numbers and should be able to go through the rest of the units fairly quickly."

"Very good, Ted. Hang on and I'll get Al Briscoe on the line. He's the R&D VP of Aviontrics, but don't be fooled. He's also an electrical engineer and has researched the information you'll need for this test."

"I'll be standing by." Moody said. He had served fourteen years in the Navy and developed work habits and communication styles that set him noticeably apart from his civilian counterparts. His superb attention to detail that had been a predominant requirement for the high-pressure demands of flight operations on Nimitz class aircraft carriers provided him with an exceptional maintenance and management background. Moody was an expert, all-around aircraft maintenance specialist. Capone would later realize how fortunate he was to have had this man on shift this particular night.

"Ted, are you still there?"

"I'm here, sir," the maintenance chief responded.

"I have Al Briscoe on the line in California, and he'll be talking you through this. I'll listen in."

"Ted, Al Briscoe here. I've been told Bob has been keeping you busy tonight. Don't feel alone, he's kept me awake the whole evening. We're doing something important here, so what say we move ahead?"

"I believe I'm ready. Where do we start?"

"We have three very simple checks. You'll have to read resistance across the cannon plug terminals. Then there's one voltage check. The recorder has a built-in battery and charger. We can't open the unit because it's sealed for obvious reasons. I know at this point you really don't need to know all this, but it may help answer a few questions. Anyway, are you with me so far?"

"You're doing good. Thanks for the condensed course. Keep going," Moody replied.

"Okay, great. Let's do a couple of checks. The

first thing you need to do is check the resistance across terminals two and four. You should have a reading between .02 and .07 ohms. Let me know when you've done that."

"Hold on, checking that." After about fifteen seconds the ex-Navy specialist said, "Looks good so far. Point oh four."

"All right, fine. Now do the same test across numbers one and four. You should read an open circuit."

Again, fifteen seconds passed and then the report. "Open circuit between one and four."

"So far this one looks normal; one more test. We're checking the internal battery. You should read eight volts plus or minus five percent. Read across terminals five and six. The number-six prong is B plus."

"Checking it now, hold on." Moody changed the setting on the yellow meter to allow DC voltage to be read on the digital read-out window. He placed the prongs of the red and black test leads onto the appropriate pins of the male end of the cannon fitting and read the digital face of the meter. "Eight point oh three. Looks good."

"You've just performed the entire check, Ted. That looks like one of our units, and you can return it to the aircraft. You okay with this test, Bob?"

Capone had been listening in on the three-way communication link. "I feel comfortable it's a safe unit according to what you explained earlier, Al. Thanks for your help. I think we can handle it from here. You can go back to sleep."

"Thanks, but I think I'll stay up now and grab some breakfast. Will you call me if we have any new developments?"

"You're number one on the list. Thanks again."

Moody waited patiently for the two to finish socializing but was eager to get started and put the equipment back in the tail sections of the jets.

"Ted, can you perform that test on the other units and call me back with the results?"

"This won't take more than twenty minutes. I'll call as soon as I'm done."

The conversation ended and Ted relocated his equipment and notes to the folding table outside the office where the remaining seven recorders lay in a neat row. He set his things on the table and looked around the huge hangar for Billy. Several men were working on the wing of a Boeing 727 thirty feet away. The rest of the mammoth building was eerily silent. Occasionally, a dropped tool or part clanged noisily, the sound rebounding off the high ceiling and distant walls with a clear echo. Billy was in hiding, but Ted was undaunted. He preferred to do this test himself to make sure the results got recorded accurately.

He cleared an area on the folding table and proceeded to perform the three tests on the remaining seven flight data recorders. The first two tested out almost identical to the one he had checked in the office. On the fourth unit, he tested the voltage of the internal battery first. The reading was within limits.

Ted was becoming convinced the night would be a waste. He wondered, *how many other airlines have been asked to spend valuable hours testing perfectly good equipment?*

He rotated the selector switch on his meter to read resistance, placed the leads on the terminals marked two and four, and began to jot the indicated measurement on his note page, but the circuit appeared to be open, indicating infinite resistance. At first, he assumed he had mistakenly placed the leads on the wrong terminals and referred back to his notes. He tried the same check again, being careful to place the leads at the correct points. The digital meter face again identified an open circuit.

He made a note of the different reading and then checked the meter to make certain the problem wasn't with the test equipment. Satisfied that the meter wasn't malfunctioning, he performed the last check between pins one and four, looking for an open circuit. This time, he read thirty ohms, an obvious discrepancy. *Maybe there was a good reason for these checks after all,* he thought. Setting the recorder with the unusual readings off to the side of the table, he finished testing the remaining boxes. He found two more that were unsatisfactory. All three recorders had almost identical readings on the terminals tested. *What's going on?* he wondered. *Three recorders couldn't fail with identical readings. That would be too coincidental.*

He reached for the phone.

CHAPTER 27

War Room, FBI Headquarters
Washington D.C.
04:40 Eastern Standard Time
February 2, 2007

The agents had spent the last half-hour brain storming and offering opinions on where to focus their efforts. The big question had not been answered to Capone's satisfaction. *What will likely happen during next few hours?* A number of possibilities had been offered, but none more plausible than any other.

The quiet room awoke with the sonorous ring of Capone's phone.

"Capone"

"Mr. Capone, this is Ted Moody in Dallas."

"Ted, right on time. What did you find?"

"Well, sir, I must admit that I thought you were wasting my time, but three of the eight recorders I checked were bad."

"What do you mean bad?"

"Well, two of the three readings on three of

the units I checked disagreed with the parameters that Mr. Briscoe provided."

"Two out of three readings? Does this definitely confirm the boxes aren't recorders? I assume the last reading was within range?"

"The reading that seemed okay was the battery voltage. The two different units seem to have the same internal battery, but the resistance I recorded between the terminals on the other two tests was considerably different from the good recorders. Each of the faulty ones read identically. Whether or not you have a recorder on the inside, I can't say. It's very suspicious to me that they each have the same readings. Could be there's a recorder inside but it has simply malfunctioned, maybe shorted out, or maybe suffering from some sort of identical failure. Maybe there'a bad component that's prematurely failing."

"I think I understand, Ted. You've helped a lot. I believe we need to get Al Briscoe on the line and sort this out. Can I call you back in a few minutes to discuss this with him on the line?"

"I'd like to help out, but I need to start putting the recorders back in the planes. I don't want to cut this too close. If a flight is delayed because I had these things removed, it'll be my ass. Tell you what, I'll have my crew start reinstalling the recorders, and I'll stay in the office and wait fifteen minutes for your call. How's that?"

"I'd appreciate that, Ted, but I wouldn't re-install the three bad units."

"I don't think I can hold the flight up just because of that test, Mr. Capone. The only requirement we have for flight is for the power light to be on, which was the case prior to removing them for the test. I agree that it may be possible the recorders won't function as intended if the plane crashes, but that's a big if. It's also a highly unlikely possibility. I don't believe it warrants canceling a flight. Airworthiness isn't affected here, and a malfunctioning flight recorder isn't a justifiable reason to ground a plane. I'm not even sure we have spares on site. I have two planes not scheduled to go out. If, and I want to repeat this, if I have time, then I'll check the recorders in those two planes. If they're good, I'll replace two of the bad ones I tested with those."

While Moody explained his position, Capone was calculating how to handle the situation. He was convinced there was something very wrong and felt certain it was serious. None of the Empire planes should be allowed to take off. He also realized that without something concrete, he wouldn't be able to convince the mechanic to make that decision. He would have to go higher on the chain of command.

"Okay," Capone sighed, "I understand, but I'd appreciate your standing by the phone while I locate Briscoe. Take a couple minutes to get your crew started."

"I'll do that, sir, and I'll be back in the office in just a few minutes."

Capone hung up the phone and immediately dialed Briscoe's home number.

A listless voice answered. "Hello."

"Al, this is Bob Capone. Sorry to wake you but I need your help. This is urgent."

"I take it Ted found some bad flight recorders."

"Well, I guess the question is, what's bad. Would you mind talking to him and diagnosing his findings? I'd like to have as much informed knowledge as possible about those recorders, before I go further."

"Sure, Bob, I'll do what I can. Can you hook us up?"

"Stand by."

Capone connected the conference call and Moody described to the electrical engineer his exact findings. Briscoe seemed to grasp the situation.

Capone broke in after the information was exchanged. He said, "Ted, you've been extremely helpful and have done an excellent job for us. I'll see that Dan Murphy is made aware of your efforts. You can get your planes ready to fly, but please, do your best to replace any bad recorders with some that meet Briscoe's specifications."

"I'll do my best, Mr. Capone. Good luck with whatever it is you're working on. I guess I'll find out more when all this is history."

"That could be very soon, Ted. Thanks again."

Briscoe remained on the line with Capone. "What do you think?" Capone asked.

"I think there's about a ninety percent chance that someone has tampered with the flight recorders. I've never seen readings like the ones Moody just described. The likelihood of three units having identical numbers makes it more suspicious. Finally, the readings don't fit the argument that the units are damaged or have failed. I can't imagine a condition that would result in those values. My guess is, there's something inside those three packages that wasn't made by Aviontrics, but I'd have to open them up and look inside to be sure."

"Al, I don't think I'll need you for a while. I can't tell you how much you've helped. I'll get back later and fill you in."

Capone looked at his associates who had been listening in. No one spoke. They stared at Capone with expressions of disbelief.

"Okay, you all heard what Briscoe said. It's four fifty-five. In just a couple of hours, hundreds of Boeing 727s filled with passengers will be taking off. We don't know for sure that anything will happen. However, we do know there's a good likelihood that someone has tampered with Empire's equipment.

We've connected Kiley to the fake recorders.

Nicholson's unusual interest in electronic disturbance places him on the same bus with the others. There's very good reason to believe that Nicholson's inventive mind has found an outlet. I fear everything will unfold in the next several hours. This new information could be the missing factor we've been looking for."

He looked to the back of the room where the mustached engineer sat engrossed, reading Nicholson's manuscripts. "Thermond, having any luck? Got anything new we can use?" Capone asked.

Thermond looked up and removed the glasses from the tip of his nose. "Bob, these works are quite dated. I'm sure that if Nicholson has broadened his ideas, the new model could be notably different. However, I did find one interesting thing that might be relevant."

"What, Thermond? You don't need an invitation here. You need to let us know if you come up with anything, anything at all."

"Well, I just ran across this in the last fifteen pages or so where Nicholson describes a unique method to enable his device. All of the electromagnet wave generators I've read about, or in the one case, the video clip I saw, were large individual units which were operated locally from the wave generator itself. Nicholson suggests a method he believes terrorist organizations will use in the future, which is now. This formula uses many small generating devices that are activated from a single remote location. When I read that section, it made me think of the one box that was important enough to be kept in the captain's safe. Jim gave me the impression this unit is on its way to the Bennettis. Could this be the activating device? Nicholson refers to the trigger mechanism as an ACU, or Activation Control Unit."

"Thermond," Capone said, "that makes a lot of sense. You could be onto something. That box in the safe has bothered me. Why is it so special? If that unit is indeed the activating mechanism, how would it be used? Could it be used from any location? What kind of range do you think it has?"

"That's all very speculative, Bob, but my guess is that it's probably line of sight, meaning the distance would be reasonably short. Fifty, maybe a hundred miles under ideal conditions. If we're talking about the wave generators living in the aircraft, the obvious place from which to enable them would be from another plane. If you were to take a location, such as a busy airport with a lot of infected planes circling around, then one plane high above the others could trigger the units. It would be devastating."

Everything was coming together at once. For the first time, Capone was visualizing what he had been trying to unravel the entire day. Nicholson's own words had betrayed him.

Jim Everett was listening closely. "Bob, if

Thermond is right about the initiating device being in the plane, then wouldn't the aircraft Nicholson's flying be the best place to look? He'd want to be the one to push the button. If he's the one who'll be activating the attack, he'd be able to have some control over where and when it happens."

"I agree, Jim. Dusty, find out Nicholson's schedule. Do we know where Nicholson's flight is right now?"

Meg spoke up. "They ended yesterday's trip in Chicago, Bob."

"Everything is just too perfect," Capone said, becoming animated as the bits of information started to connect. Like metal filings pulled by a powerful magnet. The bits of data were literally leaping into the central story line, logically linking each to the other.

"Okay, Nicholson's in Chicago, and I'm sure we'll find he's due out first thing this morning. He'll be in the O'Hare area, one of the busiest pieces of atmosphere in the world. We've got our work cut out for us," Capone said.

Jim said, "That's an understatement."

"Capone continued. Dusty, you still need to find out what flight he's on this morning, and when it leaves. Before we can think about doing anything, we have to know his flight number, and when it's scheduled to leave."

"We have a lot of circumstantial evidence." Meg stated. Then asked, "Probably not strong enough for us to force Empire to ground the flight, or search Nicholson at the plane. Do we?" Indicating she wasn't certain of the full scope of FBI authority.

Jim said, "Ouch, that's touchy. What do you think, Bob?"

Capone responded, "Jim's right. There are situations when the courts have recognized an exigent circumstance to allow an exception to the Fourth Amendment's warrant requirement. It's not perfectly clear in some cases."

Jim said, "He's right. It requires a situation where there's a reasonable belief that someone is in immediate danger. Some type of emergency. For example, there's a house fire, and an officer needs to kick a door in to save someone inside. The officer has to be certain that the person is in danger before he can enter without a warrant."

Capone agreed, "Right. And additionally, the only thing the officer can do once he's inside is provide rescue. He can't use the opportunity to conduct a quick search on the way out."

Meg asked, "So, can we use that exception to bypass the warrant process? Can we consider the passengers to be in danger?"

"That might be possible under different circumstances. If we had positive evidence of a serious threat, maybe. In the case of the burning house, it's undeniable that people inside are in danger. It's indisputable. With our situation, I would hate to argue in court that we were positive about anything. That's the problem," Capone responded.

Jim added, "Making our case even worse, is that we actually believe that Nicholson's plane is probably the safest one to be on."

Capone said, "If we're thinking about searching Nicholson to recover the control box, it's the same thing. We have no real reason to think he has something dangerous in his possession. In fact, even if our assumption of his device is correct, we don't have good reason to believe he's the one who will control it. As we said earlier, anyone could have it. The person wouldn't necessarily even be on the same plane."

Capone said, "You're right. I think we have enough to get a warrant later today, but I don't believe it falls under the exigent circumstance exception. I believe the best chance of holding the plane on the ground is to get Sheffield to do it voluntarily."

Meg said, "Will he do that?"

"He's hard-headed, but I think with this new information, he'll help us. Meg, get him on the line. I have to talk to Connelly first."

"Is he in the building?" Jim asked.

"I think he went home," Capone said.

Meg walked away to call Sheffield.

Capone dialed Connelly's home.

Connelly answered, "Hello."

"J.R., I hate to wake you, but there's developments."

"Not good?"

"No, not good. We've tested some of Empire's flight data recorders. They almost certainly have been tampered with. Redmond has a plausible theory of what Nicholson might be up to."

"Nicholson?"

"Right. We have a lot of circumstantial suspicions that suggest Nicholson is up to something rather hellish. I think there's a good chance he's involved in some type of terrorist effort against Empire."

"Explain."

"We have good reason to believe he's invented a device that will disable aircraft engines during flight. I think he's planning to cause multiple crashes. There's not time to explain it now. You better come in."

"You've got me worried. I'm on my way."

Capone walked over to Meg's desk. She was finishing up a conversation and hanging up the phone.

"You don't look happy, Meg."

"I'm sorry Bob. I called Sheffield. He's not home. I talked with his wife."

"And?"

"They'll be leaving in a few hours for their daughter's wedding in New York. It seems Sheffield had some business at the office he wanted to take care of. He had just left the house when I called."

"Do you have his cell number?"

"His wife gave it to me. I tried it. No answer."

Capone said, "At this hour he probably isn't expecting anyone to call. He might not have it turned on."

"My thinking, too. Or, if he's like me, he may have left it at home. I'll keep trying, but we might have to reach him at the office. I have the number. No answer there yet either."

"I'm sure it's too early to expect any of the staff to be there. I expect he's going in early to get some work done before leaving on his trip. Keep trying."

"Okay."

CHAPTER 28

Chicago Downtown Regency
Chicago, Illinois
03:44 Central Standard Time
February 2, 2007

Tony and Jack arrived at the Chicago Hyatt at 3:44 A.M. Nicholson's plane wasn't scheduled for departure for a good four hours. Tony was feeling secure about having the ACU in hand and knowing that all the major hurdles had been overcome. All they had to do now was hand the unit over to Nicholson and drop the captain off at the terminal. In a few hours, the months of preparation would be realized as, one by one, Empire jets begin to drop out of the sky.

The carefully prepared plans had been somewhat marred with the late arrival of the ACU, Mick being laid up in the hospital, and of course, the murder of the old couple in Mauston. Otherwise, everything was moving along perfectly. In a few short hours the entire operation would be over and well over fifty million dollars would be deposited into accounts that Robert Bennetti had established at various locations throughout

Europe and the Bahamas.

Three unsuspecting souls would occupy seats on Flight 867, departing Chicago O'Hare at 08:15, using tickets in the names of Robert, Tony, and John Bennetti. The plane would crash and the Bennettis would be presumed dead. Before the day was through, a "safe" car with the real Bennetti brothers inside would be on Highway 65 headed for Miami. From there, the brothers would board a flight to Rio de Janeiro to assume new identities established months earlier. The plan was perfect.

The heavy snow stopped several hours before Tony and Jack arrived in Chicago, and only isolated flakes could be seen drifting near illuminated signs and streetlights. Even though the night had been long, the two were alert and energetic, thanks to an ample supply of prescription drugs provided by the Bennetti physician. Jack was feeling no pain. His finger had been nearly severed but Tony had given him several capsules of Oxycodone. To stay awake, he took a couple of blue mollies, amphetamines that were passed around like chewing gum in the fraternity of thieves.

They got out of Tony's car and entered the deserted motel lobby, carrying the ACU. Jack hadn't shaved since seven o'clock the previous morning. He wore the same pin-striped suit he had left Chicago in three days earlier. The two men strolled through the lobby looking like gangsters out of a Martin Scorsese film. The only difference was, they weren't actors.

At the elevator, Tony encouraged Jack by telling him how well he had done and suggested that a bonus would be forthcoming. They rode quietly until the small room jolted to a stop with a metallic clang.

As Jack stepped onto the crimson carpeted hallway, Tony held the rubber bumper on the door to prevent it from closing, and flashed his trademark grin. "Everything's working out fine, Jack. Sleep late in the morning and get some rest. I'll bring your money down before I leave and get the doc over to look at that hand."

"Sure, Tony."

"Look, Jack, you'll be on your own, pal. I've got you set up with Mark Fisher in Phoenix. He'll put you to work when things settle down. Don't mess up and do something stupid. If you're wise, you'll invest your money in that diner you've always talked about and get out of this life. You're not smart enough to stay out of trouble. If the cops haven't found that old couple in Mauston yet, they will soon, and you'll be the number one debutante on their dance card. Get some rest, and we'll talk in the morning."

"Thanks, boss. I appreciate what you're doing for me."

Tony released the bumper, and the elevator continued upward. He was undecided about Jack. His hardened survival instincts told him to kill Jack during the night and eliminate the chances of him being caught and possibly talking too much. He struggled with this dilemma. There was a natural law of the streets, a code among thieves, which was as strong as the bond between him and his brothers. The kind of bond that was necessary where the violent nature of their work required absolute trust and honesty. The alternative usually meant a bullet to the temple or a short ride on the hood of a Lincoln.

In John and Robert's world there was no love lost between contract principals. These executive lawbreakers protected their own butts and wasted no time eliminating anyone in the way of closing a deal. Robert and John thrived in the cutthroat factory of power trading and high-leverage deal making. They used enormous wealth to buy what they needed. Loyalty, honesty, and integrity were words with no practical use to the two brothers who performed their crimes with ink and paper.

Tony had difficulty contemplating killing Jack. This problem would have to wait, or be handled by John or Robert.

Tony entered his hotel room and set the ACU on the bed. He picked up the phone and called Short Eddie, his two brothers, and Nicholson.

Within fifteen minutes the group was gathered in Tony's room.

John Bennetti spoke. "Mike, I know you've had time to look at the ACU. What's your assessment?"

"I believe everything's okay, John. Until I activate it, we won't know for sure, but then that would be the case even if we hadn't forced it open. It looks fine."

"That's good news. Now, this will be the last time we see each other. If there're any questions or concerns, this is the time."

There was silence. Each individual had gone over the details of John's plan numerous times during the last few months. Every possible situation had been planned, and all possible scenarios anticipated.

"Okay, then," John stated, "let's go over this one last time."

Looking bored, Nicholson exhaled through his mouth.

John looked his way and spoke. "Once comfortably airborne and climbing out," pointing to Nicholson, "you'll yaw the plane fairly violently and act as though the rudder shifted on its own."

"Right," Nicholson said.

John continued, "You'll ask Ted if he accidentally kicked it in. He'll act surprised, and you two will discuss the problem. Then you'll cause it to reoccur, and that should convince Lawrence that the controls are erratic and malfunctioning. At that point you'll suggest going into holding to check the controls before continuing. You're sure this will get you in holding, Mike?"

"I'm positive. I've told you, I'm responsible

for the plane. If I feel I need to enter a holding pattern to evaluate a problem, it's my prerogative. Air Traffic Control has to grant me that request. Ted will agree with my reasoning. This part of the operation is guaranteed."

John continued, "At eight twenty-five, five minutes after Flight 867 is due to depart, you'll activate the ACU for fifteen seconds. Flight 867 should be directly below you and its PSDs should begin shutting down the engines. It's during these few minutes that all our work becomes dependent on how we perform individually. My brothers and I will monitor the media. I'll be in communication with my personal pilots in the area who'll be monitoring emergency frequencies. If a plane goes down, we'll know it within minutes. You'll continue to hold, Mike."

John turned toward Eddie Dumbrowski and said, "Eddie, can you explain to us what'll be happening at this point?"

The small man known as Short Eddie was barefoot and wore a pair of khaki Dockers and a badly wrinkled white tee shirt. His thin blond hair was flattened on one side from being pressed against a pillow, and his eyes were bloodshot from the smoke-filled bar downstairs where he had stayed until closing.

He said, "I'll use my cell phone, or if necessary, the Airphone, to call Tony after hearing Nicholson's expected turbulence announcement. Mike will wait a few minutes and then come to the back. I'll give him a go or no-go signal, depending on whether or not a plane, or planes, have been reported down. If we failed, then we repeat the process and Mike will activate the ACU again. This time for thirty seconds. I call Tony every fifteen minutes until the first allotment is confirmed in the bank. After that, Mike will begin to systematically enable the ACU at fifteen-minute intervals."

"Excellent, Eddie. You're to continue to check in during the entire flight. Mike will occasionally walk through the cabin to check with you."

The group continued to discuss the remaining portion of the flight. All three Bennettis were convinced that nothing could go wrong. They finished the meeting at five-thirty, and departed to their respective rooms.

CHAPTER 29

War Room, FBI Headquarters
Washington D.C.
07:47 Eastern Standard Time
February 2, 2007

Shortly after Connelly arrived back in the building, Capone had briefed him on the latest developments. Connelly was astounded by the work that Capone had done during the night, yet unnerved. He, too, was troubled about Nicholson's morning flight. He concurred with Capone's understanding of the exigent exception to the warrant laws and agreed that dealing with Nicholson's early flight warranted a more creative solution. Connelly remained upstairs to call the Secretary of Homeland Security.

Capone's team grouped in the war room, still discussing different courses of action.

To no one in particular, Capone said, "It's decision time." He looked toward Everett, and asked, "What's your assessment?"

Jim said, "It's seven forty-seven. Six forty-seven in Chicago. Flight crews will be arriving to the terminal any time."

Meg said, "If they're not there already."

Jim continued, "There just isn't time to do a whole lot. We still might reach Sheffield before Nicholson departs. Have we tried his office again, Meg?"

Meg said, "I've been calling his cell and office every fifteen minutes. Nothing."

Jim said, "There has to be one of his assistants in the office any minute. Keep trying." He added, "Bob, we've started on a couple things we talked about earlier. As offices open today, we may have better luck. I hope it won't be too late."

"What do we have in motion, Jim?"

"Well, you know Connelly has started on the principal concerns, working with Homeland Security and the FAA. Other than that, Dean Jones left for the O'Hare terminal over an hour ago. Haven't heard from him yet. It's iffy he'll make it in time. If he gets there early enough, and if a seat is available, he'll purchase a ticket and get on the plane."

Capone said, "Good. So long as he doesn't attract attention? Keep the badge in his pocket. If Nicholson gets word that one of our agents is on the flight, he'll be unpredictable."

"Right. It looks doubtful that Jones will get there before the plane departs. Possible though."

"Bob, our first consideration was to try and get someone on the plane who can help us. If Jones doesn't make it, there might be other options."

"I'm listening."

"We should be able to communicate easily using cell phones and Empire provides Airphones in first class. If there was anyone, other than Jones, who could fill that need, we have to make it happen."

Capone said, "You're saying, if planes start to drop, we may be able to intercede at the source and overtake Nicholson?"

"I think it's possible. It's a long shot, but that's about all we have." Jim paused to look around the room at the others.

Dusty provided support with a slight nod.

Capone asked, "And who do you have in mind if Jones doesn't make it?

Jim said, "I was thinking, maybe it would be possible to contact one of the other crewmembers, another pilot, and use him as a contact on the plane."

"It would be good to be able to communicate. Worst case, another pilot might have to intercede physically," Capone said.

"Meg said, "We're not positive that Nicholson will be the one on the plane who'll be initiating the failures. It could be any passenger, or even someone on another plane."

Capone said, "I know. We've been through all that. But as a precaution, and going on the information we have, we need to have some type of plan in place. It makes sense to have someone on the plane we can talk to."

Jim said, "Bob, they'll be taking off in just over an hour."

Capone said, "Do we even know how to reach any of the crew? That seems like something the FBI should be able to handle."

"We don't think we'll be able to find anyone in the next hour who'll have that information, Bob. We simply don't know where they are."

"You got to be kidding me. We don't know how to contact anyone working that plane?"

"Unfortunately, no. We don't. Not this quickly. There just isn't any time. If we had an hour or two, and if offices were open, yeah, sure."

"Well, shit."

"We've tried a number of angles." Jim started to explain, trying to justify why he hadn't been able to locate the flight crew. "We've called everyone who's awake at Empire. Their operations department obviously works around the clock. There's a logistics coordinator. I've got the guy's name, who's responsible for all that, but he works nine to five."

Capone asked, "How about the ticketing people in Chicago? Maybe someone there is familiar with the usual arrangements for the flight crews."

"Tried that. No one that we talked with could help. We've started calling every hotel in the area. I'm sure it won't be long before we locate them."

Capone was emphatic. "There's no excuse for this Jim. Put someone on this and find out where the pilots are staying."

Meg said, "Bob, I've been going over the personal data on each crewmember. We've got a fortunate coincidence here."

"How so?"

"One of the flight attendants has a father who lives in Chicago. Arlington Heights. Her personnel folder lists his address and phone number. If I happened to be laying over at an airport located a few miles from my dad's house, I think I would not only give him a call, but he'd pick me up and I'd spend the night at his home."

"Excellent, Meg. That's sounds like a worthwhile undertaking. We don't have much time. Do we want to discuss this with the flight attendant, and if we do, how can she help us?"

"Bob, let me quickly finish. I don't have much more. Then we can talk about the flight attendant. We may want to go that route." Jim said.

"Go ahead, Jim, quickly."

"We believe it's paramount that the FAA is prepared. I assume J.R. has taken care of that."

Capone said, "He has. Connelly will be providing us with a contact for the FAA and Homeland Security. They been told to be geared up for possible air disasters this morning."

"Emergency rescue services need to be forewarned," Jim advised.

Capone responded, "I'll confirm that has happened."

Capone added a notation to the bottom of his list. "Anything else, anyone?"

There was no response.

"Let's talk about the flight attendant."

Dusty jumped in. "I think we need to call her father right away. If we can contact her, she'll know where the rest of the crew's staying. We may still be able to reach McIntyre or Lawrence. At the very least, we can brief her on what may be coming down. She can get help from one of the other two pilots after she gets to the plane."

"Good suggestion," Capone said. "Anyone else have a feeling on this?"

"I agree with Dusty, Bob," Jim Everett said. "We absolutely need someone on that plane that knows what's going on if things go south. We won't be able to talk across the normal aircraft channels because Nicholson will be listening in. The flight attendant is the perfect choice since she's in the back, away from Nicholson. She can use her cell phone and check in with us periodically. If she gets a chance to brief one of the other two pilots beforehand, all the better. Nicholson may have to be restrained, and the other pilots need to be ready for that eventuality."

"Okay, I'll call the flight attendant's father in Chicago. I want a continued effort here to determine what we haven't considered. Keep working on this. Meg, will you give me that number again?"

Meg handed him the folder and pointed toward the bottom of the page. Capone quickly memorized the number and left to make the call.

The phone in Arlington Heights rang twice and Richard Elliott answered. "Hello."

"Is this Mr. Richard Elliott?" Capone asked.

"Yes, it is. Who's this?"

"Mr. Elliott, please excuse the early morning call. This is Special Agent Bob Capone, FBI, out in Washington, D.C."

"Good morning, Mr. Capone. This is highly unusual. Should I be nervous?"

"No, Mr. Elliott, this is not in connection with you or your affairs. Please don't be alarmed. There is, however, a fairly serious matter that I'm presently dealing with, and you may be able to assist me."

"Go ahead, I'd like to hear more."

Capone said, "I assure you that this has nothing to do with you or your business. The project I'm working on is totally disassociated from you. Let me qualify that somewhat. There is an association only in that it involves Empire Airlines, the company your daughter works for. She's not involved in any way. The matter concerns the airline and a possible act of aggression against one or more of the company's planes. Your daughter's well-being is not in jeopardy, and you have no reason to be concerned with her

safety. Please hear me out before jumping to con-
clusions on this."

"I'm listening."

"We suspect, and I wish to emphasize, that
they are only suspicions at this point, that one
or more of Empire Airline planes are being tar-
geted in some way by an individual who cur-
rently works for the company."

Claire's father said, "Ah...that's alarming."

Capone continued, "The individual in question is the captain of Claire's flight. We're sure
he'll do nothing to expose himself or his own
plane to danger, but we think he could affect
other planes from his position in the cockpit.
I'm afraid I can't tell you more than that. We're
very pressed for time, as you might guess. The
morning flights will be departing soon."

"Agent Capone, I don't want my daughter
placed in a dangerous situation."

"Mr. Elliott, what I'm proposing is that she
act only as a link, to provide us with communication with the cockpit using her cell phone. We
have no way of locating the other crewmembers
in the few minutes available. I believe she can
provide an added degree of safety to her fellow
Empire associates in other aircraft by doing this
and I think she'd welcome an opportunity to
help. If you know how we could reach her to
discuss this, I'd greatly appreciate your cooperation."

"I believe you wouldn't be calling me at this

hour, Agent Capone, if there wasn't a need and if this weren't the only option. Claire's here, getting ready for her flight. We were just about to leave. I'll discuss this with her and call you back if that works for you. No offense, but I'd like to confirm that you are who you say you are."

"I understand, and I appreciate your cooperation. I need to ask you to please expedite your talk with your daughter."

Capone gave him two numbers he could use to contact the Hoover Building in Washington directly. "Punch in my extension 5413 when the recording prompts you. You'll be transferred directly to my desk. Can you call me back in, say, five minutes?"

"I will, Mr. Capone, as quick as I can."

Claire's father was torn between his duty to help law enforcement authorities and his deep devotion to his daughter, the most important thing in his life. He knew what he had to do. Claire would have it no other way. If he failed to allow her to make the decision herself, she'd never forgive him.

CHAPTER 30

Arlington Heights, Illinois
06:55 Central Standard Time
February 2, 2007

Richard Elliott moved quickly up the stairs toward the bedroom that Claire had claimed as her own nearly a year ago. He desperately wanted to prevent her from going on the trip, but he knew she would have to decide. He hesitated only for a moment before continuing down the hall to her room. The door was open, and she was lifting her travel bag from the bed.

"Dad, are we ready? We better hurry. I hate to be late."

"Claire," her father said somberly. "We have to talk for a minute. Something important has come up."

He sat on the bed taking her hand.

"What is it? We'll really be late if we don't hurry."

"Claire, this is important. An FBI agent just phoned me from Washington. He's made an unusual request that involves you and your flight to Minneapolis."

Claire remained silent. She could tell that her father was serious, and so was the message he had brought. She looked at him inquiringly.

Her father paused and took a deep breath. He found it hard to speak. She waited patiently giving him time.

"There's a man on your flight," he finally said. "One of the pilots who may be involved in something that could be dangerous to some of the other Empire jets. Not to your flight. The man who called from Washington wants you to help him by relaying information using your cell phone. This situation apparently has just developed. You seem to be their last resort for dealing with it. They don't know how to reach the other crewmembers. He wants us to call him back."

"Did you say they suspect one of the pilots on my flight?"

"They suspect your captain. They think he may be up to something, and I understand it may take place on your flight."

Claire blanched. What her father had just told her sounded like something out of a cheap novel. She released his hand and covered her eyes, desperately hoping the news was not what it seemed. Surely there had to be a mistake.

Lowering her hands, she looked to him in confusion. "What are they talking about, Dad?"

Her father wasn't sure if she had misunderstood what he had said, or whether she was reaching out for him to alter the meaning, to somehow make it different. "I know it sounds unbelievable, honey, but I'm sure the FBI has suspicions about your captain. I don't know exactly what he's done, or is intending to do, and I don't think they can give you the full details. It sounds very serious. He wanted us to call him back immediately."

He could see that she was shocked and needed more time to digest things. "You don't have to do this," he said gently. "In fact, I don't think you should. You're not a secret service agent, and no one expects you to put your life in danger. This isn't a job for a twenty-three-year-old flight attendant."

"I know you're worried, dad, but it sounds like I'll be in a safe position. I have to think about my friends on the other planes, and about the passengers. I don't know what's happening, but if I can help, then I should. I need your support, so let's call the man back and see what he has to say. Let's hurry. We have to go."

Richard Elliott could have predicted her decision. She was adamant and there was no time to deliberate the pros and cons. He carried her things downstairs and dialed the Washington number for her.

"Mr. Capone, this is Claire Elliott. My father has discussed your problem with me. Can you tell me exactly what it is you want me to do?"

"We have very little time. Your captain, Mike Nicholson, may be involved in a conspiracy that could possibly result in serious problems for some of your sister flights. I want to emphasize that we have no solid proof, and right now we only suspect him. I can't tell you more, except that we feel it would be wise to let one of the other pilots know, just in case. We also think that being in communication with you could be very helpful if things do go awry. Are you willing to help us? We have to move fast, Claire."

"I'll do what I can, Mr. Capone. What do you want me to do?"

"Glad to hear that. I know you have a plane to catch. "

"I wish we had more time. Claire, if there was any other way, I assure you I wouldn't be asking you to do this. How much time do you have before you have to leave for your flight?"

"I'm late now, Mr. Capone, but I can show up at the last minute as long as they haven't pulled the Jetway back and closed the forward door."

"Okay. We'll move fast. How long will it take you to get to the airport?"

"About fifteen minutes."

"This won't take long. The FBI strongly suspects Captain Nicholson will attempt to do something from the cockpit of your plane. It could seriously affect other flights. I don't want to panic you, but if the worst happens, you may have to help us deal with the situation. At this point I'm only contacting you as a precautionary measure."

"You're making this sound like something terrible's going to happen."

"We have to treat this as if it will, but again, your flight is safe. Is there any way you'll have a few seconds to discuss this privately with one of the other pilots before takeoff?"

"It'll be difficult, but I can try."

"Select either Lawrence or McIntyre and tell him what's happening and do it as soon as possible. Decide which one of the two you trust the most. We have an agent on the way to the airport but I'm not sure he'll make it in time. His name is Dean Jones."

"What do I tell the pilot?"

"Tell him that we're concerned Nicholson may have a small box or device which he may use to activate systems detrimental to other aircraft. I don't have time go into details. I want you to call me after you get airborne, and every ten minutes afterwards, if you can. We can monitor what's happening with the other planes and I'll give you directions. You with me?"

"I think so. I'll tell one of the other pilots, probably McIntyre, that the FBI suspects Nicholson, and that we may need to intervene. Mr. Capone, I don't think Mac's going to believe this."

"Do the best you can, Claire. Do you have a pencil?"

"Yes."

"Take down these numbers. Either will ring directly in my office. I'll be standing by.

She copied the telephone numbers down and placed them in her travel bag. "Anything else, Mr. Capone?"

"No, Claire, get going now. Time's running short."

CHAPTER 31

Mauston, Illinois
07:33 Central Standard Time
February 2, 2007

Every few minutes a car or truck drove by the familiar farm on the road connecting I-94 with eastern parts of the county, a mile north of Mauston. Some of those driving by were long-time residents of the area and took notice of the unusual activity near the house. A Wisconsin Highway Patrol car was parked just inside the tree line. Not far beyond, in the front yard, was an orange-and-white ambulance. Other vehicles, well behind the thick tree line, couldn't be seen easily by those passing by. Had the murders occurred during the summer months the foliage would have obstructed the house entirely. Some of the people driving by would guess that a family gathering was in progress. Others wouldn't be concerned, and a few would think that maybe one of the old people who lived there passed away during the night. None were aware of the tragic double murder that had been committed the day before.

The activity around the house included all the normal elements of a big city crime scene. At the end of the drive, behind the tree-lined perimeter of the yard, two state patrol cars were parked on opposite ends of the lot. An ambulance had backed in close to the front steps, and the coroner's green Taurus wagon was parked next to it. Three paramedics tugged a loaded gurney. Taking care not to slip and drop their cargo, they worked the cart across the footprinted snow to the open doors of the ambulance. A police officer pointed toward the ground directing them away from crime scene evidence.

In the back of the house, two police officers inspected the side of the white Ford pickup. One of the officers wrote notes on a clipboard while they talked.

Inside the house, the coroner stood in the living room discussing the gruesome scene with a fourth member of the Wisconsin State Patrol. Sitting silently alone at the far end of the small parlor was an elderly lady, the niece of the old man who had just been removed in the plastic bag. She had discovered the bodies only an hour earlier.

The medical personnel returned to the parlor with the gurney. Norma was sprawled out in the center of the room and had just been declared officially dead by the coroner. The coroner handed paperwork to a white-smocked young man fumbling with a new body bag. Nora Neumiller lay sprawled on the floor. Her skin was grayish white, and her flower print dress was twisted tightly around her hips and legs. Rigor mortis had set in and the awkward way the woman had been left, with her arms extended from being dragged into the house, made it difficult to tuck her body into the bag. After wrestling with the corpse for several minutes, it finally slid into the thick polyurethane pouch. One paramedic held the end of the bag tight while a second ran the zipper closed in one long sweep. The loud whining sound, amplified by the taut plastic, caused everyone to turn and stare at the source of the noise. Three men knelt and hefted the sealed bag onto the gurney.

As the doors to the ambulance closed, a third squad car slid in behind the blue and white blocking the drive. A uniformed officer, Harry Dodd, exited the cruiser. Dodd moved quickly to the front of the house to survey the evidence found earlier by the first team of cops. They had noticed a red tint to the fresh snow around the area of the front walkway and used a straw broom to sweep away the top layer of powdery snow. Large amounts of frozen blood appeared and exposed the extent of the bloody murder. Dodd made a mental note and continued to the back of the house where he performed a quick examination of the white pickup. He pulled a small notepad from his shirt pocket and wrote down the license number. Entering the house from the back door near the woodpile, he moved through the mudroom to join the others in the parlor.

"Hey, Harry, 'bout time you joined the party," one of the officers said, forgetting the woman in the corner of the room.

"Brian," Dodd said, in a manner that was meant to silence the other cop. Dodd looked in the direction of the niece and then gave the officer who greeted him a withering look, expressing his disapproval about the party comment. The room remained silent for a few moments until Dodd asked, "Has anyone called the FBI?

"What for?" Brian replied.

"What for?" Dodd repeated incredulously.

"We called in the pickup as the one that was stolen from those kids back in Black River yesterday afternoon, if that's what you're talking about."

"Didn't you read the call sheet? Did you read block ten?" Dodd said, referring to the special instruction sheet on the missing car notice. The pick-up had been listed as stolen and every cop on I-94 had been looking for it since yesterday afternoon. The patrolmen speaking to Dodd had reported on shift at six-thirty and received a watered-down summary of the search. They had failed to study the entire notice explaining that when the pickup was discovered, the FBI needed to be notified. Dodd couldn't believe it. Four patrolmen were on the scene, and not one of them had properly reviewed the available information regarding the stolen truck. Only an hour had elapsed since the niece phoned in the murders, and sure, the officers had been busy processing the bodies and securing the crime scene, but still . . .

Dodd shook his head in disappointment. He calmed down and bit his lip, not wanting to appear too critical of his fellow officers.

"That's okay," he said, after carefully considering his words. "The driver of the pickup was involved in that wreck yesterday afternoon down by Black River. I ended up talking with the FBI. I was expecting to find the pickup. I already knew the driver was wanted by the Feds. You guys weren't aware of all that. I'll give him a call."

Seated in an overstuffed chair near the niece, who continued to sit quietly in the corner, Dodd held the phone to his ear and dialed Washington.

"Agent Capone," he said, "this is Harry Dodd, Wisconsin State Patrol. We talked yesterday about your two boys in the accident."

"Yes, Dodd, how's the weather up your way?"

"Frigid, but that crazy idiot of yours who left the accident yesterday is keeping my stretch of highway pretty warm. He's been acting up again."

"Tell me about it."

"We got a report about an hour ago from a

lady who stopped by to check on her aunt and uncle here in Mauston, about a half hour south-east of Black River Falls. They'd been dragged into their home after being murdered. The stolen pickup we've been hunting is in the back yard. Your man took the old couple's Buick and split. I'm guessing not long after the accident yesterday. He's probably in Chicago by now, but you can add two counts of murder to whatever you had on him before."

"Thanks, Dodd. I'm real sorry to hear about the lady's aunt and uncle. I wish we had done better yesterday."

"Yeah, I know how you feel, Bob. Look, I'll send you the report when we get done. I guess you're through with us now."

"I think so. Hey, heard anything about the other one in La Crosse? Mick Mallory?"

"No, I'm afraid I haven't checked on him today. He was still unconscious about six yester-day afternoon. That's all I know."

"Thanks. If you get any more news, give me a call. Good luck."

CHAPTER 32

O'Hare International Airfield
Chicago, Illinois
07:45 Central Standard Time
February 2, 2007

There was still no word on Kiley. I was unable to find any reference of a missing Empire captain in the morning edition of the Chicago Herald. I wasn't particularly fond of Kiley and really wasn't broken up about him being gone, but I was concerned. It seemed strange how Nicholson responded so coldly yesterday when I asked about what he had learned, as if he were disinterested. For some reason that I couldn't pinpoint, I was beginning to feel a little uncomfortable around Nicholson. He was an excellent pilot and didn't have any of Kiley's contemptible qualities, but there was something aloof and odd about his manner. Ted was his normal jovial self and had been ribbing me about Claire since he showed up at the plane. I had made the mistake of telling him about dinner with her and her father but fortunately didn't mention the late-night call I received. Otherwise the trip home would be a long one.

Having arrived before the rest of the crew, I completed the pre-flight inspection early. I hoped to see Claire but figured she had probably eaten breakfast with her father and would be running a little late. The other flight attendants arrived shortly after me and began preparing the back of the plane. After finishing in the cockpit, I took my usual stroll through the passenger section, checking out the cabin and making sure the girls hadn't identified anything unusual.

The first thing I noticed as I entered first class was the fresh smell of the recent cleaning. It was good to get a different plane than the one we had used to slaughter geese the day before. Karen was brewing fresh coffee in the forward galley.

"Everything okay?" I asked.

"Everything's fine, Mac. How are you this morning?"

I thought I detected a hidden implication to her question and wondered if she knew of my rendezvous with the Elliott's last night.

"I'm great. Looks like a good plane, and the weather is perfect everywhere. We should have an easy trip. They're predicting it'll reach forty degrees in Minneapolis today."

"You're kidding," she replied with genuine amazement.

The temperature had been in the low twenties the day before. Forty degrees in Minneapolis the first week in February was considered by the natives to be balmy. Any convertibles on the road would probably have their tops down.

"Did you hear what the forecast is for tomorrow?"

"Colder again. High around eighteen."

"Are you serious?" she asked, not sure if I was putting her on. I wish I were, but the one-day heat wave was moving through rapidly and a more typical mass of cold air was rumbling down from Canada. It would be arriving in Minneapolis about the same time we were due to land.

She offered me a cup of coffee, which I accepted and carried toward the back of the plane while she continued checking her equipment up front. I said hello to Julie, who was inspecting the overhead compartments, and looked at the wings out of habit. Erin was in the back, near the rear exit, fighting with one of the rest room doors. She seemed to be having trouble getting it to open.

"Need some help?" I asked.

"Hi, Mac. This door seems to be jammed or something. I didn't realize there was anything wrong until I tried to use it."

She kept pulling at the handle and pushing the door in and out to jar it loose. Then she threw her hands in the air in defeat and rolled her eyes. "Should we call someone to look at it?"

I eased up close to the door and allowed her to move around behind me so I could check it out. I tried to turn the handle, which seemed stuck or locked. The only way to lock it was from the inside, and in order to get out of the small water closet, the locking lever had to be released. There wasn't much time to call a mechanic, and I hated to leave with one of the rest rooms out of service. I tried harder to turn the knob. It remained stuck. Placing both hands around the handle and using considerably more force, I tried to move it again. There was a loud snap and whatever had been jamming the door released. The handle turned and the door swung open.

"Way to go, Hercules," Erin remarked.

"I hope I didn't break it." Looking inside the latch, I tried turning the knob in both directions. Then I slid the locking lever back and forth. Everything looked normal, but I thought I should give it a functional test to make sure. I went inside and closed the door.

"If I get locked in, Erin, you'll have to try and force it like I did. Otherwise, I may have to sit in here all the way to Minneapolis."

I slid the lock over to the latched position and asked Erin, loud enough to be heard through the door, "Did the occupied sign show up in the window?"

"Yep."

I slid the lever back and it seemed to move normally, then turned the knob and stepped out. Inquisitively, she asked, "How did you do that?"

"Don't know, but it seems to be fixed. Let's leave it alone before it locks up again."

"Mac, have you seen Claire, she's really late. It's not like her. I know she stays at her dads place when we're in Chicago, but he always has her here on time."

"I was going to ask you the same thing. We had dinner last night. She went home early and she seemed fine. I'm sure she'll be here soon."

"You know, Mac, this is scary. This reminds me of what happened in Midland when Kiley disappeared."

"Now you are really over-reacting, Erin. She's just a little late. If she doesn't show up, I'm sure there's good reason."

"Well, I think it's weird."

The passengers had been boarding for several minutes. I realized I had stayed too long in the back of the plane and would have to fight my way to the front.

"I better get back."

"Thanks for helping with the door."

I worked my way toward the front, excusing myself at every encounter. I could see Ted through the cockpit door. Karen was adjacent to the opening and was greeting the boarding passengers. She reached out to grab my arm as I approached.

"Where's Claire," she said in a mild state of panic.

"I don't know. Erin asked me the same thing.

I know she stayed at her father's place last night. Can just the three of you handle this crowd?"

"That's no problem, Mac. I'm just concerned about Claire."

"Me too, but I think she'll be along soon."

I entered the cockpit and took my seat behind Ted.

"Sorry I'm late, I had to help Erin fix the rest room door in the back. There's something wrong with the lockset. I'll write it up and get someone to look at it in Minneapolis. It seems to be okay now."

Nicholson's absence this close to departure gave me concern.

I said, "Where's Mike?"

"I just got a call from ops, they said he called in sick last night. They've got someone on the way. Spooky."

"I'll say, must be your breath."

"Thanks."

"Something else though, Claire isn't on the plane yet either. I've never been on a trip where so many people got lost."

"Claire's not here either. That is strange."

We started getting the cockpit lined up without the captain and got halfway through the checklist before he showed up.

"Morning guys, sorry I'm late. I guess you kept Mike out too late last night."

"You know Mike?" I asked.

"Sure, haven't seen him in a few years

though, it seems. He'll be alright. I was told he had the flu or something and headed home. By the way, I'm Skip Willis."

In response to Skip's request for the pre-taxi checklist, I began to read through the items, and we started our switch-turning and button-pushing routine to prepare for pushback. I had forgotten all about Claire. The orange light on my panel, that indicated the position of the rear cargo door, extinguished, telling me the caterers were finished servicing the back galley. I informed our new captain that the door was closed, so he could start the engine when he was ready. It was five minutes before departure and the passengers were nearly all seated and buckled in. Claire entered my mind again and I wondered if she was in the back.

The cockpit door opened, and Karen tapped my shoulder. "Mac." She seemed to be trying to get my attention without disturbing the other two.

I removed my earpiece and rotated the seat to better hear what she was saying. "What?"

"Claire's in the back. She needs to talk to you right away."

I couldn't leave my position at this critical moment to go back and talk to Claire. *What could she need that was so important*, I thought? *Did it have something to do with her being late?* The only thing I could think of was that it was personal. That seemed very sweet, but she must know I

331

couldn't leave now. This was strange. The last two days had been strange. The plane was moving back, and I turned to see the large glass windows of the terminal getting smaller. I couldn't leave.

"Karen," I said, "I can't now. Tell her I'll be back as soon as I can."

CHAPTER 33

J.R. Connelly had just arrived to the war room. He, Capone, and Everett, gathered together around Capone's desk to rehash the latest developments. Connelly had set up response plans with the FAA and Homeland Security. It seemed Capone had done everything possible to stop the Bennettis, however, if he was correct about Nicholson, then the entire night would have been a failed effort. Dean Jones hadn't reached the airport in time.

Connelly approved of everything Capone's team had done and later would use much the aggressive, preventative tactics as examples during training sessions. Even if all efforts failed to stop Nicholson, at least they had done everything possible to try to prevent the disaster. The clock had ticked down to the final hour. There was every indication Nicholson would get airborne.

Capone finished a thorough, but condensed, report to the director and waited for a response.

"Bob, you and everyone here have made amazing progress, especially considering the rather obscure missing person's report on Kiley I gave you only yesterday. I can't offer any suggestions from this point. You seem to have everyone in place. How much help will you need this morning?"

"J.R., we're all tired. Jim and I are staying, at least until we see what happens during the first few hours. I want to send everyone else home after they've had a chance to brief some fresh bodies. I think I'll need at least six people to start with."

"You've got it."

"Thanks."

Bob, I've got the FAA and Homeland working out contingencies. Use the contacts I gave you if you need help from them. The FAA will be able to prepare emergency services at some of the larger airfields. They may come up with some other ideas. I want to listen in to your conversations with the flight attendant. What's your take on her?"

"I think she'll do well. We had only about ten minutes to talk. We were lucky to reach any of the crewmembers before departure. At least we have someone on the plane who knows what could happen and who'll serve as a communication link. She may be our only hope if Nicholson starts to act. She's supposed to call us in the next few minutes. We've contacted the Chicago Control Center and confirmed that they'll call us immediately if they field any emergencies."

Connelly looked at his watch. It was just a few minutes after eight o'clock in Chicago, and Flight 855 would be rolling in position for take-off any minute.

"Have you decided exactly how we should handle Ms. Elliott if a crash is reported?" Jim asked.

Capone's expression was abnormally blank. "I was hoping to've had more time with her. I'm not even sure she's been able to speak with McIntyre or Lawrence yet. If she hasn't talked with either of them, then she'll have to set up a situation requiring one of them to come to the back of the plane. At that time, we'll be totally dependent on the pilot she confides in. I believe the first thing he should do is try to find the box. If Nicholson has it, someone must take it from him."

"Of course, someone else might have it."

"Right, that's possible, but I don't think it would have been as desirable for Nicholson. First, the Empire 727 can get to altitude much faster than a smaller plane. By activating the wave generators from his plane while flying a scheduled trip throws out a red herring. No one would suspect an Empire plane or pilot when it's Empire's planes that are being attacked. Remember, he has no idea that we suspect him. If we hadn't stumbled onto his college papers, we wouldn't have had a clue to look in his direction. I'm sure he never believed he would be under suspicion."

One of the phones in the room rang, and a few seconds later Meg called over to the area where Capone and Everett were talking. "It's Claire Elliott."

"Claire, how're you doing?" Capone asked in his best bedside manner.

"Mr. Capone, I'm sorry. I got to the plane late and haven't had time to talk with Mac yet. We're climbing out now. What should I do?"

"Claire," he said reassuringly, "I want you to stay calm. You're doing good. I'm glad you called us. So far, there's nothing to worry about. Here's what I want you to do. Set up a situation that would require Mac or Ted to come to the back. Maybe a problem in the galley, or you've badly burned your hand, anything. Is there anything that's happened in the past that required one of the pilots to come back to investigate?"

Claire thought for a moment. "Yes, I think so. Erin, one of the other flight attendants, said there was a problem with one of the bathroom door locks during the cabin check this morning. Mac managed to fix it temporarily. I can tell him it's stuck again and ask him to come back and fix it."

"That's very good. If for some reason Nicholson comes back, you can just say it must have just broken loose on its own. Before you do that, tell your senior attendant what's going on, if you haven't already. If Nicholson comes to the back, she can then go to the cockpit and explain the situation to McIntyre, and Lawrence too, if necessary. It would be best to bring only one of the other two pilots in on it at this time, if possible. But we'll have to improvise. Does that make sense?"

"Yes, I can do that. I'll call you back when I'm done."

"Thank you, Claire. Good luck."

Claire had already discussed the situation with Erin, who had been seated next to her on climb out, but she hadn't had a chance to talk with the other flight attendants who were working the first-class section. She picked up the intercom phone and pressed the button that alerted Karen.

"What's up?"

"Karen, this is Claire, I don't know how to tell you this...."

Claire continued, and with a condensed version, was able to fill Karen in on the situation. She asked Karen to go to the flight deck and ask Mac to come back and fix the restroom door.

At a window seat toward the front of the first-class section, Short Eddie watched the flight engineer walk by and wondered, *if that pilot could only listen into my conversation with*

Robert, he wouldn't look so calm. He was at a window seat and spoke into his cell phone with his left palm cupped around his mouth so the businesswoman seated to his left couldn't hear.

"Robert," he said anxiously, "we've been airborne about five minutes. I just wanted to check in to make sure we had a good line. Can you hear me okay?"

"Yes, Eddie, you're coming in loud and clear. It's too soon to tell if anything has happened yet. Call me back in a few minutes and be careful what you say. Just tell me what I need to know. Otherwise, make this sound like a normal conversation."

"I understand, boss. I'll call you back in five minutes."

CHAPTER 34

Chicago Downtown Regency
Chicago, Illinois
08:15 Central Standard Time
February 2, 2007

Robert Bennetti answered on the second ring. "Hello."

"Robert, it's me, Eddie."

"Damnit, Eddie. Who the hell else would it be? Is everything okay?"

"I don't know. Nicholson hasn't come to the back like we planned. One of the pilots has been back here an awful lot."

"Eddie, I don't like the sound of this."

Tony rose from his seated position on the bed. The others froze. No one spoke.

Robert returned to the phone. "Nicholson hasn't been in the back since you took off?"

"No. We've been airborne maybe ten minutes. There's been a lot of talking between the flight attendants and that other pilot."

"Hang on."

Robert turned toward his brother. "John, Eddie says Nicholson hasn't been out of the cockpit. He said one of the other pilots has been doing a lot of talking with the cabin attendants."

John's eyes closed tight while he considered his brother's words.

"John, did you hear what I said?"

"Yeah I'm thinking."

Tony spoke, "More than ten minutes now. He should have gone to check with Eddie by now. Something has to be wrong."

Robert Bennetti spoke up, unable to contain his anger. "I can't believe this. It's incredible. Fifty million dollars on the line and we're working with idiots. I knew this Nicholson bastard was insane. If he's changed his mind now, or is trying to get away with something, he'll spend several days wishing he was dead."

"Robert," John said in his usual mild tone, hoping to keep the situation in check. "Let's not panic. Let's find out what's happening and go from there? Any number of things could have delayed Nicholson temporarily."

"What next, then?"

"Tell Eddie to give Nicholson five more minutes and call us back. We'll all discuss this before someone screws everything up," John said calmly.

"Eddie," Robert spoke firmly into the phone. "Give Nicholson five more minutes, then call back. We'll have instructions." He jabbed the 'end' button and laid the phone on the desk next to the television.

"Eddie might need to find a way to get into the cockpit, to see what's up," Tony suggested, looking first to John, then over to Robert.

"I agree," John said. looking to Robert for his approval.

"I think there's no other choice if Nicholson doesn't come out. But how's Eddie going to get into the cockpit? And what'll he do once he's there?"

Robert said, "We've already transferred money into Nicholson's account. I hope we didn't underestimate him."

John shook his head. "I don't think so. He knows we'll be waiting for him when he lands. He's not that stupid."

"What do you think is holding him up?"

"Don't know. Could be anything. Either he has some real problem with the aircraft that he's trying to work out or he's had a heart attack or something. I don't believe he's backing out."

John said, "Robert, if we don't start dropping planes, Arbari will get nervous. I don't want him on my ass. I'd much rather have the FBI looking for me than that lunatic."

"Yeah. We'll work it out."

The phone rang.

"Eddie?"

"Okay, he's still in hiding. What now?" Eddie asked.

Robert responded, "We don't know. Could be a number of things. We're thinking."

Eddie said, "Okay, then. What do you want me to do?" He wasn't as calm as when things were going smoothly twenty minutes earlier. His heart was pounding more rapidly and his voice shaky. He couldn't get comfortable in the cramped seat. Sweat formed on his forehead, and his eyes darted back toward the cockpit door, searching for Nicholson.

"Sit tight for a few minutes. We're thinking. Call us back in five."

Eddie hung up. He looked out the small porthole to his right and suddenly realized the plane had lost considerable altitude. He hadn't noticed when the change took place, but the engine noise was gone. The plane was totally silent. *What the shit?*

CHAPTER 35

Chicago Air Traffic Control Center
Chicago, Illinois
08:18 Central Standard Time
February 2, 2007

"Mayday . . . Mayday . . . Mayday! This is Empire Flight 867. We've lost all engines. I repeat, we've lost all three engines."

The departure controller instantly sat upright in his chair and keyed his microphone. "Roger, eight six seven. Can you turn back to the field?"

"Negative, Chicago, not enough altitude, no control. We're going in straight ahead."

The controller's name was Bob Siskel. He felt complete helplessness. This type of emergency wasn't practiced, or for that matter, even discussed. It just didn't happen. Large commercial jets just don't lose all three, or four, engines at once. The controller's heart beat wildly as he quickly located the distressed plane's blip on the nearly yard-wide, neon-green radar screen. The target continued straight ahead, heading three two zero off the end of Chicago O'Hare's longest runway. The ex-Air Force controller raised his hand and yelled to his supervisor, Ray Vick.

"Ray, get over here quick! We've got one going in."

The supervisor left the screen he was monitoring a few stations away and quickly ran to the unsettled controller.

"What's happening, Bob?"

"867. Right here," he said, between broadcasts while pointing to a small bright dot on the round screen. "He just reported complete engine failure. All three gone. He's going straight in."

About that time the bright yellow dot disappeared.

"Shit, I think he bought it."

"Keep working your traffic, I'll call O'Hare."

The supervisor picked up the phone on the console and pressed the O'Hare control tower button.

"Tower," came the voice at the other end.

Ray said, "This is Ray Vick. Did you get a report on Empire 867? He called in total engine failure off the departure end of three-two. He's off the screen. I think he may have gone in, about eight miles out. Do you have a visual?"

The tower controller on the other end of the line looked to the northwest through the enormous angled glass window of the control tower. An American DC9 was rotating near the departure end of the active runway. The tower chief didn't immediately respond to the caller. In his twenty years of experience in the air traffic control profession, he had never witnessed a disaster like this. He initially saw a small puff of black smoke beyond the DC9, similar to what one would expect from a house fire. But within seconds, it began to grow and billow higher until there was no mistaking what it was. Bright-red and yellow flames boiled from the ground, the fireball pushing the black smoke skyward.

All the controllers in the tower were transfixed by the growing inferno. Only a few seconds elapsed before they regained their composure and began to react. As a result of years of recurrent training, each person instinctively responded according to established procedures. The tower chief began to spit out orders like an NCAA basketball coach in the final seconds of a final four game. The landing and departure controllers continued to direct their planes while broadcasting advisories of the incident. A departing Delta flight reported observing the crash. Other pilot reports would follow.

The tower chief instructed someone to call nine-one-one and get help to the crash site. Another was told to report the accident to the airport fire crew. Local hospitals were also called. All this happened within the first minute. The man who had received the call from the en-route supervisor had already confirmed the crash and dialed the airport manager's number.

Radar controllers are known for their ability to handle pressure. They have years of experience working under stressful conditions. Most of the men and women in the dimly lit room responded to the disaster professionally and calmly. Having owned responsibility for Flight 867, Bob Siskel's initial response was more personal. He was understandably unnerved. Now, however, he was hysterical.

He screamed. The radar experts in front of the other screens turned in unison toward the high-pitched cry emanating from the fat man working O'Hare departures. Ray Vick had walked to the desk at the long end of radar stations and was about to begin his emergency notification procedures in response to the crash. He looked up from his desk in sync with the young trainee next to him, toward the scream. It was Bob Siskel again.

Bob continued to stare at the radar screen and was speaking into his microphone, his right hand held high above his head waving. Signaling to anyone that he needed help.

Ray and the trainee were behind him immediately.

"What is it, Bob?" Ray asked as he put a comforting hand on his shoulder, in an effort to calm him.

"I've got another one! What the shit is going on? Why me, for Christ's sake? Get me some help over here!"

Ray pulled up a chair and plugged his headset into one of the holes just below the edge of the brown Formica counter. He looked at the portly man who, just moments ago, lost his first plane and said, "You work the other traffic, Bob. I'll take this one."

Bob slid a slip of paper toward his supervisor and turned it around so he could read it. "This is it, Empire 855, lost all engines. I was just about to hand him over. He's at 13,000, two niner zero, direct Rockford, he may be able to make it..."

Before Bob could finish, the pilot of Flight 855 broke in. "Departure, eight-five-five, unable to restart, dead stick, very little control. Passing 12,000 keep me informed here, where's the field?"

"I'll take it, Bob. Work your planes."

"Thanks."

"Empire eight-five-five, turn left thirty degrees. You're twenty miles from runway two seven at Rockford. They're expecting you. Do you want foam?"

"Affirmative, Departure. Foam the runway and get some trucks out there. This could get messy."

"Roger, eight-five-five. Hang in there, you're do'n good. Fourteen miles now. Say altitude."

"Passing ten-thousand seven-hundred. Twelve hundred feet a minute." We won't be cranking the gear down, not enough time. We'll be coming in hot, wheels up."

"Roger, eight-five-five. Turn left five degrees. Say heading."

"Rolling out on two-five-five."

"Thank you, Empire. Maintain heading two-five-five. The airport is at your twelve o'clock, niner miles. Rockford tower is giving you a white light. Report the light in sight."

"Got the light now. Thanks, departure. I can take it from here."

"Good luck, Empire. Rockford has you on 118.1."

"Roger, one eighteen point one, thanks."

The captain fought hard to maneuver the aircraft without hydraulic assist. He had both legs extended and was nearly standing on the right rudder to maintain runway alignment. Both hands clenched tight to the yoke and the plane continued to roll slightly.

With some anxiety, but calm considering the circumstances, he said to his flight deck crew, "Ted, help me with these ailerons. Mac, make sure they're braced in the back. How's the fuel dump coming?"

CHAPTER 36

Downtown Regency Hotel
Chicago, Illinois
08:24 Central Standard Time
February 2, 2007

Tony Bennetti sat at the round table near the window. Robert leaned against the headboard of his queen-size bed with two pillows behind his back. John slouched in a chair near window. They watched the local news broadcast, just beginning the sports segment. The attractive young blond sports reporter had their attention, but they became more alert as her image was replaced by the figure of a man behind a desk holding a sheet of paper.

An announcement preceded his voice. "We interrupt this program for a special bulletin. Here from the news desk of WGWP is Phil Edwards."

The man behind the desk began to read from the script on the teleprompter. "Ten miles north of Chicago O'Hare airfield, an Empire Airlines jet crashed shortly after takeoff. News of the disaster was confirmed only minutes ago. The crash happened at approximately eight-twenty. Reports indicate that the scene is one of total devastation as the Boeing 727 exploded on impact and erupted into a tremendous fireball. We have no reports of survivors. It's believed the plane had just taken off from Chicago O'Hare Airfield and carried a full load of passengers. The departing flight was filled with aviation fuel, contributing to the enormous explosion. Emergency rescue personnel fear there is little likelihood of survivors. Empire Airline representatives have been unavailable for comment. The crash site was in the outlying community of Iverness, and it's believed that a number of residential homes have been destroyed due to the crash and resulting fire. We will continue to report on this tragedy as information is received."

Tony's clenched fist hit the table hard. "Yes. He did it! It's started."

"Hot damn, this is it. Let's give Arbari a call."

John used his cell phone to dial the long distance number where the leader of the World Liberation Alliance awaited their call.

The connection was made and there was the familiar, thick-throated voice of the foreigner. The man spoke in broken English that was difficult to understand.

"Hello," he said, with no evident emotion.

"Arbari, have you received the report from your operatives?"

"Yes, Mr. Bennetti, I have wait for you call."

Robert Bennetti was amazed by how quickly the terrorist leader had gotten word of the crash on the other side of world. "Have you begun the transfer?"

"Yes, you will receive confirmation with your bank. You have done excellent job. You know soon you get report of second jet crash?"

Arbari's people were monitoring all the aviation broadcasts, especially the emergency frequencies that the pilots normally switched to when reporting in-flight emergencies. Arbari had established a sophisticated radio-receiving station just outside the Chicago city limits, which utilized a two-hundred-foot tower to receive aircraft transmissions. A similar facility was set up in the Minneapolis area.

Robert was surprised by Arbari's knowledge of the pending crash. He wondered how the terrorist leader across the Atlantic could have gotten this information so soon.

"I didn't know that, but I'll track the reports closely and will check with my associates to make sure the funds are distributed in the accounts we've set up. If the money doesn't appear in a reasonable time, I'll stop Nicholson. His fuel is limited, so it's to your benefit to make the deposits quickly."

"I understand. I know immediately when aircraft makes Mayday call. You get money and I get many airplane crashes. Is true?"

"Yes, Arbari, that is true."

The two business partners ended the call. Robert Bennetti turned to his two brothers who were listening intently. "His communication network is very sophisticated. He already knew about Flight 867 and told me of another one in progress. We should hear about the first deposit within minutes. Tony, if Eddie calls, tell him to signal Nicholson for a go. I don't want to risk losing opportunities. I know Arbari has made the transfers. We'll have that confirmed in a few minutes.

Robert said, "I've already transferred Nicholson's money into his account. His people should be able to confirm the deposit any time."

"Good."

"Nicholson should be making an appearance in the first-class section about now and Eddie will signal him to continue. As well as this initial attempt worked, I expect that Nicholson will be able to bring down quite a few planes on the next round," Robert said.

Tony pumped a clenched fist in the same fashion that Tiger Woods celebrates a long putt and said, "Yessss."

CHAPTER 37

War Room, FBI Headquarters
Washington D.C.
09:28 Eastern Standard Time
February 2, 2007

Now, nearly 24 hours after the disappearance of Bob Kiley, the search had grown into a full-blown investigation. Homeland Security had issued a RED alert. Several agents were pulled in to assist the original team.

Redmond continued to study Nicholson's manuscripts. Capone knew the next few hours were critical, and that whatever calls came in during this period would certainly be pivotal. His phone rang.

"Bob Capone."

"Bob, this is Brandon Sheffield, got a minute to talk?"

"Brandon. We've been trying to reach you."

"Sorry, I haven't been available. I came in early today to fire off a few memo's before leaving to New York. I hadn't been here long and a situation arose that required me to call an emergency executive meeting."

"Okay."

" Bob, I have some things you need to know. I had intended on getting up to New York at 12:15 to make it to my daughter's wedding this evening in SoHo. I've changed my plans."

"Oh?"

"I was finishing up my work when my assistant came into my office. She had received information on Captain Kiley. At the same time, it was brought to her attention that Mike Nicholson was assigned to Kiley's trip."

"I'm aware of that."

"Bob, I'm so certain that this might relate to the threat against my fleet, I felt the need to cancel my New York trip. I need to remain here in case there's an incident. That's why the emergency meeting this morning."

"I'm not sure I understand," Capone said.

"Several years ago, I became personally involved with an issue regarding Mike Nicholson."

There was a pause in Sheffield's delivery and Capone said, "That is interesting. Tell me more."

"Well, Nicholson is an extremely bright individual, somewhat of a genius actually. A few years ago, he developed a software program that uses quite a large data base of information to program our routes. This is an extremely complex task. One that has previously been done by an entire team, and even then, was far from perfect. Determining the most efficient routes for a large airline like Empire is much more complex than one would think. Establishing routes and departure schedules involves dealing with many dynamic factors. It's also an undertaking that affects profits in a large way. There's much more to this, but you get the idea. Using Nicholson's software saves us millions of dollars a year."

"We're aware of Mr. Nicholson's intellect. How does this tie into our problem?"

Sheffield replied, "Nicholson, understandably, wanted to secure a patent and sell his program to other carriers. Naturally, we balked at that idea. He hadn't realized that he had signed an assignment of inventions, or property assignment, clause as part of his employment. This clause is somewhat unusual for our industry but not unheard of. I'm pretty sure few of our employees are aware of the particulars. It's something that, quite honestly, never comes up. In this case however, we just couldn't allow other airlines to benefit from Nicholson's work. This is the main reason a property assignment clause exists. It's not at all unethical."

Capone asked, "It sounds like Nicholson may have put a huge effort into developing this program, expecting to make money on it. Then, Empire pretty much yanked the rug out. Is that about it?"

"You could say that."

"How did Nicholson handle your position?"

"The clause is very clearly worded in the contract. Each employee has to initial that they've read it when signing employment documents.

"It seems like your employees may not be fully aware of what they agreed to in their contract," Capone said.

"That's probably true. Anyway, unfortunately I became personally involved in the dispute with Nicholson over ownership of the software. Nicholson finally acquiesced, but not after considerable legal haggling. He was very bitter the last time I had contact with him. I know he spent a huge sum of money on representation. During that period, Nicholson exhibited extreme emotional outbreaks. On several occasions he totally lost control, to the point it worried me. I'm all but certain that this factors into your investigation."

Capone's mind was racing, and he said, "I have to agree. Is there anything else you can add right now that might help?"

"No. If something definite regarding my planes comes to light, I would like to know about it immediately. Just so you know, I do have a contingency plan in place and I'm meeting with my team again this morning to enhance that effort."

"Thanks, Brandon, I appreciate you cancelling your trip to New York to deal with this. I'll be in touch if anything develops."

Capone was now approaching certainty of what was just a few hours ago more of a guess. He scanned the room and noted the change in activity, and different agents now involved.

One of those individuals sat at a desk near the back wall. Capone didn't take note. The man was average size, mid-thirties, and wore a plaid jacket and a red flowered tie. His name was Jeff Telbert. He was reading through one of the documents left by Redmond when his phone began to ring. He answered. "Jeff Telbert, FBI."

"Mr. Telbert, this is Rick Simpson, manager of the Chicago Radar Control Center in Joliet. I was directed to contact your office immediately if we experienced emergencies in our area."

"Yes, Mr. Simpson, that's correct. Have you got something to report?"

"I'm afraid so. Just a few minutes ago, an Empire Airline 727 suffered multiple engine failures and crashed off the departure end of Runway three two at O'Hare. We have a second Empire jet descending into Rockford with apparently the same problem. I want to know what's happening. We have two, large commercial jets crashing in our area with identical catastrophic engine failures and it seems your office had prior notice. Why wasn't I informed earlier that this might happen? Why were these flights allowed to take off?"

"Mr. Simpson," Jeff said, slowly and with authority, "I understand your concern. We're all concerned. We'd hoped that you wouldn't call this morning. We'll tell you everything we possibly can. I'm going to hand you over to Chad Christian. He's been working closely with the FAA representatives who provided you with the information you've already received. He'll answer your questions and set up a conference call with Bill Riley, the FAA coordinator appointed to this project by Director Adams. We hope that there'll be no additional incidents. You should, however, prepare for further disasters. Heads of various agencies are enacting response plans as we speak. Now here's Chad. Good luck."

Jeff moved quickly to where Capone, Connelly, and Everett were seated and interrupted without waiting for an opening. "I just got a call from a Mr. Simpson, manager of the control center in Joliet. One Empire jet just crashed departing O'Hare. A second one is going in near Rockford with engine failures."

Capone said, "Our worst fears."

Everett added, "We've done all we can. The FAA should be redirecting Empire planes."

Capone was stunned, "I've known all along that this might happen. I just didn't want to believe it. I wrongly thought that maybe we could stop it."

Capone was devastated. The stricken expression on his face clearly expressed his anguish.

Everett reached out to clasp his shoulder in comfort. "Bob, we have to try to prevent Nicholson from continuing."

Capone nodded in agreement. "Yes."

He turned to face Connelly but spoke to all the agents who were gathered around.

"A few moments ago, I talked with Brandon Sheffield. He told me something important. Apparently, Nicholson and Sheffield had a rather serious falling out. I believe Nicholson was left with a very good reason to hold a grudge, even a hatred for Sheffield. It may be the primary motive we've been looking for. Sheffield thought it was so important that he cancelled his trip this morning to New York. He'll miss his daughter's wedding this evening."

Meg said, "That's right. He was leaving this morning."

"He was. Not now. He seemed certain Nicholson was involved," Capone said.

"That explains a lot," Meg said.

Capone continued, "Apparently, Sheffield, actually Empire, was responsible for assuming ownership of a very valuable software program developed by Nicholson. What the airline did was legal, but still left Nicholson with very unpleasant feelings toward Empire. A hatred. We may be witnessing his vendetta."

Connelly responded, "Thanks for filling me in, I know we don't have time to fully evaluate this now. We'll discuss it more later. Let's deal with the problem at hand. I have to call the White House and discuss what's happened. I'm sure the President will want to know more."

"You're right, J.R., we may even need our

military pilots. Do we consider shooting down Nicholson's plane?"

"Bob, I believe, at the very least, we'll have to launch some of our jets in the area and be prepared. I don't think at this point that I want to discuss bringing down a plane full of innocent people. That will be the President's decision, but he'll want our input. I'll make the call."

Connelly left the room as Capone continued to think of a way out. He looked to his friend for help but received only a blank stare.

Jim remarked, "Our hands are tied. I wish we could've had two more hours. We may have been able to stop this."

"I know, Jim. You did the best you could with what we had. We all did. By now, the FAA's initiating the procedure we discussed with them. They'll be directing Empire planes to return or land at the nearest airfield. They'll be doing everything possible to get those planes on the ground. Sheffield told me he had a contingency plan. I assume he's put in place some sort of company directive and hopefully has his pilots responding."

Everett said, "Nicholson won't be expecting a prepared action from the FAA and it'll take some of his sting away."

Capone said, "We should be getting a call soon from Claire Elliott. She's bright, and I believe she'll make good decisions. I wish we had one of our men on the plane."

Chad Christensen, the agent who had been speaking with Jolliet Control Center, grabbed Capone's elbow to get his attention. He said, "Boss, didn't you say that Nicholson's plane, the one with the flight attendant, is Flight 855?"

"Yeah, she should be contacting us any moment. Do you have her on the line?"

"Sorry boss, I've got some bad news."

"What."

"Flight 855 is the second one going in. They've just crashed at the Rockford, Illinois airport."

"How bad?"

"I think they were lucky, or Nicholson's a good pilot. They're okay, I guess. It was a controlled crash, wheels up landing with no power. No explosion or fire. No word on injuries, but it sounded like everyone is probably okay. I've got a task force all over the plane. We'll nab Nicholson as he deplanes."

"Good, Chad, good. I don't get it though. Why did Nicholson bring down his own plane?"

"Good question."

Capone placed his hand on Chad Christensen's shoulder, to hold him in place while he thought.

Shortly, Capone spoke, "We don't know that Nicholson is on that plane, do we?"

"I guess not. I just assumed..."

"So did I. Could be our first big mistake. Find out immediately who's on that plane, specifically, I want to know were Nicholson is, and Claire Elliott."

"Will do, Bob."

Capone spoke to the room in general, knowing that everyone needed an update. "Jake, I want you to get a briefing from the FAA. Find out if they're being successful in redirecting Empire equipment. Meg, find Sheffield, I want to talk with him immediately. You can tell him what it's about, but I'm sure he's aware by now that two of his planes have gone in. I assume he's busy getting his equipment on the ground. If he needs to speak with me, let me know."

"Right on it."

CHAPTER 38

War Room, FBI Headquarters
Washington, DC
09:55 Eastern Standard Time
February 2, 2007

Capone leaned back in his chair and became aware of his exhaustion. He rubbed his face and realized he hadn't shaved or brushed his teeth for over twenty-four hours. Everett noticed Capone had finished his telephone conversation and approached him.

"You okay, Bob?"

"Tired, but okay."

"Connelly called while you were on the phone. He managed to get through to the Vice President who is briefing the President now. He expects a call back soon. He said to press on."

Capone turned to take in the room. Six members of the new team were working diligently on their assignments. Four were on the telephone and two pounding away on keyboards. On his way to the rest room one of the agents waved him over, holding up a telephone receiver.

Capone moved quickly and reached out to

accept the phone.

The agent handed him the headset, and said, "Richard Elliott."

Capone nodded and accepted the phone. He sat on the agent's desk. "Mr. Elliott, this is Bob Capone."

"Bob, I'm glad you were able to reach me. I've been worried about how your problem is evolving and particularly about how my daughter's doing."

"I understand, Mr. Elliott. That's why I called. I have a son, and I know how you must feel. I want you to know that Claire is a very impressive young lady."

"I heard the news this morning. I know the crashes were not the flights that Claire was on, but I'm also aware that they were both Empire planes. I'm very concerned."

"Your concern is understandable, but I have to be straightforward. We miscalculated."

"What do you mean?"

"I was just informed that one of the two planes that have crashed was Flight 855, the one your daughter was on. Please don't..."

"You bastard. You..."

"Mr. Elliot, please."

Claire's father was nearly hysterical. Capone heard the phone go dead. He turned to the agent who handed it to him and said, "Call Mr. Elliott back, he knows about Flight 855 but I wasn't able to explain that it was a controlled crash, and that his daughter is okay. Call him back. Get someone over to his house. Let me know if you can't reach him."

"Yes, Sir."

Capone closed his eyes and could only think of what may still be occurring in the air over Chicago. Images began to play out in his mind. He saw hundreds of burning fires and black clouds of smoke scattered across snow covered fields.

He almost nodded off. Meg Gerrity tapped his shoulder and he turned quickly as though poked by a cattle prod. The startled look on his face and his lightning response to her touch, caused Meg to jump back reflexively and stumble over a chair.

Recovering, she said, "Sorry, boss. Are you okay?"

"Meg, what are you doing here? You should be home in bed."

"Are you kidding? I went down to my office and got a nap. I'm fresh as a daisy. Are you okay?"

"A little tired."

"What can I do?"

"Sit down, I'll fill you in. It's not good."

"You look awful."

"Thanks. I feel awful, but that's another matter."

She slithered slowly into a nearby chair. "How bad is it?"

"Two planes have gone in. One is in flames.

Everyone's dead. Claire Elliot's plane lost its engines, but the pilot managed to crash land in Rockford. I don't believe there were injuries there."

"Thank God for that." She shook her head in disbelief. "What can I do?"

"I need someone to work on the flight manifests for Nicholson's plane, and also for 867. I don't know what else to do."

"Do you have something in mind?"

"I can't help you. We're fishing, Meg. Try to find some common denominator or maybe a passenger with a connection to the Bennettis or Nicholson. I don't know, maybe some association with a radical group... anything."

"I'll get right on it," she said.

She stood, placed a hand on Capone's shoulder, and said, "There's still a chance. Hang in there, Bob."

She scooped her notes from Capone's desk and left.

Turning toward Jim Everett, Capone moved across the room, oblivious to the activity around him. Numerous agencies had been alerted, and everyone was actively pursuing critical assignments. Senior FAA officials were being consulted. The President had been contacted and his advisors were speaking directly to Connelly. Air Force pilots were in the air, standing down for the time being.

Jim Everett was within arms' reach. Their

eyes met and they spoke simultaneously.

"Now what?"

"Any ideas?"

Capone spoke first, not sure which question was his. "Jim, I'm out of steam. I can't believe I let that girl get on the plane this morning. I hope she's okay. I was positive that if Nicholson was going to do anything, it would be from the cockpit of his plane."

"Everything pointed to that. It was the only reasonable conclusion."

CHAPTER 39

War Room, FBI Headquarters
Washington, DC
10:30 Eastern Standard Time
February 2, 2007

Capone finished a fresh cup of coffee. He glanced up instinctively and saw Meg moving quickly in his direction. She landed in the chair next to him. He gave her a quick look and saw that her make-up was hastily applied, and her short dark hair was disheveled. Her eyes were crisscrossed with red lines and the green silk blouse that several hours earlier had appeared hanger-fresh was now rumbled and haphazardly tucked into the tight-fitting skirt.

"Meg, you need to go home. Get some rest."

"Not yet, I've still got work to do. I've found something that might help a little."

"What?"

"There's a passenger on the plane. His name's Eddie Dumbrowski. They call him Short Eddie. He's been with the Bennetti gang for years. He's in the first-class section."

"How did you …?"

"I had a feeling, a hunch someone was on that plane that had a history. I was working on the wrong flight though. The first manifest I received from Empire was for Flight 867. I started looking on that flight while I waited for an email of the 855 passenger list and got hung up with some surprises I didn't count on. I'll explain that in a minute."

"Keep going."

"Anyway, I remembered you wanted me to check out the passenger list for Nicholson's plane. I had this feeling we were missing something, and you got me thinking."

"How's that?"

"I first received the manifest for 867 and looked it over. It took about ten seconds. You wouldn't believe who was there. All three Bennettis. I couldn't figure it out at first, but I think I know why they were on the flight."

"Why?"

"They weren't on the flight."

"What?...Okay... I'm with you," Capone said, catching on to what she meant. "They sent three people on that flight using tickets made out in their names. They knew the flight was going to crash and that they'd be reported as victims. Their worries would be over."

"Exactly. But that doesn't help us with the problem at hand, so I took some time to check on Flight 855's passenger list. I ran the names through the computer. Dumbrowski was easy to find. The printer kicked out eleven pages on'm. He's been working for the Bennettis for fifteen years."

"Oh Meg! How could I have been so stupid?"

"You weren't, you were the one who pointed it out. You asked me to review the passenger lists."

"Meg, this is a big help. What seat is he in?"

"3E"

"First class seat."

"I guess."

"Anything else you can tell me?"

Meg handed Capone a sheet of paper containing a description and criminal history of Eddie Dumbrowski. "Here's Dumbrowski."

"If we can pick up Dumbrowski, maybe he can lead us to Bennettis, and more importantly now, to Nicholson."

Meg offered, "It seems clear that they plan on bolting and setting up new identities."

"Right. I think we still have a little time. We've got people at the crash site in Rockford. Make sure they immediately snatch Dumbrowski and get him to lead us to the Bennettis."

She smiled and winked, "Got it".

"Jim, can you come here a minute"

Capone's angular partner left his computer terminal, grabbed a small notepad and pencil, and took the shortest route between the line of desks toward Capone. "I'm all ears."

Everett always had a way to divert his partner's attention from the serious nature of the job. In this instance, his reference to his ears made Capone's concentration slip. *He really is all ears*, Capone thought. *I've never seen a human appendage that more resembles the ears of an elephant.* Capone's fatigue added to the confusion and he lost his train of thought.

He shook his head in an effort to regain some alertness and shake off the image of the unusual ears. He shifted his gaze back to Everett. "Jim, Meg just gave me a news flash. Flight 855 has one of the Bennetti boys on board, Eddie Dumbrowski. The Bennettis were listed as passengers on Flight 867."

Jim's ears got larger. "Impersonators?"

"Right." Capone continued, "Work with Meg and make sure we get information from Dumbrowski as soon as he gets off the plane, then work the Bennetti angle. Keep me informed."

"How did we place him in the plane?"

"Meg found him on the manifest"

"Listen, Jim, Nicholson isn't on Flight 855 like we expected, but otherwise, everything else is going down as we anticipated. Two planes first thing this morning, maybe more any minute."

"That's what scares me."

"Our first priority has been to remove Nicholson from the equation. Nothing's changed, except his location. We have to find him."

"You're right. Any thoughts about where he

371

is?

"I don't know, we're missing something."

"I've got the same feeling. I'm still not sure about what's driving Nicholson. I know he hates the airline. He must have lost millions. I guess that's a lot of motive."

Capone said, "That's a fact. He hates the airline and I'm sure Sheffield. You know, Sheffield stole his software patent. He might as well have walked into Nicholson's bank and withdrew his life's savings. That seems like a pretty good reason to be pissed off"

"Jim, what was that you said."

"What?"

"You said Sheffield stole his software patent. He hates Sheffield. You didn't say Empire stole it. It may be Sheffield that's he's after. I mean Sheffield personally, not his company. He may be misdirecting us, and the Bennettis."

"How so, I don't follow."

"Well, we thought he would be using his ACU from the air, from his plane. That may have been the original plan, and he might be thrilled to be destroying the Empire fleet, but obviously something has changed."

"Meaning?"

"I don't know, maybe causing a few crashes might not be enough."

"Keep going."

"He might want to go after Sheffield himself."

"How do you figure?"

Everett sighed and thought, then said, "Isn't Sheffield flying today? A wedding?"

Several others had gathered nearby and were listening, trying to follow along. Meg pulled up a chair close to Everett. She made no attempt to pull her short skirt down as it rose abnormally high up her thigh, exposing the upper band of her hose. Dusty noticed the view, but only momentarily, and looked back to Capone.

Capone was still speaking. "Sheffield was planning to fly to New York this morning, but he cancelled. Nicholson might believe he's still making that trip."

"Would Nicholson have been aware of Sheffield's travel plans?"

"I'm sure it was common knowledge within the company," Capone said.

Meg asked, "Do we know when Sheffield was scheduled to land in New York?"

Capone answered, "He told me he had planned to arrive into LaGuardia at around noon, I think. I assume Eastern Time. But, he cancelled that trip to deal with this crisis."

Meg said, "Nicholson wouldn't be aware of that. He would still assume Sheffield is flying into New York."

Capone said, "That's right."

Meg observed, "So that Flight to New York would probably be...maybe... halfway there by this time. If Sheffield had taken it?"

Capone said, "Maybe. This might factor in, but his original trip wasn't actually a scheduled Flight. Sheffield has his own 727, same plane as the rest of his fleet, but he reserves it for his own use."

Meg said, "I wasn't aware of that. Must be nice."

"It's not unusual for the CEO of a large corporation to have a private jet," Capone added.

Everett said, "Using a 727 like the rest of his fleet would simplify maintenance. He could use some of the company pilots also, I suppose."

Capone said, "Probably."

Meg said, "And if Sheffield's personal plane has a PSD, Nicholson would be assured the ACU will bring it down."

"And it would have been easy for either Nicholson or Kiley to access Sheffield's plane. One of them could have installed the PSD month's ago. Nicholson could have just waited for the right opportunity. He would be certain that Sheffield is on an altered plane."

Meg said, "Absolutely. Even if it doesn't work for him today, he could do it later."

Everett said, "But today would be much better. If Sheffield's plane crashes the same day as the others, it may not appear to have been directed at him."

Capone said, "Sheffield being in the air today was strangely fortunate for Nicholson, though."

Everett said, "I'm sure we'll know more

about that later, but we need to stop Nicholson."

Capone continued. "So, if Nicholson is focused on bringing down Sheffield's plane, he could activate the ACU when he's near New York, from a passenger seat of any airplane, as long as he is in the same airspace."

Everett said, "His plane lands immediately after the incident, he deplanes, and flies off on another flight to who-knows-where."

Meg said, "Just too perfect."

Capone said, "I want you and Dusty to check schedules. Find flights that are leaving, or have left, which will arrive at LaGuardia around noon."

Dusty said, "I have a thought about that."

"Go ahead."

"Well, I guess, depending on how much prior planning Nicholson did, and how many of the Empire planes have PSDs, Nicholson might risk taking out the plane he's on. But if he flies United or Northwest then he's guaranteed to get on a plane without a PSD."

Everett added, "Excellent point. You may be right, but either way we can't be sure. We have to check all the flights and find him. But start with the other carriers."

Dusty said, "I hate to keep throwing wrenches into this, but I believe he has cockpit privileges with other airlines, just as he does with Empire. He may hop a ride in the cockpit on any of the airlines, and I'm not sure he would be listed as a passenger. Anyone know about that?"

Capone said, "Thanks dusty, we need to consider all of that. Meg, you and Dusty need to get started, find out how Nicholson might be listed or tracked. Get as many people looking for him as you can round up. We need to work fast."

CHAPTER 40

Rockford Airfield
Rockford, Illinois
10:56 Central Standard Time
February 2, 2007

I finished the checklist from my normal position at the engineer's panel and looked over to Skip Willis, Nicholson's replacement who had landed the plane. We had been on the ground less than two minutes and the first priority would be to get the passengers out safely. I could see from my panel that the emergency exits were already opened.

Tower advised us that rescue teams were in place and that our emergency slide chutes were deployed. Ted wrapped up his conversation with them quickly. I had been securing the various systems to make sure we had properly shut down the aircraft and that it was ready to be evacuated. Skip made one last announcement to the exiting passengers. We finished the checklist quickly but carefully, knowing that the voice recorder would retain every word. What we did and said during these minutes will be scrutinized by a variety of agencies, and later, the public. Skip said to Ted and me, "Nice work fellas. Now the fun starts."

I knew what he meant. There will be an investigation. Lots of paperwork, newspaper reporters, probably finger-pointing, accident boards, and for sure much aggravation. All this will go down on our records and remain there the rest of our lives. None of us had a clue what happened to our plane. Pilot error was on the back of my mind. Did we forget something? We hadn't run out of gas. Of course, there wasn't time for too much troubleshooting on the way in, but we sure didn't have a clue as to why our engines suddenly quit. I was out of my seat first and opened the door to see how things were going in back. It was hectic, but the girls had things under control.

I said to Skip, "They're mostly out already."

He responded, "Mac, I want you to go back and check on things, make sure everyone gets out. Ted and I will be right behind you."

I left my things, knowing that the authorities will check the plane out thoroughly and it would be some time before the passengers, and the rest of us, would get our belongings. Safety, of course, is the first priority. Getting everyone clear of the plane, including us, was paramount. "Right," I said.

It wasn't long before all the passengers were on the ground and clear of the aircraft. I advised the remaining flight attendants to deplane, and I followed. I saw Claire near the crowd, which had gathered a few hundred feet away. Some passengers were being loaded into ground transport. As I approached her, she was wiping a tear from her cheek, but she smiled.

"You okay," I said.

She nodded, smiled some more, and then surprised me with a big hug.

"I was fine until just now when things started to sink in," she choked. Then she pushed herself away. "I'm sorry. I'm okay now."

Members of the fire crew were pulling us toward a van. One said to me, "Sir, they're waiting."

I grabbed Claire's arm, looked back and saw Skip and Ted walking toward us. They waved us ahead.

We walked away without talking.

CHAPTER 41

Minneapolis Minnesota
12:47 Central Standard Time
January 6, 2008

The recent dusting of snow was less than an inch, and the driving conditions were good, at least for Minneapolis. The heavy traffic leading down Cedar Avenue from the airport had worn parallel black paths in the pavement. Dirty rows of packed crusty snow filled in the areas between. The rush hour traffic was heavy. A white Saturn sped by and darted between him and the car ahead, splitting the gap with precision and avoiding contact by inches. *This is worse than Washington*, he thought. But the day was special, and he had plenty of time to make his appointment with the residents of the small house in Richfield, about ten minutes away.

Capone had retired early from his fast-paced life at Bureau headquarters following the Bennetti indictments just two months ago. At fifty-five, he was far from finished with detective work but was ready for a change. The months following Nicholson's capture were the busiest he had experienced during his time with the FBI. The long hours and stressful conditions had led to a mild heart attack that fortunately left no side effects. Through strong encouragement from his wife, Janet, and after deciding to open a private investigative agency with Dave Blake, he chose to hang up the federal badge.

Although his official departure from the FBI was nearly a month old, the Bennetti trial continued to demand much of his time. He had, in fact, been prevented from leaving town by the state attorneys. Recently he called in some favors that provided him a two-day amnesty to visit Minneapolis. He would meet with Blake tomorrow and discuss their new partnership before returning home. Today's business was his primary concern.

Richfield was less than a half-hour drive from the Minneapolis Airport, and Capone had twenty minutes to make the appointment. He was eager to find the house and meet the young lady he had come to know through the ordeal back in February of 2007. The continued relationship during the final stages of the Bennetti case had brought the two even closer.

He tried to picture the house. *Probably much like the one we first bought back in North Carolina*, he thought. It seemed so long ago. Now he was retired and would basically be starting all over. He and Janet had discussed their next home and opted for a small, cozy cottage that they could purchase for cash. He could get by with less income until his full retirement kicked in. *Funny how the beginning of the circle comes back around*, he thought.

The clock radio read 12:47. Still a little early.

There was a silver mailbox with the numbers on the side, 725. Before turning into the drive, Capone sat quietly and studied the small residence. It was an older, two-story home with a gray stucco exterior, white trim, and a single-car garage in the back. Large leafless oaks lined both sides of the street.

A narrow sidewalk had been shoveled recently in front of the house, but the downhill side in the opposite direction was still snow covered. White smoke billowed from the chimney.

He saw a figure in the window. *That must be Claire*, he thought, seeing a mental image of the girl he pictured months ago, but still had not met in person. He felt like he was about to see an old friend.

He didn't have to ring the bell. The door flew open before he reached the last step, releasing a vibrant young woman with long wavy brown hair. She jumped out stocking footed, with outstretched arms and a huge wide smile. She engulfed the ex-federal agent with sleeveless arms.

"Bob, I'd know you anywhere."

"Claire, you look wonderful, just as I imagined. How have you been?"

"I've been just fantastic. I'm on a leave of absence from Empire you know."

"Yes, I've spoken with your father. He told me about your engagement to Mac. That's exciting news. Where is he?"

CHAPTER 42

Richfield, Minnesota
13:15 Central Standard Time
March 27, 2008

Claire and Capone entered the house laughing, and I wondered what I had missed. He didn't look like I imagined. He shook his coat free and Claire held the collar as it slid loose. He glanced up in my direction and offered a bright set of teeth framed by course black whiskers. His smile reminded me of Yogi Berra, but his eyes were Humphry Bogart.

"Agent Capone, at last," I said, as I took his coat from Claire.

"Ex agent Capone. I'm retired now and Bob works just fine. Hi-ya, Mac."

He stuck out a paw the size of my foot. I shook it. "Come in."

Claire led Capone to an overstuffed chair near the fire. She sat on the couch across the room from the picture window, where I joined her. Cookies that Claire made yesterday filled a plate on the coffee table between us.

"I like your place," he said.

"Would you like some coffee or a something to drink, Bob?" I offered, as he reached for a chocolate chip cookie.

"Coffee would be fine, I'm still thawing. I thought snow and cold were pretty much the same everywhere, but this town of yours is an ice box."

I got up to go to the kitchen for the coffee, moving quickly, so I wouldn't miss what was being said.

"You'll have to adjust," Claire advised. "I understand we're going to be neighbors."

"I'm looking forward to it. Dave Blake's a fine investigator and also an all-around great guy. He's going to take me to some of his secret fishing holes in the spring."

"You'll have a terrific time. I spent a lot of time on the lakes up north," I said, while pouring coffee into the cups that Claire had placed on the counter earlier.

Claire asked, "Bob, your business seems very exciting to me. I've wondered about all the information you gathered in the short time you had after Kiley disappeared. Is the FBI really full of all that cloak-and-dagger stuff we read about? Can you guys really read a newspaper on a bench in Central Park from a satellite thirty miles up in space?"

I sat down and handed Bob his coffee while he formulated an answer for Claire.

"I'd love to tell you some of the sensitive

things about the government's capabilities, but you hit on the key word. Secret. Maybe I can answer you without breaking my oath of silence. The satellites can do a lot more than most people think, and there's a lot of incredible equipment. If you're seriously interested in detective work, especially with the FBI, I know some well-placed people. I'm aware of your excellent scholastic record. In fact, Mac should be humbled by your college achievements. Sorry, Mac," he said, looking at me and grinning.

"That's okay, Bob, she knows about my less than impressive grades in college. But you should both know that I had to surmount unusually difficult and overbearing distractions. My years at St. Cloud were demanding beyond belief, and I had to carry the yoke of unbearable encumbrances weighted down by activities that prevented my full attention to the erudition to which I aspired."

"Oh, God! Did you bring a barf bag from your flight, Bob? I can't take it any longer. He's making me sick again."

"Is he always this desperate?"

"It gets worse," she teased, then asked, "You know, we never did hear the whole story about how you finally nailed the Bennettis, and how you caught Nicholson before he caused any more planes to crash."

"That was easy. Eddie Dumbrowski led us to the Bennettis."

He paused and looked down. "Stupid, really stupid," he said while shaking his head. "When we picked Dumbrowski up at the Rockford airport, naturally we searched him. He had a hotel matchbook in his pocket. We had agents there within minutes and found all three Bennettis in the same room. They had no idea we were on to them."

"What about Nicholson? I know that when he called in sick for our flight he stayed in the area. That's how he caused our plane to lose power, and those poor people on Flight 867. How did you figure out what he was really up to?"

Capone was still chewing, and we waited while he swallowed and took a sip of coffee.

He smiled and said, "We guessed. The first time we guessed we were wrong. We were certain he would be on your plane, Claire. When that turned out to be wrong, and we discovered Skip Willis had taken his place and that Nicholson had called in sick the night before, well, we really were confused."

I had heard parts of the story and encouraged Capone to fill in the blanks. "How did you figure out what he was up to, and more to the point, how did you prevent him from continuing?"

"Like I said, a lot of guesswork. Fortunately, we had gathered a lot of information. We eventually came to know that he hated Empire, but particularly Sheffield. We initially failed to realize that Sheffield was the key. He was the focus of Nicholson's ire, not the Empire fleet. Of course, the Bennettis had a different plan. For them it was about money and avoiding prison. Anyway, once we came to that conclusion, we identified what plane Nicholson was on. We were fairly certain that Nicholson intended to activate the ACU over New York, knowing that Sheffield's plane was in the same airspace."

"Without knowledge of Nicholson's magnetic pulse theories, you would never have realized what was happening. It seems that was the key to catching him?" I said.

"Of course, knowing about his early fascination with EMPs was definitely what brought our attention to him."

"It seems they had things figured out pretty well," Claire said.

"Actually, they did."

Capone used a napkin on the table to dab his mouth and continued, "He had convinced the Bennettis to transfer eight million dollars into an offshore account. That's why he had to start with the two planes in the Chicago area, to convince the Bennettis and start the money rolling in."

"How did he manage shutting down the engines on Flight 867 and on our plane when he wasn't in the air? I thought his device only worked in fairly close proximity. Line of sight?"

"Right, Mac. Line of sight was the limiting

factor. That's why there were only two planes affected. Nicholson activated his ACU from the end of Concourse C, which extends out toward the runway you were using that day. He enabled it just as Flight 867 took off. Because you had taken off a few minutes earlier, you had much more altitude, and were able to make Rockford. We figured if he had waited another minute, you would have been safely away, any sooner though and you wouldn't have had the altitude to make Rockford."

"So that explains that, but how did you know where to look for him?" I asked.

"We knew he hated Sheffield, and Sheffield was set to fly into New York at that very time. It was too convenient, even though Sheffield had cancelled and stayed in Dallas, Nicholson didn't know it. On a hunch we checked all the flights leaving Chicago that had comparable ETA's, or close to the same arrival time as Sheffield's original schedule. It didn't take long to find Nicholson listed on a Northwest flight. Of course, he believed no one could be suspecting him. He felt completely safe."

Claire was on the edge of her seat, literally. I thought she was going to slip off her chair and fall on the floor. She asked, "This is fascinating. Okay, so now you know that Nicholson is on a flight to New York. But you don't have any way to disarm him. Did you call up the flight crew and have them overtake him?"

"No, although that did occur to us. Good idea Claire, and of course the first thing that would come to mind. However, that would have taken time to set up. Too complicated."

"We came up with a simpler solution."

"Well don't keep us in suspense." Claire slid further off the cushion. *She's gonna drop any second,* I thought.

She continued to prod Capone. "What did you do?"

"It really was quite simple. I wish I could take credit for the idea, but actually, my partner, Jim Everett, made the suggestion. Someday I'll have to tell you about it."

Capone reached over and lifted his coffee cup from the table and sunk back into the big chair.

I was sure this would send Claire tumbling. I was a little disappointed when she too settled back. She took her cup, sipped, and said, "Oh well."

I knew this was for my benefit. I said, "Okay, you both are aggravating me. Come on, Bob, tell us the rest."

"I don't know," he said, now enjoying our misery.

Claire threw a rolled-up napkin at him.

"Okay," he said, shielding his face from the projectile, "it's strictly top-secret FBI information, but here's what we did. We had the FAA redirect all Empire flights away from the area. We didn't have to worry about the other air carriers and there were only three Empire flights that were affected."

He settled back again and folded his arms across his chest.

She said, "That's it. That's the big secret. That's the big amazing trick the FBI used to ensnare Nicholson?"

She gave Capone a 'shame-on-you look and pointed her finger at him accusingly.

"Now think about it," he said, sitting up and reaching for another cookie, "a good plan doesn't have to be complicated, in fact, usually the less complex the better. Jim's suggestion was so simple that it almost slipped by the rest of us. And, I might add, by you two as well."

Claire acted hurt. "Well, I really didn't spend much time on it. I think I would have come up with that."

Capone said, "I'm sure."

"Okay, okay, I get it," Claire relented, "you divert a few of the Empire jets around New York, let Nicholson land, and grab him as he deplanes."

Capone said, "That's how it worked out."

I was curious about how Nicholson's invention actually worked, and asked, "How did Nicholson come up with the idea for the device he used? Are there more like it?"

"We don't think so, at least not as sophisticated as his. Nicholson was the father of the science that uses pulsating magnetic fields to stop electrical devices. His knowledge in this area is still years ahead of everyone else. We're fortunate to have caught him before he was able to pass his secrets on to others."

"Bob, can you explain. . . I mean... can you tell us in simple terms how exactly the energy works to affect something like a jet engine from miles away?"

"One thing to remember is that the PSD's that were planted in the tail sections of your airplanes only had to have an effect of a hundred feet or so. They only needed to send pulses far enough to travel from the tail section to the engines, or actually to the electronic chips that controlled the engines. They were simply triggered from a further distance, from the ACU that Nicholson had. His ACU could activate any PSD within about a twenty-mile range. Originally, Nicholson thought he could affect PSDs as far away as a hundred miles."

"That seems to be part of what made his device unique. Am I right?" I asked.

"Exactly. He was a philosopher as well as a physics and electronics genius. He wasn't always the deviant that we came to know. What he was able to do with electronic interference isn't new. In fact, it is a widely understood phenomenon. The most common example is probably an incidental effect that results from a nuclear blast. It's referred to as an Electro-Magnetic Pulse or EMP. This type of pulse can easily span continent-sized areas. It's not common knowledge, but our country, as well as several others, have developed an electromagnetic bomb, an E-bomb, specifically for that purpose. Physics students know this phenomenon as the Compton Effect."

This was all new to me, and I must admit, very disturbing, especially in my line of work. "Would an E-bomb affect commercial jets?" I asked, but then realized that was a pretty stupid question.

"Do you have any computers or electrical systems on your planes?" he replied.

I was expecting him to say, *does a bear shit in the woods*. I knew the answer to my question before he gave it.

"Wonderful," I said. "I'm more worried though about the type of device Nicholson used. Something that could be used by terrorists. Something small and portable. How probable is it that we'll be faced with that again?"

"Not probable, but possible. Now that we know about, and have experienced the reality of it, the government is taking steps. We're being much more guarded."

"Exactly how did the thing work?" Claire asked, and then said, "I guess it was similar to a nuclear blast, but we didn't have the explosion."

"You're right. Same result on a small scale, directed at your plane's electronics, but it didn't use a nuclear blast. It's very technical and would take a while to explain. I have some interesting reading on the subject that I'll send you. One very similar device is called a Flux Compression Generator, or more commonly an FCG."

"Like the flux capacitor on Marty McFly's DeLorean?" Claire asked.

Capone laughed, and shaking his head he said, "No, a little different. The real FCGs all work by causing a rapidly accelerating magnetic field to be pulled across a copper coil. There's more to it, but a propagating ramping pulse results, enhancing the effect. The resultant flash has been compared to a thousand lightning bolts."

He paused. "Maybe the one on *Back to the Future* was similar."

"Traveling magnetic pulses," I said, "that's all it was?"

Claire lowered her head and said sadly, "He was an evil person."

Capone said, "Nicholson had a name for the magnetic field he created."

"What was that?" I asked.

"He called it a death pulse."

ABOUT THE AUTHOR

Greg W. Peterson is a prior naval aviator, air traffic control specialist, commercial airline pilot, and flight instructor. During his naval service he was a certified air traffic control specialist and flight instructor. He served as Control Tower, Radar, and Flight Planning Officer at NAS Norfolk, Norfolk, Virginia. Mr. Peterson graduated from St. Cloud State University in Minnesota with a BS in Engineering Technology. He is married, has two children, and lives in northern Georgia during the winter months and the Brainerd Lakes area of Minnesota in the summer.

Made in the USA
Monee, IL
29 May 2020

32183440R00216